ADMINISTRATION OF
Justice
AND
Constitutional Law

Larry Vick

Fayetteville Technical Community College

Kendall Hunt
publishing company

Cover image © Shutterstock, Inc. Used under license.

publishing company

www.kendallhunt.com
Send all inquiries to:
4050 Westmark Drive
Dubuque, IA 52004-1840

BRIEF CONTENTS

CONTENTS

*C*HAPTER 6   Police Procedures 137
By Robert Aberle 137

PREFACE

For as long as I can remember, I've had a love of reading. Some of my best memories are of spending quiet time under an elm tree on my college campus in New England and studying the causes of the French or Russian Revolutions, how representative government was instituted in third world countries, or why jazz is considered distinctly American. Without access to books, I would never have been exposed to such diverse subjects or made it out of East New York Brooklyn to law school and to rewarding careers as an Army officer, courtroom attorney, and college instructor. And while I realize that textbooks cannot alone ensure academic or professional success, they certainly play a critical role when used properly by well-trained and motivated educators.

My deeply held belief in the value of good books is why I undertook the challenge of assembling a customized textbook for use in teaching the *Administration of Justice* and *Constitutional Law*. I've taught both of these subjects at the college level for twenty years and feel that I have developed a reliable sense of what engages students and what does not. Like anything that's not built for a specific purpose, generalized textbooks are going to require compromise in their use. And when it comes to textbooks on the Administration of Justice or Constitutional Law, it's extremely hard to find one book that contains 100% usable material. Most of the time, there's too much emphasis on some topics and not enough on others. For the reasons I'm about to explain, this customized textbook goes a long way toward meeting this challenge.

First, it combines under one cover, the collective wisdom of three different subject-matter experts. The most extensively used author is Robert Aberle as well as chapters from his book, "The Administration of Justice: An Introduction to the Criminal Justice System in America." The five chapters from his book not only focus on the Constitution as the underpinning of criminal justice in America; they also focus on the courts as a unique system of people, laws, and structures; trials as complex entities; police procedures; and sentencing. Another selected author is Gregg Ivers. Two chapters are used from his book entitled, "Constitutional Law: An Introduction." Specifically included are one chapter on the US Supreme Court and Constitutional Interpretation and another on Freedom of Speech, Assembly, and Press. Lastly, there are two chapters from Craig D. Harter's book which is entitled, "Introduction to Fundamental Concepts in Criminal Justice." There's one chapter on the law of search of seizure and another on custodial interrogations.

The above chapters are organized in a logical sequence, beginning with an examination of the Constitution itself and how the US Supreme Court interprets it. These two foundational chapters are followed by an exploration of the American Court System, which is followed by in-depth analyses of First Amendment and Fourth Amendment constitutional law issues. These chapters are then followed by an examination of police procedures, custodial interrogations, pretrial activities, and sentencing. As you can see, an attempt was made, not only to cover all relevant topics, but to assemble them in an easily understood order.

Lastly, but certainly by no means less importantly, this customized textbook will save money and time. No longer will students have to buy separate textbooks for each subject and no longer will instructors have to familiarize themselves with multiple textbooks instead of just one. As mentioned above, because the textbook is organized in the way described, Administration of Justice instructors will have no problem extracting material needed for teaching Constitutional Law and vice versa. This streamlining of textbooks is also consistent with the present-day trend away from being heavily reliant on "the book." Today's tech savvy students want to roam the Internet and use social media to learn and interact. This customized text, by being specifically tailored to course needs, complements the desire to reach out and explore other available avenues to learning.

THE CONSTITUTION: THE BASIS OF CRIMINAL JUSTICE IN AMERICA

BY ROBERT ABERLE

Chapter 1

CHAPTER OVERVIEW

© Onur ERSIN, 2011. Used under license from Shutterstock, Inc.

The United States Constitution is the basis of all laws in this country, and therefore is the basis of our entire criminal justice system. It is only appropriate that any textbook that is intended to give an overview of the criminal justice system in America begin with a discussion about the U.S. Constitution and its applications to justice. A student of Criminal Justice needs to have a working knowledge of how the government is set up, how this structure directly affects how our laws are made, how society influences our laws, and how our individual rights shape our society.

This chapter provides a summary and analysis of the first ten amendments to the U.S. Constitution, commonly referred to as the Bill of Rights. The majority of citizens are at least familiar with most of the rights afforded to them under these amendments, but this chapter will look at how they are applied to the administration of justice. We will also discover that none of these rights are absolute; there are exceptions and limitations to each of them. One of the primary functions of the United States Supreme Court is to interpret the U.S. Constitution, and over the course of the past 220 years the Court has interpreted it in a variety of ways. These interpretations change with each session of the Court, and criminal justice professionals need to stay abreast with these changes because many of the rulings from this Court have a direct effect on, and constantly change, the procedures for each of the three sub-sections of criminal justice: police, courts, and corrections.

CHAPTER LEARNING OBJECTIVES

After reading this chapter you will be able to:

1. Describe the three branches of government and their relation to the criminal justice system.
2. Understand the system of checks and balances within our system of government.
3. List the individual rights associated with the proper amendments of the Bill of Rights.
4. Understand the function of the United States Supreme Court in the interpretation of the U.S. Constitution and the Bill of Rights.
5. Explain why the rights afforded by the U.S. Constitution are not absolute and why their interpretations change over time.

KEYWORDS

United States Constitution
Legislative Branch
Judicial Branch
Bill of Rights
Capital Crime

Amendment Process
Executive Branch
Checks and Balances
Exceptions and Limitations

© Rich Koele, 2011.
Used under license from
Shutterstock, Inc.

THE PREAMBLE TO THE UNITED STATES CONSTITUTION

We the People of the United States, In Order to form a more perfect Union, establish Justice, insure domestic Tranquility, provide for the common defence, promote the general Welfare, and secure the Blessings of Liberty to ourselves and our Posterity, do ordain and establish this Constitution for the United States of America.

INTRODUCTION

The **United States Constitution** is the basis of criminal justice in America.  This remarkable document was completed on September 12, 1787 and was ratified and became the law of the land on June 21, 1788. The U.S. Constitution has become one of the most important and influential government documents ever written.

The original United States Constitution is a hand written document that consists of seven Articles (or sections). Since its ratification, the Constitution has been modified and added to, by the use of the **amendment process**. Article V of the Constitution provides that an amendment may be proposed either by the Congress with a two-thirds majority vote in both the House of Representatives and the Senate or by a constitutional convention called for by two-thirds of the State legislatures. None of the twenty-seven amendments to the Constitution have been proposed by constitutional convention. The Constitution currently contains twenty-seven amendments.

United States Constitution

The United States Constitution is the basis of all laws in the United States and was ratified and became the law of the land on June 21, 1788. The Constitution also set up the framework of our government and defined the roles of the three separate branches.

Amendment process

The amendment process is the procedure used to modify or add to the United States Constitution. The Constitution has been amended twenty-seven times since its inception.

BRANCHES OF GOVERNMENT

© Songquan Deng, 2011. Used under license from Shutterstock, Inc.

© kropic1, 2011. Used under license from Shutterstock, Inc.

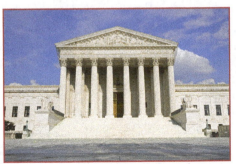

© Gary Blakeley, 2011. Used under license from Shutterstock, Inc.

CHECKS AND BALANCES

The United States is divided into three branches of government: legislative, executive, and judicial. These branches were set up by the United States Constitution. Article I established the legislative branch, Article II established the executive branch, and Article III established the judicial branch.

The **legislative branch** of government is responsible for making the laws of the country. The legislature of the United States is housed in The United States

Legislative branch

The legislative branch of government is responsible for writing and passing all laws. Each level of government (federal, state, and local) has a legislative branch. The United States Congress makes the laws on the federal level. Each state has a legislature that makes the laws for each state. Local governments have a legislative process which is typically comprised of a city council or county commission.

Congress, which is made up of the House of Representatives and the Senate. There are 435 members of the House of Representatives and one hundred senators in the Senate. The **executive branch** of government is responsible for carrying out the laws; and the **judicial branch** of government is responsible for interpreting the laws, and the highest court is the United States Supreme Court which has the authority as the interpreter of last resort.

The framers of the Constitution wanted each of these branches to work equally and in concert with each other and did not want any one branch to become more powerful than another. It was for this reason that a system of **checks and balances** was built into the Constitution itself. Each of the independent branches of government has the power and responsibility to keep the other two branches in check.

The legislative branch of government has the power to override any vetoes that the President may place on laws that it has passed (with two-thirds majority). They also have the power to control the spending of the government and, in extreme cases, have the ability to impeach and remove the President from office. The Senate must also approve presidential appointments, which is one of the checks the legislative branch has over the judicial branch since it also approves the appointment of all federal judges.

The executive branch has the power and authority to check the legislative branch by vetoing laws that they passed. The check of this branch over the judiciary is that they appoint all federal judges, including those who serve on the Supreme Court.

The most powerful check of the judicial branch is the ability to interpret the laws passed by the legislative branch and declare them to be unconstitutional.

APPLICATIONS TO THE CRIMINAL JUSTICE SYSTEM

To put the branches of government into perspective within the Criminal Justice System, the legislature makes the laws that the police and courts must enforce. The police fall under the executive branch and enforce those laws, and the judicial branch tries the cases that the police initiate through arrest.

© Vince Clements, 2011. Used under license from Shutterstock, Inc.

This separation of powers applies to all levels of government: federal, state, and local. On the state level, the governor oversees the executive branch and controls the state public safety functions. The legislative branch makes the state laws; and the judicial branch is responsible for interpretation of the state constitution, and the trial of offenders who violate the laws and are apprehended by the police.

On a local level the legislative function is performed by city councils and county commissions which are responsible for making local laws (or ordinances). The executive branch is headed by a mayor, city or county manager, or other elected official who is responsible to the community for running the government. The judicial role is assumed by the local court system, whether it is city (municipal) or county (justice court or equivalent).

*T*HE BILL OF RIGHTS

The **Bill of Rights** is the common name given to the first ten Amendments to the United States Constitution. These amendments establish the basic rights and liberties that all citizens of the United States enjoy.[1] The Bill of Rights was ratified on December 15, 1791, three years after the U.S. Constitution. The actual amendments contained in the Bill of Rights contain only 462 words, yet thousands of volumes of court decisions over the past 220 years have been based on these words. These decisions make it clear that none of these rights are absolute since the courts have applied many **exceptions and limitations** to them and some of these exceptions are discussed in the following section.

The United States Supreme Court (see Chapter 8 for a comprehensive discussion on the workings of the court) has never applied the rights of the first eight amendments[2] uniformly to the states. When it was ratified, the individual rights afforded by the Bill of Rights (arguably) applied only to the federal courts, not the state courts. To put this simply, this means that a person charged with a federal crime would have been granted all of the rights enumerated in the Bill of Rights while a person charged with a state crime would not necessarily be given the same rights. The person charged in the state court would be granted those rights as adopted by the individual state.

The United States Supreme Court has adopted a process of "selective incorporation" of the rights afforded under the Bill of Rights to the individual states.[3] The dates and the U.S. Supreme Court cases that applied each of the individual rights to the states, and therefore to everyone under every circumstance, are cited in the discussions of the selected amendments which follow. It is important to note that four of the rights stated in the Bill of Rights have never been fully incorporated or specifically applied to the states:

1. The Third Amendment's protection against quartering of soldiers.
2. The Fifth Amendment's grand jury indictment requirement.
3. The Seventh Amendment's right to a jury trial in civil cases.
4. The Eighth Amendment's prohibition on excessive fines.

Bill of Rights

The Bill of Rights is the common name given to the first ten amendments of the United States Constitution. The Bill of Rights was ratified on December 15, 1791, three years after the Constitution was ratified.

Exceptions and limitations

The rights afforded all Americans by the Bill of Rights are not absolute. Over the past 220 years, the United States Supreme Court has recognized the need to apply exceptions and impose certain limitations on the constitutional rights granted by amendments to the United States Constitution. The court has the power to do this through its use of judicial review and its authority to interpret the Constitution.

_____ FIRST AMENDMENT _____

*C*ongress shall make no law respecting an establishment of religion, or prohibiting the free exercise thereof; or abridging the freedom of speech, or of the press; or the right of the people peaceably to assemble, and to petition the Government for a redress of grievances.

OVERVIEW AND RELEVANCE TO THE CRIMINAL JUSTICE SYSTEM:

The First Amendment contains some of the most basic rights that all persons in the United States enjoy. The rights to express ourselves in our speech, our writings, and our religion are so basic to Americans that we tend to take them for granted.

RIGHTS AFFORDED UNDER THE FIRST AMENDMENT:

1. Establishment of religion and not prohibiting the free exercise of it.
2. Freedom of speech and of the press.
3. Right to peaceably assemble and to petition the government for a redress of grievances.

EXCEPTIONS AND LIMITATIONS OF THE RIGHTS AFFORDED UNDER THE FIRST AMENDMENT:

1. Establishment of religion and not prohibiting the free exercise of it.

© Christy Thompson, 2011. Used under license from Shutterstock, Inc.

The courts have consistently affirmed that the Free Exercise Clause of the First Amendment protects religious beliefs[4]. This means that Americans are free to *maintain* their religious beliefs without interference by state or federal legislation, or other authority. How you think and what you believe is a basic freedom. There are no 'thought' police. This freedom is not always extended to how we act on these thoughts and beliefs. The courts have stepped in and limited some conduct that has been associated with religious beliefs. They have ruled that some religious practices so patently violate the standards of conduct in our society that they have taken action to restrict them.

One of the first and most famous of these restrictions involved the Mormon Church and its practice of polygamy. The U.S. Supreme Court, in the 1890 case of *Davis v. Beason,* stated that "Bigamy and polygamy are crimes by the laws of all civilized and Christian countries." The Court went on to say that "To call their advocacy a tenet of religion is to offend the common sense of mankind."[5]

The 'Establishment Clause' which allowed for the establishment of religions, was applied to the states in 1947.[6] The 'Free Exercise Clause' which gives us the right to worship whatever way we want, was applied in 1940.[7]

2.   Freedom of speech and of the press.

The right to express ourselves both orally and in the written word is one of the basic freedoms that separate the United States from much of the rest of the world. Americans can be rightfully proud of their ability to express their feelings without fear of governmental reprisal. Over the years, the U.S. Supreme Court has been very cautious when facing challenges to these basic freedoms. The Court takes many factors into consideration when limiting these rights, including the vagueness of the individual laws and the impact that any restriction will have on our society as a whole. The Court has stated that the government may not restrict speech "because of its message, its ideas, its subject matter, or its content."[8]

There are situations where the courts have imposed restrictions on these basic freedoms. "The most stringent protection of free speech would not protect a man falsely shouting fire in a theatre and causing a panic."[9] The Court has also ruled that a person cannot use "fighting words,"[10] which are "words ... [which] have a direct tendency to cause acts of violence by the person to whom, individually, the remark was addressed."[11] Restrictions have also been imposed on the use of libelous statements[12] (libel is the making of false or malicious statements published to hurt or damage a person's reputation). The U.S. Supreme Court has also held "... that obscenity is not within the area of constitutionally protected free speech or press."[13]

While the United States Supreme Court has ruled that there are compelling exceptions to the First Amendment freedom of expression, it has consistently stated that some acts, even some that offend many people, are not prohibited. "While flag desecration ... like virulent ethnic and religious epithets, vulgar repudiations of the draft, and scurrilous caricatures ... is deeply offensive to many, the Government may not prohibit the expression of an idea simply because society finds the idea itself offensive or disagreeable."[14]

Freedom of speech was applied to the states in 1925[15] and the freedom of the press was applied in 1931.[16]

3.   Right to peaceably assemble and to petition the government for a redress of grievances.

The rights to peaceably assemble and to petition the government have been merged over the years into the basic First Amendment right to freedom of expression. The courts have not interfered very often in this area except to allow for governmental regulations related to obtaining permits and restricting specific areas that may not be used for demonstrations.[17]

The right to peaceably assemble was applied to the states in 1937.[18]

SECOND AMENDMENT

A well regulated Militia, being necessary to the security of a free State, the right of the people to keep and bear Arms, shall not be infringed.

OVERVIEW AND RELEVANCE TO THE CRIMINAL JUSTICE SYSTEM:

Probably one of the most controversial amendments in recent years has been the Second Amendment right to bear arms. There has been heated debate on both sides of this issue. Gun rights advocates argue that individuals have the absolute right to own guns without restrictions imposed by the federal or individual state governments. Opponents argue that the government has the right to regulate all weapons. The debate has also focused on the wording of the amendment and its reference to "a well regulated Militia" and the implications in a modern society.

This amendment is of particular importance to the police throughout the United States. The police are the ones who must regulate firearm laws in this country and must be thoroughly versed in the laws that govern firearms within their jurisdictions. The police must also be aware at all times that, while law-abiding citizens have a right to possess and carry weapons, so do the not so law-abiding. What makes this even more concerning to police is the fact that, according to the National Rifle Association, there are about 300 million legal firearms in this country and about 100 million of these are handguns.[19]

RIGHTS AFFORDED UNDER THE SECOND AMENDMENT:

1.   The right to bear arms.

EXCEPTIONS AND LIMITATIONS OF THE RIGHTS AFFORDED UNDER THE SECOND AMENDMENT:

Like most rights, the Second Amendment right is not unlimited. It is not a right to keep and carry any weapon whatsoever in any manner whatsoever and for whatever purpose: For example, concealed weapons prohibitions have been upheld under the Amendment or state analogues. The Court's opinion should not be taken to cast doubt on longstanding prohibitions on the possession of firearms by felons and the mentally ill, or laws forbidding the carrying of firearms in sensitive places such as schools and government buildings, or laws imposing conditions and qualifications on the commercial sale of arms. The U.S. Supreme Court has held that the sorts of weapons protected are those "in common use at the time" and finds support in the historical tradition of prohibiting the carrying of dangerous and unusual weapons.[20] Private citizens may not possess most military weapons such as hand grenades, bombs, and cannons. It has also been well established that the government can regulate such things as fully automatic guns as well as sawed-off shotguns.[21]

The United States Supreme Court did not apply the rights afforded under the Second Amendment to the states until 2010.[22]

FOURTH AMENDMENT

*T*he right of the people to be secure in their persons, houses, papers, and effects, against unreasonable searches and seizures, shall not be violated, and no Warrants shall issue, but upon probable cause, supported by Oath or affirmation, and particularly describing the place to be searched, and the persons or things to be seized.

OVERVIEW AND RELEVANCE TO THE CRIMINAL JUSTICE SYSTEM:

A thorough understanding of the Fourth Amendment is essential to all police officers (as well as prosecutors, judges, criminal defense attorneys, and almost all criminal justice practitioners) in the United States. This is the basis of all searches and seizures conducted by the police and includes the laws of arrest. Police officers at every level receive extensive training concerning this amendment and all of the exceptions that have been associated with it.

This amendment includes the provisions for an arrest. An arrest is a seizure of a person and must be based on probable cause (see Chapter 5 for definitions). An arrest can be made with a warrant or without a warrant if it is based upon probable cause, or if the suspected criminal act occurred in the officer's presence. The Fourth Amendment does not allow warrantless arrests of persons within their own home unless there is some exigent (emergency) circumstance that would make the obtaining of a warrant unreasonable.[23]

RIGHTS AFFORDED UNDER THE FOURTH AMENDMENT:

1. Right against unreasonable searches and seizures.

EXCEPTIONS AND LIMITATIONS OF THE RIGHTS AFFORDED UNDER THE FOURTH AMENDMENT:

1. Right against unreasonable searches and seizures.

There are probably more Supreme Court and other appellate court decisions dealing with the Fourth Amendment than all of the other amendments combined. The United States Supreme Court has decided many cases that have expanded the interpretation of this amendment. Below is a list of some of the exceptions that have been decided (these will be examined in more detail in Chapter 5).
Exceptions to this amendment include:

2. Consent searches
3. Vehicular searches
4. Border searches
5. "Open Fields" searches
6. Abandoned property searches
7. "Plain View" searches
8. Public school searches
9. Prison searches
10. Searches incident to arrest
11. Probation and parole searches
12. Detention and "Stop-and-Frisk"

The United States Supreme Court applied the freedom from unreasonable searches and seizures to the states in 1949[24] and applied the warrant requirement in 1964.[25]

FIFTH AMENDMENT

$\mathscr{N}$o person shall be held to answer for a capital, or otherwise infamous crime, unless on a presentment or indictment of a Grand Jury, except in cases arising in the land or naval forces, or in the Militia, when in actual service in time of War or public danger; nor shall any person be subject for the same offence to be twice put in jeopardy of life or limb; nor shall be compelled in any criminal case to be a witness against himself, nor be deprived of life, liberty, or property, without due process of law; nor shall private property be taken for public use, without just compensation.

OVERVIEW AND RELEVANCE TO THE CRIMINAL JUSTICE SYSTEM:

The Fifth Amendment contains the rights of persons and is broken into several different categories of rights, and includes one that deals with the non-criminal right of the government to take your property for eminent domain[26]. The amendment also contains some language that needs explanation in today's terms.

"*No person shall be held to answer for a capital, or otherwise infamous crime* ..." A **capital crime** is a crime for which the accused could get the death penalty if convicted (capital punishment). An "infamous" crime is generally accepted as a crime for which the punishment would be imprisonment in a state prison or penitentiary.[27] Today, this category of crimes is called felonies.

Capital crime
A capital crime is any crime for which the penalty can be death.

One of the most well known U.S. Supreme Court cases is based, in part, on the Fifth Amendment right against self-incrimination. The *Miranda* decision in 1966[28] has had far-reaching effects on the criminal justice system. One of the foremost changes involves the procedures that police officers use when interrogating suspects and obtaining confessions.[29]

The concept of double jeopardy is also addressed in this amendment. This right is one that prosecutors and the courts must be aware of at all times in criminal cases.

RIGHTS AFFORDED UNDER THE FIFTH AMENDMENT:

1. Right to a Grand Jury hearing.
2. Right against double jeopardy.
3. Right against self-incrimination.

EXCEPTIONS AND LIMITATIONS OF THE RIGHTS AFFORDED UNDER THE FIFTH AMENDMENT:

1. Right to a grand jury hearing.

"The grand jury is an integral part of our constitutional heritage which was brought to this country with the common law. The Framers, most of them trained in English law and traditions, accepted the grand jury as a basic guarantee of individual liberty; notwithstanding periodic criticism, much of which is superficial, over-looking relevant history, the grand jury continues to function as a barrier to reckless or unfounded charges. ... Its historic office has been to provide a shield against arbitrary or oppressive action, by insuring that serious criminal accusations will be brought only upon the considered judgment of a representative body of citizens acting under oath and under judicial instruction and guidance."[30]

The grand jury is generally comprised of twenty-three citizens who are subpoenaed for jury duty and serve for a designated amount of time on the jury. Unlike a criminal trial jury, these jurors hear evidence presented by witnesses called by the prosecuting attorney to establish whether or not probable cause exists to prosecute a defendant or to issue a warrant of arrest. The actual procedures vary from jurisdiction to jurisdiction but in most cases the defendant is not even present for the hearing.[31]

The right of a defendant to have a grand jury indictment has never been incorporated or applied by the courts to the states. This constitutional right remains a requirement within the Federal Court System but not a requirement for the individual States. Many of the States have adopted the grand jury system of indictments for felony cases; however, some have adopted other procedures in its place (see Chapter 7).

2.   Right against double jeopardy.

"… nor shall any person be subject for the same offence to be twice put in jeopardy of life or limb;"

The concept of double jeopardy protects individuals from being convicted twice for the same crime. Once an individual is prosecuted for a criminal offence, this Fifth Amendment right guarantees that the government cannot prosecute the person again for the same criminal act.

To put this constitutional right in perspective, if a person is tried for burglary in a state court and found not guilty, the state is barred from prosecuting the person again for that same crime.[32] This would be true even if additional evidence is later discovered that would tend to prove that the person was guilty of that crime.

The right of double jeopardy, like all rights, is for the benefit of the accused, not the prosecution. The prosecution is not permitted to appeal an acquittal (a verdict of not guilty).[33] Once a person is found to be not guilty in a criminal court, the prosecution is barred from appealing the decision. On the other hand, if the defendant is found guilty in court, they have the right to appeal the decision to a higher court. This is true even though one of the results of that appeal could be a retrial on the same charges. This is not double jeopardy because the defendant is the one who initiates the request for appeal and therefore is constructively waiving their right to another trial if they win their appeal.[34]

There have been many instances of a person being found not guilty in a criminal court and then being sued in civil court using the same witnesses and evidence and subsequently having the civil court finding against them.[35] The language of the Amendment states that a person cannot be put in "jeopardy of life or limb." Since a person is not put in jeopardy of criminal punishment (capital punishment, imprisonment, or punitive fines), the courts have held that double jeopardy does not apply in noncriminal proceedings.[36]

The double jeopardy clause was applied to the states in 1969.[37]

3.   Right against self-incrimination.

Shutterstock

"... nor shall be compelled in any criminal case to be a witness against himself ..."

The right against self-incrimination means that a person cannot be forced or required to make any statements that could be used against them in any criminal proceeding (present or future) or to be used as a basis to discover any other incriminating evidence against them. This privilege is applicable in criminal court proceedings, as well as while being questioned by the police in an interrogation situation.

A defendant is not required to take the stand and testify in their own behalf in a criminal proceeding or trial and the prosecution is prohibited from commenting to the jury on this lack of testimony.[38] If the defendant does take the stand and testify, they then waive their right against self-incrimination and are required to answer questions under cross-examination. The defendant can be impeached when they take the stand because the courts will then allow the prosecution to introduce any prior criminal record and can comment on the defendant's prior silence during police questioning.[39]

The right does not apply to "routine" booking questions. When a person is arrested, the police (and/or the jail) may ask questions required to properly book the person without asking for a waiver and are not violating this right. Such questions include asking the suspect their name, address, date of birth, and other identifiers.[40] The court has also determined that requiring a person to submit to a blood alcohol test is not a violation of this right, even though refusal to submit to the test may be used as evidence against them.[41]

Probation revocation hearings have also been ruled by the courts to not be criminal proceedings, so a probationer is required to answer questions during the hearing even though the questions may be incriminating in nature and may result in the revocation of probation.[42]

This right is the basis of the *Miranda* decision, where suspects must be advised that they have the right to remain silent (the right against self-incrimination) and that if they do waive this right, that anything they say can be used against them in court.

This right does not, however, apply in civil cases or in situations where a person does not face criminal or other significant penalties (other than just monetary).

The privilege against self-incrimination was applied to the states in 1964.[43]

4. Due process of law in criminal prosecutions.

This right guarantees that a person who is accused of a crime will be given the opportunity to have their case heard in a court of law, and will be afforded all of the constitutional rights that are applicable to their case and situation. The Fifth Amendment originally applied this right to those cases that were in Federal Court and it was applied to everyone in all cases with the adoption of the Fourteenth Amendment.

© Gina Sanders, 2011. Used under license from Shutterstock, Inc.

SIXTH AMENDMENT

In all criminal prosecutions, the accused shall enjoy the right to a speedy and public trial, by an impartial jury of the State and district wherein the crime shall have been committed, which district shall have been previously ascertained by law, and to be informed of the nature and cause of the accusation; to be confronted with the witnesses against him; to have compulsory process for obtaining witnesses in his favor, and to have the Assistance of Counsel for his defence.

OVERVIEW AND RELEVANCE TO THE CRIMINAL JUSTICE SYSTEM:

The Sixth Amendment encompasses those rights that a person has when they are accused of a crime and formally enter the criminal justice system. While all persons in the United States have the rights afforded under this amendment, they do not become applicable until a person is actually accused of a criminal offense. Once accused, a person enters the court system of the United States, whether it is on a federal, state, or local level. The Sixth Amendment protects the accused throughout this process. The amendment guarantees that the process will be fair and impartial and is the basis of due process. The Sixth Amendment rights are read to the accused in court as a part of the arraignment process.[44]

RIGHTS AFFORDED UNDER THE SIXTH AMENDMENT:

1. Right to a speedy trial.
2. Right to a public trial.
3. Right to a trial by an impartial jury.
4. Right to be informed of the charges against you.
5. Right to confront witnesses against you.
6. Right to have compulsory process for obtaining witnesses in your favor.
7. Right to have an attorney.

EXCEPTIONS AND LIMITATIONS OF THE RIGHTS AFFORDED UNDER THE SIXTH AMENDMENT:

1. Right to a speedy trial.

The right to a speedy trial "is one of the most basic rights preserved by our Constitution."[45] The purpose of this guarantee is to prevent long delays before trial for an accused person who may have to remain in custody before going to trial. It also affords the defendant with the opportunity to go to trial without the concern that witnesses may not be available to come to court or that their memory may not be as fresh if there is a long delay.

While the constitution does guarantee a "speedy" trial, it does not specify a specific time frame in which it must take place. Title 1 of the Speedy Trial Act of 1974[46] (amended in 1979) specifies the time restrictions that must be followed in criminal proceedings in Federal Court. This statute states the information (or indictment from the grand jury) must be filed within thirty days from the date of arrest or service of the summons. The trial must then begin within seventy days from the date the information or indictment was filed, or from the date the defendant appears before an officer of the court in which the charge is pending, whichever is later.

States do not have to establish a firm time line; however, most states have adopted time frames that are similar to those established by the federal Speedy Trial Act.

This right was applied to the states in 1967.[47]

2.   Right to a public trial.

With very few exceptions,[48] court hearings and trials are open to the public. The openness of our trial system is a safeguard against any attempt to employ our courts as instruments of persecution.[49] Open trials also assure that the criminal defendant receives a fair and accurate adjudication of guilt or innocence. It also provides a public demonstration of fairness and discourages perjury. The Court has also stated that open trials enable the public to see justice done and the fulfillment of the urge for retribution that people feel upon the commission of some kinds of crimes.[50]

The right to a public trial was applied to the states in 1948.[51]

3.   Right to a trial by an impartial jury.

The Sixth Amendment gives us the right to a trial by an impartial jury. Originally, this meant that a person accused of any crime had the right to have their case heard before a jury comprised of twelve impartial citizens. Over the years, the Court has reexamined this right and has limited the requirement to serious crimes (generally felonies) and has stated that juries can be comprised of less than twelve jurors,[52] but had to be made up of more than five.[53]

While the Court applied this right to the states in 1968,[54] the individual states are still free to limit jury trials to felonies only and can reduce the size of the jury from the traditional twelve to six.

4.   Right to be informed of the charges against you.

Every defendant who is accused of a criminal offense has the Sixth Amendment right to have the charges against them be properly explained and given to them.

This allows the defendant to be able to prepare a proper defense to the charges and to protect them once a judgment has been rendered against any additional prosecution on the same charge (double jeopardy).[55]

It is important to note that the charges that the defendant is informed of under this amendment are not necessarily the same charges that the person was arrested for. A person could be arrested by the police and charged with the crime of burglary. After review by the prosecutor, the charge may be reduced prior to trial to the crime of grand larceny. The person would then be informed in court (usually during the arraignment) of the charge of grand larceny, not burglary, and this would meet the Sixth Amendment requirement.

5.   Right to confront witnesses against you.

This constitutional provision was included to give assurance to defendants that they may question anyone who accuses them of a crime. The U.S. Supreme court has said criminal accusations should not be by written affidavits (sworn documents) only. They further stated that an affidavit is not to be used "… in lieu of a personal examination and cross-examination of the witness in which the accused has an opportunity not only of testing the recollection and sifting the conscience of the witness, but of compelling him to stand face to face with the jury in order that they may look at him, and judge by his demeanor upon the stand and the manner in which he gives his testimony whether he is worthy of belief."[56]

Most of the exceptions to this right deal with the testimony of child witnesses when the welfare of the child outweighs the right of the defendant to confront them in court.[57] The U.S. Supreme Court has also made exceptions when dealing with child sex crime victims.[58]

The right to confront witnesses was applied to the states in 1965.[59]

6.   Right to have compulsory process for obtaining witnesses in your favor.

Every defendant in a criminal trial has the right to present a defense. Part of this defense may be the presentation of testimony from witnesses who may have evidence favorable for the defendant. Many defendants do not have the money or resources to find and subpoena these witnesses and get them into court. This constitutional right guarantees that these witnesses will be brought to court (if applicable) even when the defendants cannot afford to do so for themselves.[60]

This part of the Sixth Amendment was applied to the states in (1967).[61]

7.   Right to have an attorney.

The Sixth Amendment gives all persons in the United States who are charged with a criminal offense the right to have an attorney represent them at every stage of the criminal process. This premise was solidified in the landmark U.S. Supreme Court decision in *Gideon v. Wainwright*.[62] The Court stated in this case "that in our adversary system of criminal justice, any person haled [sic]

into court, who is too poor to hire a lawyer, cannot be assured a fair trial unless counsel is provided for him.'' *Gideon v. Wainwright* is also the case that applied this right to the states.

The assistance of counsel applies to all criminal defendants who potentially face imprisonment for the crime they are charged with, even if the charge is a misdemeanor.[63] This right has also been extended to juveniles.[64]

If a person accused of a criminal offense cannot afford to hire an attorney themselves, then the government entity that is prosecuting the case must provide an attorney for them at no cost to the defendant.[65,66] This Court has also gone so far as to say that the counsel appointed must be "effective" counsel.[67]

EIGHTH AMENDMENT

Excessive bail shall not be required, nor excessive fines imposed, nor cruel and unusual punishments inflicted.

OVERVIEW AND RELEVANCE TO THE CRIMINAL JUSTICE SYSTEM:

The Eighth Amendment is a continuation of the rights given to defendants, and subsequently to those convicted of a crime, who become a part of the court and correctional systems. Although this is the shortest Amendment to the U.S. Constitution, it has far-reaching implications, particularly the right against cruel and unusual punishments.

RIGHTS AFFORDED UNDER THE EIGHTH AMENDMENT:

1. Right against excessive bail.
2. Right against excessive fines.
3. Right against cruel and unusual punishments inflicted.

EXCEPTIONS AND LIMITATIONS OF THE RIGHTS AFFORDED UNDER THE EIGHTH AMENDMENT:

1. Right against excessive bail.

One of the most important legal premises in a free society is the presumption of innocence. In our system of justice, just because a person is arrested and brought to trial on a criminal charge does not mean that they are guilty of that crime. The presumption is that the person is innocent of the charge and will be afforded full due process of law. The burden of proof to prove guilt rests firmly on the shoulders of the prosecution. With this in mind, it would be unfair to keep the accused in jail while awaiting trial. We do not incarcerate innocent people. The right to reasonable bail insures that the accused has an opportunity to be free prior to conviction. The Court has said that: "Unless this right to bail before trial is preserved, the presumption of innocence, secured only after centuries of struggle, would lose its meaning."[68]

There are times when the safety of society outweighs the need to offer bail to a suspect. Certain crimes have been deemed to be so serious, that even the presumption of innocence does not allow the person arrested to be granted bail. Murder, sexual assaults, high level drug trafficking, and crimes involving serious bodily injury are all examples of crimes that the courts have determined (on a case by case basis) that the assignment of no bail may be warranted. The courts may also consider such variables as flight risk and possible attempts by the suspect to commit additional serious crimes.

Excessive bail has been held to be an amount that is higher than what would be "reasonable" for the circumstances.[69] The term "reasonable" is one that the courts have intentionally left vague. It would be unreasonable to set a bail of one million dollars for a person who has been arrested for shoplifting, but it may not be considered unreasonable for a person who was arrested for smuggling twenty million dollars' worth of drugs into the United States.

The right against excessive bail was applied to the states in 1971.[70]

2.   Right against excessive fines.

The United States Supreme Court has had very little to say about this clause to the Eighth Amendment. The Court has ruled, however, that a person who does not have the ability to pay a fine because they are indigent cannot be given a jail or prison sentence because of this inability.[71] The Court has never applied this constitutional right to the states.

3.   Right against cruel and unusual punishments inflicted.

The Court has never given a precise definition of what "cruel and unusual" actually is. In the 1800s the Court did give some insight by stating: "... it is safe to affirm that punishments of torture [such as drawing and quartering, embowelling alive, beheading, public dissecting, and burning alive], and all others in the same line of unnecessary cruelty, are forbidden by that amendment to the Constitution"[sic].[72]

© Linda Bucklin, 2011. Used under license from Shutterstock, Inc.

The Court has, over the past two hundred years, ruled that the various techniques used to legally carry out the death penalty in the United States have passed the legal scrutiny and have been ruled not to be cruel and unusual. Firing squads[73] and electrocution[74] are examples of types of executions that have been ruled acceptable. The Court even went so far as to rule that it was not cruel and unusual when the State of Louisiana had to electrocute a man a second time when a mechanical failure during the first execution only injured but did not kill the condemned man.[75]

In 1972 the Court, in the landmark case of *Furman v. Georgia,* looked at the way the death penalty was administered (as opposed to the actual mechanisms of putting a person to death) and ruled that the death penalty violated the cruel and unusual clause of the Eighth Amendment.[76] This decision effectively suspended executions in the United States for several years. Following this ruling, thirty-five states redid their death penalty statutes to conform to the *Furman* decision, and resumed executions in their respective states.

Since the *Furman* decision, the Court has made several rulings that have put limits on who may be executed. In 1977, in *Coker v. Georgia,* the Court held that rapists could not be executed if they did not take the victims life during the commission of the crime.[77] The Court stated that "... rape cannot compare with murder in terms of moral depravity and of injury to the person and the public."[78]

The Court has also ruled that the Eighth Amendment prohibits the execution of a person who is insane,[79] but does not specifically prohibit the execution of juveniles who commit crimes when sixteen or seventeen years of age[80] who have been certified as adults (but does prohibit the execution of fifteen year olds[81]).

The cruel and unusual punishment clause of the Eighth Amendment was applied to the states in 1962.[82]

FOURTEENTH AMENDMENT

Section. 1. All persons born or naturalized in the United States and subject to the jurisdiction thereof, are citizens of the United States and of the State wherein they reside. No State shall make or enforce any law which shall abridge the privileges or immunities of citizens of the United States; nor shall any State deprive any person of life, liberty, or property, without due process of law; nor deny to any person within its jurisdiction the equal protection of the laws.

Section. 2. Representatives shall be apportioned among the several States according to their respective numbers, counting the whole number of persons in each State, excluding Indians not taxed. But when the right to vote at any election for the choice of electors for President and Vice President of the United States, Representatives in Congress, the Executive and Judicial officers of a State, or the members of the Legislature thereof, is denied to any of the male inhabitants of such State, being twenty-one years of age, and citizens of the United States, or in any way abridged, except for participation in rebellion, or other crime, the basis of representation therein shall be reduced in the proportion which the number of such male citizens shall bear to the whole number of male citizens twenty-one years of age in such State.

Section. 3. No person shall be a Senator or Representative in Congress, or elector of President and Vice President, or hold any office, civil or military, under the United States, or under any State, who, having previously taken an oath, as a member of Congress, or as an officer of the United States, or as a member of any State legislature, or as an executive or judicial officer of any State, to support the Constitution of the United States, shall have engaged in insurrection or rebellion against the same, or given aid or comfort to the enemies thereof. But Congress may by a vote of two-thirds of each House, remove such disability.

*S*ection. 4. The validity of the public debt of the United States, authorized by law, including debts incurred for payment of pensions and bounties for services in suppressing insurrection or rebellion, shall not be questioned. But neither the United States nor any State shall assume or pay any debt or obligation incurred in aid of insurrection or rebellion against the United States, or any claim for the loss or emancipation of any slave; but all such debts, obligations and claims shall be held illegal and void.

*S*ection. 5. The Congress shall have power to enforce, by appropriate legislation, the provisions of this article.

OVERVIEW AND RELEVANCE TO THE CRIMINAL JUSTICE SYSTEM:

© JustASC, 2011. Used under license from Shutterstock, Inc.

The Fourteenth Amendment to the United States Constitution was ratified on July 9, 1868. The amendment is divided into five sections but Section 1 is the one that is most applicable to the criminal justice system. Together with the Fifth Amendment, the Fourteenth guarantees all persons in the United States the right to due process of law in all criminal proceedings.[83] Section 1 of the Fourteenth Amendment has been commonly referred to as the "due process clause" and the amendment is referred to as the "equal rights amendment."

REVIEW QUESTIONS:

1. The basis of all laws in the United States is the _____.

2. The three branches of government are: _____, _____, and

    _____.

3. The first ten amendments to the U.S. Constitution are commonly called the _____.

4. The system of _____ and _____ within the government keeps each
    branch from becoming too powerful.

5. The "right of the people to keep and bear arms" is found in the _____ Amendment.

6. The right against self incrimination is found in the _____ Amendment.

7. "Freedom of speech" is found in the _____ Amendment.

8. The right "against unreasonable searches and seizures" is found in the _____ Amendment.

9. The right "to be confronted with the witnesses against him" is found in the _____ Amendment.

10. The right protecting us against "cruel and unusual punishments" is found in the _____
    Amendment.

CRITICAL THINKING QUESTIONS:

1. Discuss in your own words the concept of checks and balances, and how it is used in the United
    States. Make sure you include all three branches of government in your discussion.

2. Explain why there are so many exceptions to the rights that are afforded us by the Bill of Rights.
    How did these exceptions come about?

3. Select one of the amendments from the Bill of Rights that was NOT discussed in this chapter
    (see Appendix A) and discuss the rights or guarantees that are presented in it.

4. Discuss the importance of the Fourteenth Amendment and explain how it applies to the criminal
    justice system.

—————————————— NOTES ——————————————

CHAPTER 1

[1] It should be noted that the Fourteenth Amendment (see later in this chapter) guarantees that all "persons" shall be denied neither due process nor equal protection of the law. There has been some controversy as to whether this includes every person who is in the United States (visitors, persons on visas, and illegal aliens) or to just "citizens" of the country. The practice of our courts has, at least over the recent past, been to grant all of these rights to all persons regardless of their status.

[2] Some scholars attribute the Bill of Rights to the first eight amendments only. The Ninth and Tenth Amendments do not establish any individual rights. See Appendix A for the full text of the U.S. Constitution and all twenty-seven of the amendments.

[3] Gideon v. Wainwright, 372 U.S. 335, 341 (1963).

[4] Findlaw, "Free Excercise of Religion." Accessed 2010 at http://caselaw.lp.findlaw.com/data/constitution/amendment01/05.html#2.

[5] Davis v. Beason, 133 U.S. 333 (1890).

[6] Everson v. Board of Education, 330 U.S. 1 (1947).

[7] Cantwell v. Connecticut, 310 U.S. 296 (1940).

[8] Police Department v. Mosley, 408 U.S. 92, 95 (1972).

[9] Schenck v. U.S., 249 U.S. 47 (1919).

[10] Chaplinsky v. New Hampshire, 315 U.S. 568 (1942).

[11] Ibid. at 573.

[12] Beauharnais v. Illinois, 343 U.S. 250 (1952).

[13] Roth v. United States, 354 U.S. 476 (1957).

[14] United States v. Eichman, 496 U.S. 310, 313-319 (1990).

[15] Gitlow v. New York, 268 U.S. 562 (1925).

[16] Near v. Minnesota ex rel. Olson, 283 U.S. 697 (1931).

[17] Hague v. Committee for Industrial Organization, 307 U.S. 496 (1939).

[18] De Jonge v. York, 299 U.S. 353 (1937).

[19] National Rifle Association, "Firearms Fact Card, 2011." Posted January 20, 2011, accessed July, 18, 2011 at http://www.nraila.org/Issues/FactSheets/Read.aspx?ID583.

[20] District of Columbia et al. v. Heller, 554 U.S. 290 (2008).

[21] United States v. Miller, 307 U.S. 174 (1939).

[22] McDonald et al. v. City of Chicago, Illinois, et al., 561 U.S. _____ (2010).

[23] Payton v. New York, 445 U.S. 573 (1980).

[24] Wolf v. Colorado, 338 U.S. 25 (1949).

[25] Aguilar v. Texas, 378 U.S. 108 (1964).

[26] "... nor shall private property be taken for public use, without just compensation." Whenever lands in a State are needed for a public purpose, Congress may authorize that they be taken, either by proceedings in the courts of the State, with its consent, or by proceedings in the courts of the United States, with or without any consent or concurrent act of the State with its consent, or by proceedings in the courts of the United States, with or without any consent or concurrent act of the State (Chappell v. United States, 160 U.S. 499 (1896)). In simple terms, this means that if the government decides that it needs to put a freeway through your home, it can condemn your house and force you to give it up, but they have to give you fair market value for it.

[27] Mackin v. United States, 117 U.S. 348 (1886).

[28] Miranda v. Arizona, 384 U.S. 436 (1966).

[29] A full discussion of the Miranda case will be presented in Chapter 5.

[30] United States v. Mandujano, 425 U.S. 564 (1976).

[31] For a more detailed explanation of the grand jury process see Chapter 7.

[32] United States v. Martin Linen Co., 430 U.S. 564 (1977).

[33] Burks v. United States, 437 U.S. 1 (1978).

[34] A full explanation of the possible outcomes of an appeal is explained in Chapter 8.

[35] Probably the most famous case involved O. J. Simpson. On October 3, 1995, O. J. Simpson was found not guilty in a criminal court in Los Angeles, California of two counts of murder. The family of one of the victims then sued Mr. Simpson in civil court for the wrongful death of their son, Ronald Goldman, who was one of the victims that he was found not guilty of killing. The civil jury, hearing the same evidence from the murder trial, found against Mr. Simpson and ordered him to pay $33,500,000 in damages on February 5, 1997.

[36] Helvering v. Mitchell, 303 U.S. 391 (1938).

[37] Benton v. Maryland, 395 U.S. 794 (1969).

[38] Griffin v. California, 380 U.S. 609 (1965).

[39] Jenkins v. Anderson, 447 U.S. 231 (1980).

[40] Pennsylvania v. Muniz, 496 U.S. 582 (1990).

[41] South Dakota v. Neville, 459 U.S. 553 (1983).

[42] Minnesota v. Murphy, 465 U.S. 420 (1984).

[43] Mallory v. Hogan, 378 U.S. 1 (1964).

[44] The arraignment will be discussed in detail in Chapter 8.

[45] Klopfer v. North Carolina, 386 U.S. 213 (1967).

[46] 18 U.S.C. §§ 3161_3174.

[47] Klopfer v. North Carolina, 386 U.S. 213 (1967).

[48] Some of the exceptions include juvenile proceedings, grand jury hearings, and times when the judge may declare the need for closure of the court (child witnesses, confidential information disclosed, etc.).

[49] In re Oliver, 333 U.S. 257 (1948).

[50] Estes v. Texas, 381 U.S. 532, 538 (1965).

[51] In re Oliver, 333 U.S. 257 (1948).

[52] Williams v. Florida, 399 U.S. 78 (1970).

[53] Ballew v. Georgia, 435 U.S. 223 (1978).

[54] Duncan v. Louisiana, 391 U.S. 145 (1968).

[55] United States v. Cruikshank, 92 U.S. 542 (1875).

[56] Mattox v. United States, 156 U.S. 237 (1985).

[57] Maryland v. Craig, 497 U.S. 836 (1990).

[58] Kentucky v. Stincer, 482 U.S. 730 (1987).

[59] Pointer v. Texas, 380 U.S. 400 (1965).

[60] United States v. Cooper, 4 U.S. (4 Dall.) 341 (C. C. Pa. 1800).

[61] Washington v. Texas, 388 U.S. 14 (1967).

[62] Gideon v. Wainwright, 372 U.S. 335 (1963).

[63] Argersinger v. Hamlin, 407 U.S. 25 (1972).

[64] In re Gault, 387 U.S. 1 (1967).

[65] Powell v. Alabama, 287 U.S. 45 (1932).

[66] The standard used by most of the courts in the United States to determine if a person is indigent (lacking the necessities of life and therefore unable to afford an attorney on their own) is based on the poverty level for the circumstances of the individual defendant.

[67] McMann v. Richardson, 397 U.S. 759 (1970).

[68] Stack v. Boyle, 342 U.S. 1 (1951).

[69] Ibid. at 4.

[70] Schilb v. Kuebel, 404 U.S. 357 (1971).

[71] Tate v. Short, 401 U.S. 395 (1971).

[72] Wilkerson v. Utah, 99 U.S. 135 (1878).

[73] Ibid.

[74] In re Kemmler, 136 U.S. 436 (1890).

[75] Louisiana ex rel. Francis v. Resweber, 329 U.S. 459 (1947).

[76] Furman v. Georgia, 408 U.S. 238 (1972).

[77] Coker v. Georgia, 433 U.S. 584 (1977).

[78] Ibid. at 598.

[79] Ford v. Wainwright, 477 U.S. 399 (1986).

[80] Thompson v. Oklahoma, 487 U.S. 815 (1988).

[81] Ibid. at 849.

[82] Robinson v. California, 370 U.S. 660 (1962).

[83] Due process will be discussed in detail in Chapter 2.

THE SUPREME COURT AND CONSTITUTIONAL INTERPRETATION

BY GREGG IVERS

CHAPTER OVERVIEW

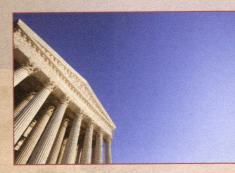

fstockfoto / Shutterstock.com

This chapter serves both as reinforcement of chapter one and as an introduction to new material. It underscores the key role the US Constitution plays in the criminal justice system while simultaneously introducing readers to new concepts such as legal formalism/realism, literalism/textualism, and natural rights.

It also goes further than chapter one in describing the role of the US Supreme Court in interpreting the Constitution and its relationship to the other branches of government. This chapter will also provide a narrative about the litigants who brought many of the cases discussed in the text and will examine the role that other entities have played in developing constitutional litigation, e.g. – interest groups, government agencies, and large corporations.

CHAPTER LEARNING OBJECTIVES

After reading this chapter, you should be able to do the following:

1. Describe the purpose and role of the U.S. Constitution in American life.
2. Identify and discuss the main components of the Constitution.
3. Describe the role of the Supreme Court and its relationship to the other branches of government.
4. Explain the separation of powers doctrine.
5. Explain the method of constitutional interpretation known as legal formalism.
6. Explain alternative methods of constitutional interpretation, including legal realism, literalism/textualism, neutral principles, and natural rights.

KEYWORDS

Brandeis Brief
Constitutional Law
Federalism
Habeas Corpus
Judicial Review
Legal Formalism
Legal Realism
Literalism
Natural Law
Necessary and Proper Clause

Neutral Principles of Law
Original Intent
Originalism
Public Law
Selective Incorporation
Separation of Powers
Supremacy Clause
Textualism
Writ of Habeas Corpus

"Constitutions should consist only of general provisions; the reason is that they must necessarily be permanent, and that they cannot calculate for the possible change of things."

—Alexander Hamilton

"The law is not an end in itself, nor does it provide ends. It is preeminently a means to serve what we think is right."

—Justice William J. Brennan, Jr.

A student preparing to study American constitutional development for the first time might experience a mix of emotions. The first encounter with judicial opinions can be a very intimidating experience for the undergraduate unfamiliar with such phrases as *ex post facto, per curiam*, and stare decisis. Indeed, the student might just wonder in what language this subject is being taught! As if this newly discovered need to brush up on Latin is not enough to cause a mild case of the shakes and sweats, the student then discovers that familiar topics such as congressional committees and political parties have been replaced by obscure subjects: appellants filing writs of certiorari, amici curiae briefs, and jurisdictional claims. It's not so surprising that a student might find the study of constitutional law a little overwhelming!

So, is it possible for the uninitiated student to learn about American constitutional development and, at the same time, find it interesting?

Certainly! Constitutional law and development is about far more than dry legal rules and their application to what seem like abstract disputes. **Constitutional law** is about how the most critical questions involving government power, social and political organization, and individual rights evolved from disputes between citizens and their government into legal rules. It is also about how the U.S. Supreme Court—the highest court in the country—has interpreted the United States Constitution and understanding what this means for the relationship between law and society. This book has two fundamental purposes:

Constitutional law
A body of law that deals with and seeks to define the relationship among the legislative, executive, and judicial branches of government.

1. to help students understand the social and political context of modern American constitutional law and how it has developed from the Founding period (the period between the Declaration of Independence in 1776 and the ratification of the Bill of Rights in 1791) to the present, and
2. to encourage students to think about the Supreme Court not only as an institution that creates constitutional doctrine based on ironclad rules of legal jurisprudence but also as one whose decisions are intertwined with social and political forces.

Students of "the Court," as it is known, and the Constitution need to know more than just the chronological development of constitutional law. This book's narrative will include references to the clients who brought many of the cases discussed in the text, the role that interest groups have played in driving the dynamics of constitutional litigation, the historical and social context in which particularly controversial cases were decided, and how the Court's decisions affect the real world. For many students, this last point is often the most important. The Court most often has the last word on what the Constitution means. But after the Court hands down an opinion, responsibility shifts to government agencies, large corporations, small businesses, college admissions directors, farmers, police departments, insurance companies, and public schools, to name just a few of the people and institutions that must apply judicial decisions to everyday life.

*L*AW AS CONSTITUTIONAL FOUNDATION

The American Constitution creates the legal foundation for our political institutions. Constitutional law in the United States, therefore, reflects a continuously evolving system of rules that has emerged after centuries of debate over what

The Constitution's timeless principles provide the foundation for our government, although new issues and questions continue to arise.

the Constitution means. Constitutional law serves as the "connective tissue" that binds the structure, substance, and culture of American constitutionalism together. (Table 2.1 offers a review of the topics covered in the Constitution.)

The decision of the Framers to create a political system in which the legislature, the executive branch, and the courts served independent purposes and were accountable to different societal interests reflected a political theory about the possibilities and limits of popular government. The idea that government should represent the wishes and aspirations of the people revealed the more optimistic side of the Framers. That the sources of political power and the motives behind such power were, in the view of James Madison, a pernicious threat to the operation of representative democracy, reflected the Framers' own experience with popular government. (Recall that it was their objections to the British monarchy's governance that prompted the American colonies to sever ties in the first place.) "The accumulation of all powers, legislative, executive, and judiciary, in the same hands, whether of one, a few, or many, and whether hereditary, self-appointed, or elective, may justly be pronounced the very definition of tyranny," wrote Madison in *Federalist* No. 47, one of a series of essays known as *The Federalist Papers*, written in defense of the U.S. Constitution's tenets prior to its ratification (as cited in Rossiter, 1961, p. 301).

Madison, and the Framers in general, believed that a proper constitutional structure was necessary to limit government power and protect individual rights. In a perfect world, no constitution would be needed because no government would be necessary to organize and channel social and political currents. But, as Madison wrote in *Federalist* No. 51, his most famous defense of the new constitutional order,

> In framing a government which is to be administered by men over men, the great difficulty lies in this: you must first enable the government to control the governed; and in the next place oblige it to control itself. A dependence on the people is, no doubt, the primary control on the government; but experience has taught mankind the necessity of auxiliary precautions. (as cited in Rossiter, 1961, p. 322)

What were—and remain—those auxiliary precautions of which Madison spoke? A constitutional government that called for separation of powers, checks and balances, federalism (a system in which government power is allocated among national, state, and local governments; see next section), and protections for individual rights against majority rule.

TABLE 2.1: OUTLINE OF THE U.S. CONSTITUTION: A REVIEW*	
ARTICLE I	**LEGISLATIVE BRANCH**
Section 1	*Legislative power*
Section 2	*Composition and authority of the House of Representatives*
Section 3	*Composition and authority of the Senate*
Section 4	*Elections of congressional members*
Section 5	*Rules governing member behavior*
Section 6	*Checks on member behavior*
Section 7	*Rules for bills*
Section 8	*Powers granted to Congress*
Section 9	*Restrictions on legislative power*
Section 10	*Restrictions on state power*
ARTICLE II	**EXECUTIVE BRANCH**
Section 1	*Qualifications and election of the president*
Section 2	*Presidential power*
Section 3	*Responsibilities*
Section 4	*Grounds for impeachment*
ARTICLE III	**JUDICIAL BRANCH**
Section 1	*Judicial power*
Section 2	*Jurisdiction*
Section 3	*Treason and its punishment*
ARTICLE IV	**INTERSTATE RELATIONS**
Section 1	*States' duties to other states*
Section 2	*Privileges and immunities as citizens*
Section 3	*New states and federal property*
Section 4	*Federal government's duties to the states*
ARTICLE V	**AMENDING THE CONSTITUTION**
ARTICLE VI	**SUPREMACY OF THE FEDERAL GOVERNMENT**
ARTICLE VII	**RATIFYING THE CONSTITUTION**

*To read the full text of the Constitution, visit http://www.archives.gov/exhibits/charters/constitution_transcript.html.

In 1789, the nation ratified its new Constitution and with it "A New Order for the Ages," or Novus Ordo Seclorum, the Latin phrase embossed on the great seal of the United States. These core principles of American constitutionalism remain vibrant and timeless. But, as will become evident over the course of this book, the transformation of those principles into constitutional law has created new issues and questions that continue to confront the participants in the U.S. constitutional system. The next section examines the basic structure of the Constitution, the government it created, and the political theory underlying American popular government.

CONSTITUTIONAL STRUCTURE

Public law
Establishes the relationship between the government and the individual.

Creating the constitutional structure of **public law**, which establishes the relationship between the government and the individual, was the problem that confronted the state representatives to the Constitutional Convention held in Philadelphia during the summer of 1787. This gathering of delegates from the 13 states was attempting to address the problems that had come up as the United States tried to operate under its original constitution, the Articles of Confederation. The opinions of the delegates varied greatly over the extent to which the Articles should be revised, and the issue was far from settled.

A painting of George Washington addressing the Constitutional Convention. The delegates at the Constitutional Convention held wildly different opinions on how the Articles of Confederation should have been revised and, even after the Constitution was completed, disagreed on what key sections truly meant.

When the Constitution was completed and presented to the public later that September, its language reflected the textual ambiguities that are an essential feature in the art of political compromise. Convention delegates and numerous others involved in the drafting of the Constitution held wildly divergent views on what it was supposed to mean. Several delegates left the convention confused over the meaning of key sections of the Constitution even after it was completed. Some of the more prominent Framers, including James Madison and Alexander Hamilton, changed their original views on the Constitution's meaning during their lifetimes. Notable opponents of ratification, such as George Mason, who refused to sign the Constitution and actively campaigned against ratification, later became more hopeful of its possibilities. If the Framers resolved their political differences through textual ambiguities and, in some cases, deliberate exclusion, should it come as any great surprise that subsequent generations continue to disagree over what the Constitution means?

This book will deal with these important issues throughout. The remainder of this section will examine the four major and interlocking components of the U.S. constitutional structure: national government, separation of powers, federalism, and civil and constitutional rights.

NATIONAL GOVERNMENT

Complaints directed at the Constitution's decided emphasis on national power by the various opponents of ratification, better known as the Anti-Federalists, were quite legitimate if one considers how the new constitutional structure altered the sources and distribution of government power established by the Articles of Confederation. In place of the loose, lateral framework that characterized the Articles, one in which the states retained their primacy, the Constitution delegated supreme legislative, executive, and judicial authority to the national government. Moreover, the Constitution provided comprehensive and specific powers to each branch that the Articles did not. Among the most dramatic changes that illustrated the Constitution's emphasis on national power were the following:

- Congress, in Article I, now had the exclusive power to regulate interstate commerce, to authorize and collect taxes, and to create federal courts and establish their jurisdiction, as well as the general authority to make all laws necessary and proper to exercise its legislative responsibilities. As will be discussed throughout this volume, since the early 19th century, the Court's interpretation of Congress's power to make laws (the **Necessary and Proper Clause**), regulate commerce (the Commerce Clause), and tax and spend has been instrumental in the expansion of legislative power at the national level.

- The executive branch, created by Article II, now consisted of a single, elected president, and not, as some Anti-Federalists had wanted, a plural council. Article II also delegated to the president the power to make judicial and cabinet appointments. In language that first appeared to be an afterthought but that has proven to be critical in the constitutional expansion of executive power, Article II reserved to the president the power to faithfully execute the laws of the United States. Article II of the Constitution grants these powers exclusively to the executive. No other branch of government has the ability to execute them.

- This book also explores how the growth of presidential power based on the "implied powers" of the executive has been enormous and extraordinarily consequential for the balance of constitutional power.

- Concurrent with the exercise of the judicial power by the Supreme Court—the sole court created by Article III of the Constitution—was the implied power of judicial review, or the Court's power to determine the constitutionality of legislative and executive actions. Judicial review remains controversial for this reason alone.

Necessary and Proper Clause

The provision of Article I that permits Congress to enact all laws "necessary and proper" to carrying out its legislative responsibility.

However, the Court's use of judicial review to advance dramatic new concepts of government power and individual rights, often in the face of popular opposition, has generated additional controversy.

■ Article VI made all laws and treaties enacted under the "Authority of the United States . . . the supreme Law of the Land," and bound the state governments to the laws created under national power. (This is known as the **Supremacy Clause**.) Disagreement continues, however, over the scope of power retained by the states in areas such as commercial and police power regulation.

Supremacy Clause

The provision of Article VI of the Constitution that makes the federal Constitution and all laws passed under its authority supreme over the states.

To secure the political and economic stability of a large, commercial republic and protect the rights of its citizens from unreasonable majority rule, Madison believed the Constitution had to quell three major threats. The first was disunion, the second was the "mischiefs of faction," and the third was the threat to the rights and liberties of individuals and political minorities regardless of whether those threats came from majorities or other minorities (as cited in Rossiter, 1961, p. 64). Madison's solution was to establish first a strong, vibrant national government, complete with the appropriate powers to allow the branches to pursue their respective ends. Such "energetic" government would need constitutional constraints to promote both the "public good and private rights," confessed "Publius," the pen name assumed by The Federalist Papers authors James Madison, Alexander Hamilton, and John Jay. Separation of powers, as the text will demonstrate, became the most important of those constraints.

Separation of powers

The principal system of government within which power is divested among different branches of government, ensuring a system of checks and balances.

President Obama signed a bill in 2013. The fact that the president plays a considerable role in lawmaking illustrates how the branches' functions sometimes overlap—while maintaining the separation of powers.

Drop of Light / Shutterstock.com

SEPARATION OF POWERS

Before the Federalists could turn their attention to how the Constitution's features would attract virtuous leaders, who would promote a good government, they had to persuade the public that it was, above all, a safe government. In *Federalist* No. 47, Madison conceded the point that the "accumulation" of all legislative, executive, and judicial power in a single branch of government could "justly be pronounced the very definition of tyranny" (as cited in Rossiter, 1961, p. 301). To soothe the suspicions of the Constitution's opponents, Madison asserted his agreement with their "objection" that governments that fail to adhere to separation of powers endanger the liberties of the people.

Separation of powers, designed to elevate the concerns of the public and allow it to guard against the false exercise of government power, could not function without each branch having the constitutional means to resist the potential intrusions of another. The Constitution creates three separate branches of the national government, each with distinct powers and responsibilities, and divides levels of government power along a federal structure, allowing state and local governments to retain appropriate legal jurisdiction and political power. These lines of division, however, are not strict. The constitutional structure outlined by the Framers can be more accurately described as one in which separate government institutions share in the exercise of their responsibilities. Each branch, as Madison states in *Federalist* No. 51, "should have a will of its own" (as cited in Rossiter, 1961, p. 321).

How and where does the Constitution put this principle into practice? Here are a few examples:

- Article I provides Congress the power to declare war, but the president, in Article II, is made commander in chief of the armed forces.
- Article III creates the Supreme Court and vests it with jurisdiction over all cases arising under "law and equity." Article I leaves to Congress the power to create inferior courts, and Article III gives Congress the power to establish the jurisdiction of the lower courts. Congress also decides how much money the federal judiciary receives each year to operate. The president appoints justices to the federal courts, and they are confirmed by the Senate.
- Article II says nothing about the president's power to make laws, but the president's constitutional responsibility to address the state of the union and recommend measures "he shall judge necessary and expedient" gives the office a considerable role in lawmaking, which is the function of Congress.
- Article II places the power to veto legislation in the hands of the president, but Congress, in Article I, has the power to override presidential vetoes with the support of two-thirds majorities of each chamber.

Difficult questions emerge from these examples. Does Article I allow Congress to create a "legislative veto" over rules made by administrative agencies it created to carry out federal law? Does the Constitution permit one branch of government to delegate its power to another? For example, may Congress delegate to agencies under the judicial branch's control the power to create and enforce sentencing guidelines for federal judges? Suppose majorities in both the House and Senate believe that the Supreme Court has erred on a major constitutional question, such as one that involves abortion rights, school prayer, or affirmative action. Does the Exceptions and Regulations Clause of Article III, which leaves to Congress the responsibility to establish federal court jurisdiction, mean that it has the right to remove the Court's authority to hear cases involving those issues? Or does congressional authority to establish federal court jurisdiction mean something more general and less intrusive as it applies to courts' core functions?

These are hard questions, indeed. They are tough not just for students encountering constitutional law for the first time but, as will become evident, for the Supreme Court as well.

FEDERALISM

Madison's conception of separation of powers was not the only departure from the established principles of popular government. The Constitution, "Publius" argued, created a republic that was a mixture of national and federal principles. **Federalism**, as it is understood in its most basic form, creates a multilevel government that permits the national and various state governments to operate in parallel fashion.

Federalist No. 51, as it appeared in the *New York Packet* on February 8, 1788. *Federalist* No. 51 emphasized the importance of checks and balances within a government.

It is difficult to know even now, as it was during the Founding period, how these general principles apply to specific problems that arise between the forces of state and national power. However, the "new" federal structure that Madison envisioned undoubtedly represented a dramatic departure from the "old" federalism of the Articles of Confederation. Madison might not have been clear about the line separating national from state responsibilities, but he did confess that the federal structure proposed in the Constitution left the states in a position subordinate to the national government. For the Constitution's supporters, a confederate structure in which the states retained sovereign power against the national government was out of the question. Madison, along with other influential Federalists, believed that the national government's sovereignty over the states was necessary to ensure the unity and effective governing of the country.

Federalism, like the separation of powers, was essential to the equilibrium that Madison believed was the basis for the Constitution's success. Placing power where it did not belong, whether on the national or state level, could doom the Constitution. This concern is similar to Madison's in *Federalist* No. 51, where he emphasized the need to diffuse the sources of unrest in the administration of government by "supplying" each branch of the national government with "opposite and rival interests" (as cited in Rossiter, 1961, p. 322). Federalism allows the national and state governments to retain control over their respective spheres of influence. States retain explicit constitutional guarantees for the right to exist and to administer their respective governments. Those guarantees include the following:

- The Tenth Amendment, which states that "the powers not delegated to the United States by the Constitution, nor prohibited by it to the states, are reserved to the states respectively, or to the people." Remember the phrase "powers not delegated to the United States," as it is important in understanding the Court's opinions on federal structure. Supporters of more state independence from federal rules and judicial decisions have pointed to those words as supportive of their position. Does that terminology support their view?

- Article V requires that all proposed amendments to the Constitution be ratified, upon approval of two-thirds of the Senate and the House of Representatives, by three-fourths of the states. Although this process gives the states the ultimate power to amend the Constitution, the Framers' decision to create a non-unanimous decision rule represented a "mixed" approach somewhere between supreme national power—congressional approval only—and state supremacy. A unanimous rule would permit one state to determine ratification or rejection. In whose favor does the balance of constitutional power over the Constitution tip, the national government or the states?

In the end, the Constitution's federal structure emphasizes the need for union through national government. Several other key constitutional provisions support the national character of the federal structure. Article IV, for example, requires each state to give "Full Faith and Credit" to the public laws of another state. It also affords citizens of other states the "Privileges and Immunities" provided to its own and empowers the United States to "guarantee" each state a republican form of government.

Despite the national features of the federal structure, assurance was needed, and the states have continued to press for more power and independence. On more than one occasion, the states have prevailed in their efforts to retain control over matters that have ranged from civil rights protection to gun control to commercial regulation. Federalism continues to remain a vibrant constitutional principle.

CIVIL AND CONSTITUTIONAL RIGHTS

Most Americans believe the Constitution's chief purpose is to protect the fundamental rights of individuals and minorities from acts of majority rule considered inconsistent with the nation's commitment to liberty and equality. Thus, it is remarkable to learn that the proposal for a bill of rights in the Constitutional Convention was considered and rejected with a little more than a snap of the fingers. Debate over the inclusion of a bill of rights was limited to the morning of September 12, 1787, less than a week before the convention completed the Constitution and adjourned. Each state present when the proposal for the Bill of Rights was submitted to the floor of the convention—including Virginia, which counted James Madison, Thomas Jefferson, George Washington, and George Mason among its more famous residents—voted against the document. What little debate took place centered on George Mason's comments that he wished the Constitution "had been prefaced with a bill of rights. It would give great quiet to the people" (Bowen, 1986, p. 243). Mason added that the convention could put together a bill of rights in no time; it would simply adopt the language of the eight states that had bills of rights of their own.

THE DEBATE OVER A BILL OF RIGHTS

The issue that concerned Mason, and later the Anti-Federalist writers in their subsequent fight against the ratification, was the potential of the national government to use its "supreme" power to declare certain rights included in various state constitutions, such as freedom of speech and religion, as incompatible with national objectives. To the Constitution's opponents, the broad powers granted to Congress under the Necessary and Proper Clause, and to the national government more generally under the Supremacy Clause, did nothing to guarantee that state constitutions would be respected.

Even when the Constitution was submitted to the states for ratification, the Federalists refused to concede that the absence of a bill of rights posed a potential problem in the protection of individual rights and liberties. Hamilton, in *Federalist* No. 84, wrote that the Constitution itself was, "in every rational sense, and to every useful purpose, A BILL OF RIGHTS" (as cited in Rossiter, 1961, p. 515). Hamilton's point here exemplifies the Federalists' initial position against the Bill of Rights. Because the Constitution vested each branch of government with no more than its textually defined power, all other rights and liberties were, therefore, reserved by the people and, where appropriate, the states. The Constitution permitted the government to exercise only those powers expressly granted in the text.

What is wrong with this argument, at least from the perspective of the Constitution's opponents? First, although the Constitution does enumerate specific grants of power to all three branches, it offers no insight as to what the "necessary and proper" exercise of congressional power might be. Such latent, broad power vested in the national government was, to the Anti-Federalists, a sleeping giant. Even now, the constitutional definition of the Necessary and Proper Clause, as well as other provisions of Article I such as the Commerce Clause, continues to evolve. The Supreme Court often becomes the arbiter of these intra- and intergovernmental disputes over what powers belong to which levels and branches of American government.

Second, the Constitution does, in fact, include several provisions that pertain to the Anti-Federalists' concerns: For example, Article I prohibits the suspension of **habeas corpus**—a person's right to seek relief from unlawful imprisonment—and Article VI prohibits a religious-oath requirement to hold public office. Their inclusion contradicted the Federalists' position that the original Constitution was a self-executing bill of rights. Nothing in the Constitution permitted the government to suspend a **writ of habeas corpus**, compel religious obedience to serve as a public official, or, perhaps most obvious, declare that the criminally accused were entitled to a trial by jury, included in Article III. Such rights, the Anti-Federalists contended, were assumed even before the Constitutional Convention began. If their inclusion in the Constitution was simply to reinforce their importance, then the Federalists had just made the Anti-Federalists' point for them: Bills of rights are essential tools in the moral and civic education of a free people.

Habeas corpus

See *writ of habeas corpus*.

Writ of habeas corpus

From the Latin "that you have the body." A petition claiming that an individual is being wrongly imprisoned and is entitled to a judicial proceeding.

RATIFICATION OF THE BILL OF RIGHTS

James Madison recognized that ratification would be a much smoother process if the Constitution's proponents promised to consider the inclusion of a bill of rights upon approval of the original document. It is also fair to say that Madison was not unsympathetic to the Anti-Federalists' desire for a bill of rights. Over time, Madison, prodded by his friend Thomas Jefferson, became a firm proponent of a bill of rights. He agreed with Jefferson that "a bill of rights is what the people are entitled to against every government on earth, general or particular, and what no just government should refuse, or rest on inference" (as cited in Boyd, 1950, p. 14). Perhaps a bill of rights would contribute to the public education of the people and reassure them that the Constitution did more than just authorize what the national government was allowed to do. By attaching an absolute negative on the exercise of government power—as the command throughout the First Amendment that "Congress shall make no law abridging the freedom of speech"—a bill of rights would declare what government could not do to its people.

In return for ratification of the original Constitution, Madison agreed to introduce a bill of rights in the opening session of the First Congress. In December 1791, Rhode Island became the final state to ratify the 10 amendments, written largely by Madison. He received considerable conceptual and intellectual guidance from fellow Virginians Thomas Jefferson and George Mason, who authored the Virginia constitution's Declaration of Rights in 1776. (See Table 2.2 for a list of these first 10 amendments and *A Closer Look: Selective*

#	AMENDMENT
TABLE 2.2: THE BILL OF RIGHTS: A REVIEW*	
1st	Freedom of religion, speech, and press; right to assemble and petition the government
2nd	Right to bear arms
3rd	No quartering of soldiers
4th	No unreasonable searches and seizures
5th	Right to due process; no self-incrimination or double jeopardy
6th	Right to counsel; right to a fair and speedy public trial
7th	Right to trial by jury in civil cases
8th	No excessive bail or cruel and unusual punishment
9th	Protects other rights not in the Constitution
10th	Limits powers of federal government; protects powers reserved to the states

*To read the full text of the Bill of Rights, visit http://www.archives.gov/exhibits/charters/bill_of_rights_transcript.html.

Incorporation and the Second Amendment for when certain provisions became enforceable against state governments.)

In light of this historical backdrop, it might seem strange that the modern construction and application of the Bill of Rights' majestic promises has been a 20th-century phenomenon, and a rather late one at that. Most Americans' perception of the Supreme Court defending fundamental rights against powerful political majorities dates from the Great Depression. Prior to the 1930s, the Court decided only a handful of cases involving claims brought under the Bill of Rights. This volume will demonstrate that as the Court began to assert its authority over the Bill of Rights, aggrieved individuals and institutions redirected their resources toward the legal resolution of problems once thought to be the province of the political branches of government. Seen in this light, law is much more than constitutional foundation. It is an instrument of social and political reform.

Selective incorporation
The process by which the Supreme Court has applied specific provisions of the Bill of Rights to the states.

A Closer Look: Selective Incorporation and the Second Amendment

In *District of Columbia v. Heller* (2008), the Supreme Court, for the first time, ruled that the Second Amendment protected the right of individuals to keep and use firearms. Previously, the Court had only addressed the meaning of the Second Amendment one time, in *United States v. Miller* (1939), holding that it protected only the right of each state to form and maintain a militia. By expanding the meaning of gun ownership from a collective right to an individual right, *Heller* marked a significant departure from *Miller*—and a milestone in American constitutional development.

For such an important decision, *Heller* affected approximately only 632,000 people, the residential population of the District of Columbia. Dick Heller, who contested a D.C. law making it illegal for individuals to own certain firearms, was a police officer who argued that, when off duty, he should be allowed to carry a firearm in self-defense. However, at the time, the Second Amendment applied only to the federal government, and the Court's ruling did not address whether the Second Amendment would apply to the states outside of the federal district of Washington, D.C.

Prior to 1925, it was the entire Bill of Rights that applied only to the federal government. In *Barron v. Baltimore* (1833), the Court ruled that the Fifth Amendment did not protect individuals from state action that devalued their property without providing just compensation. Chief Justice John Marshall concluded that the Bill of Rights "demanded security against the apprehended encroachments of the General Government—not against those of the local governments" (*Barron v. Baltimore*, 1883, p. 250).

The ratification of the Fourteenth Amendment in 1868 changed the relationship between the Bill of Rights and the states. Most scholars now agree that the original purpose of the Fourteenth Amendment was to protect the rights of newly freed slaves from the Southern states that had denied them legal personhood and disenfranchised their small free black populations. The Fourteenth Amendment was widely understood at the time to have been enacted to apply the Bill of Rights to the states—the referenced "privileges and immunities" being shorthand for the Bill of Rights. In the *Slaughterhouse Cases* (1873), however, the Court offered a very different interpretation than Congress intended, effectively holding that the Fourteenth Amendment did not bind the states to honor the Bill of Rights.

(continued)

A Closer Look: Selective Incorporation and the Second Amendment *(continued)*

In 1925, the Court, for the first time, held that a provision of the Bill of Rights applied to the states through the Fourteenth Amendment. In *Gitlow v. New York* (1925), the Court upheld the conviction of a socialist activist who had violated a state sedition law, but also held that the Fourteenth Amendment "incorporated" the Free Speech Clause to the states. Over the next 50 years, the Court gradually applied most of the provisions of the Bill of Rights to the states, a process known as **selective incorporation**. Among the few provisions excluded from the Court's selective incorporation of the Bill of Rights are the Fifth Amendment right to indictment by a grand jury, the Seventh Amendment right to a jury trial in civil cases, and the Eighth Amendment ban on excessive fines.

Until recently, the Second Amendment was on that short list. In *McDonald v. City of Chicago* (2010), the Court ruled that a local ordinance preventing individuals from owning handguns was unconstitutional under the Second Amendment. Wrote Justice Samuel Alito, "We have previously held that most of the provisions of the Bill of Rights apply with full force to both the Federal Government and the States" (*McDonald v. City of Chicago*, 2010, p. 13). *McDonald* marked the first time since 1972 the Court incorporated a provision of the Bill of Rights to the states through the Fourteenth Amendment. In the process, it made the nationalization of the Bill of Rights almost whole.

TABLE 2.3: A HISTORY OF SELECTIVE INCORPORATION

CASE	YEAR	AMENDMENT	PROVISION
Gitlow v. New York	1925	First Amendment	Freedom of speech
Near v. Minnesota	1931	First Amendment	Freedom of press
Powell v. Alabama	1932	Sixth Amendment	Right to counsel in capital cases
DeJonge v. Oregon	1937	First Amendment	Right to assembly
Cantwell v. Connecticut	1940	First Amendment	Free exercise of religion
Everson v. California	1947	First Amendment	Establishment of religion
In re Oliver	1948	Sixth Amendment	Right to a public trial
Cole v. Arkansas	1948	Sixth Amendment	Notice clause
Wolf v. Colorado	1949	Fourth Amendment	Unreasonable search and seizure
Robinson v. California	1962	Eighth Amendment	Cruel and unusual punishment
Gideon v. Wainwright	1963	Sixth Amendment	Right to counsel in felony cases
Malloy v. Hogan	1964	Fifth Amendment	Self-Incrimination Clause
Pointer v. Texas	1965	Sixth Amendment	Right to confront witnesses
Parker v. Gladden	1966	Sixth Amendment	Right to an impartial jury

(continued)

TABLE 2.3: A HISTORY OF SELECTIVE INCORPORATION (CONTINUED)

CASE	YEAR	AMENDMENT	PROVISION
Klopfer v. North Carolina	1967	Sixth Amendment	Right to a speedy trial
Washington v. Texas	1967	Sixth Amendment	Compulsory process clause
Duncan v. Louisiana	1968	Sixth Amendment	Right to jury trial in criminal cases
Argersinger v. Hamlin	1972	Sixth Amendment	Right to counsel in misdemeanor cases
McDonald v. City of Chicago	2010	Second Amendment	Right to bear arms

THE ROLE OF THE U.S. SUPREME COURT IN AMERICAN POLITICS

As observed earlier in the chapter, the Constitution's meaning has often been up for debate, even among the delegates who ratified the document. Thus, it has been left to the nine justices of the U.S. Supreme Court to interpret the Constitution. The specific powers granted to the Court will be discussed in more detail in the next chapter, but for the purposes of this chapter, it is enough to know that interpreting the Constitution is no easy task or inconsequential responsibility. In a single judicial stroke, the Supreme Court can affect people's lives on a national scale and redraw the boundaries within which U.S. political institutions make public policy. Interest groups, government agencies, and powerful private actors understand this, which is why they often turn to the courts to contest legislation or policies unfavorable to them. Litigants before the Supreme Court who have failed to secure redress for their constitutional grievances in the elected branches of government have included corporations and labor unions, slaveholders and abolitionists, abortion rights and pro-life advocates, civil rights groups, state governments, newspapers and public officials, and religious activists and civil libertarians.

The American constitutional arrangement offers multiple points of access to organized interests and individuals seeking to influence the various branches of government. The courts, however—and the judicial process more generally—are supposed to be the neutral and independent branch of government, where legal, not political or social, disputes are resolved. Judges should make decisions in accordance with what a law or constitutional provision means. They should not introduce their biases, personal experience, or other non-legal factors into the decision-making calculus. Judicial appointments should be based on merit, not politics; competence, not ideological leanings; and so on.

Demonstrators like these pro-choice advocates recognize the power of the Supreme Court to interpret the Constitution and affect public policy.

But the fact is that judges are people, not computers, whose constitutional vision is the sum of a constellation of values rooted in their life experiences, their education, their professional socialization, and numerous other factors more difficult to pin down. The process of judicial selection and confirmation is a political one, with the president, who is the figurative leader of a political party, in the position to nominate someone who can extend the interests of the executive branch in the courts. Presidents, however, are not always successful. Sometimes they guess wrong. Other times their nominees are rejected, forcing them to turn to someone less controversial. In truth, judicial appointments represent a mixture of politics and merit.

Whatever the case, one is hard pressed to escape the conclusion that the courts, and the Supreme Court in particular, are an integral part of the American political process. In December 2000, the Court resolved an intense electoral and legal dispute between then-candidates for president, Republican Governor George W. Bush of Texas and Democratic incumbent Vice President Al Gore, who had taken their arguments to court over how ballots should be counted in Florida. That dispute began on election night and wound its way through the Florida and federal courts for six weeks, until a 5–4 majority, in *Bush v. Gore*, ruled in favor of Governor Bush. The Court's action was indeed historic, as it marked the first and, in all likelihood, last time it intervened to resolve an American presidential election. And in 2012, in the spring of another presidential election year, the Court upheld the core of President Barack Obama's health care plan, turning back a constitutional challenge brought by an array of conservative activists who had hoped that a Court consisting of a majority of Republican-appointed justices would strike it down.

Interpreting the Constitution: Legal Formalism

From almost the moment the Constitution was ratified, each subsequent generation of Americans has argued over the document's meaning and application.

The range of opinions, whether of scholars or of Supreme Court justices, on what the clauses and provisions of the Constitution mean, how it divides and allocates power among the branches of government, and the limits it creates on the exercise of government power over individual rights is so wide that one unfamiliar with this debate would be stunned to discover that almost all of its participants claim to speak on behalf of the Framers' intent.

The purpose of the next two sections is to explore the various approaches to and theories of interpreting the Constitution. Because even those who believe that the Constitution means and requires different things agree that the Constitution is the authoritative source of law in the United States, the Court's decisions must have legitimacy. Constitutional theory is often bound together with the process of **judicial review,** or the power of the Supreme Court to review and decide the constitutionality of legislative and executive acts that allegedly violate the Constitution.

Judicial review

The power of the Supreme Court to review and adjudicate the constitutionality of legislative and executive acts.

For constitutional adjudication to have power and resonance, the Court must explain how and why it has reached its decision. Its decisions cannot stand if they are viewed as nothing more than raw exercises in political power. Even if the justices, regardless of their assertions to the contrary, cannot help but infuse their constitutional philosophies with their own policy preferences, those choices must bear some relationship to the more general, abstract principles of the Constitution.

What should judges emphasize in interpreting the Constitution? Some theories suggest that the Court should minimize the role of judicial review and allow legislatures and other democratic institutions wide latitude in their policy choices. Other theories suggest that the Court must remain aware of the prevailing social and political sentiments and interpret the Constitution in light of modern societal norms. Still, two broad and interrelated sets of ideas are pervasive throughout all constitutional theories. The first is that theories of constitutional interpretation often differ about the certainty of the constitutional text's meaning and the appropriate methods for discovering its meaning. The second involves beliefs about the allocation of institutional responsibilities and roles between the courts and the elected branches of government.

Keep in mind as well another important question that pervades the debate over constitutional interpretation as the chapter progresses: Is it possible to separate constitutional theory from the outcomes it produces? How the Court decides, for example, to interpret the power of Congress to regulate interstate commerce will do more than just address an important theoretical question about the separation of powers. It will mean that Congress will have more or less power to regulate the environment or the sale and ownership of handguns. The same is true for the Free Speech Clause of the First Amendment. The Court's decision to interpret free speech rights broadly will, on a much more specific level, affect rights to engage in public protest, rights to use the public schools for religious purposes, and the rights of homeowners to place objectionable signs on their lawns. In sum, the enterprise of constitutional interpretation has real consequences for public institutions and the lives of the most common of citizens. With this background in mind, consider whether it is possible to separate the rules that should govern constitutional interpretation from their real-world consequences.

It is hard to avoid categorizing complex methods to constitutional interpretation, ignoring overlapping ideas in an effort to emphasize differences. Although text, intent, and structure often provide the basic foundation for theories of constitutional interpretation, the emphasis of one factor over another results in a particular approach being labeled as interpretivist or noninterpretivist, literalist or indeterminist, activist or strict constructionist, traditionalist or postmodernist, and so on. Some scholars discount the effort to root constitutional interpretation in legal theories and instead insist that judicial behavior is an expression of ideological and policy-based values. Supreme Court outcomes can and should be understood as reflecting strategic choices justices make to advance these interests.

Categorization, despite its risks and drawbacks, does have certain advantages. Three broad categories have been created that draw the sharpest distinctions among competing approaches to constitutional interpretation: legal formalism, alternatives to formalism, and natural law. On the most general level, the differences among these approaches are greater than their similarities. A clear view of these visible differences will demonstrate the different weight accorded to constitutional text, Framers' intent, and other sources used to support different theories of constitutional interpretation. But also note the differences that exist within a particular school of thought as well as the similarities among what superficially appear to be separate categories.

Legal formalism rests largely on the assumption that the Constitution can be understood as having a specific and true meaning. The sole task of those charged with interpreting the Constitution is to uncover the historical intent of its creators. Judges should not take it upon themselves to decide what the Constitution should mean, but instead uncover the facts and historical intent that informs the Constitution's language. To suggest that the Constitution does not impart clear commands risks putting judges in the position of "creating" and not "discovering" constitutional values. Personal biases must be constrained in favor of a neutral approach to constitutional interpretation. If the Constitution no longer stands apart from politics, then it becomes just another instrument for the advancement of a social and political agenda.

Legal formalism
Theory of interpretation that assumes the Constitution can be understood as having a specific and true meaning.

ORIGINALISM

Perhaps the most stark and dramatic expression of legal formalism is found in the interpretive method called **originalism**. Advocates of originalism (or, as it is also called, **original intent**), argue that the Constitution (and the Bill of Rights) must be interpreted in a manner consistent with those who wrote and ratified it. Originalists claim that judges who favor approaches inconsistent with the intent of the Framers are legislators in disguise, creating and bending the law to suit their own version of the Constitution.

Naturally, originalism, like any theory of constitutional interpretation, has its skeptics. The most obvious question comes first: Who were the "Framers"

Originalism
Theory of interpretation that attempts to discover the original meaning of the Constitution and the intentions of the Framers; also known as *original intent.*

Original intent
See *originalism.*

Although James Madison left behind a number of notes and commentaries, they were not released until after his death and are incomplete. The inability to verify his and other Framers' intent in the drafting of the Constitution presents a problem for originalists.

and how does one know they were of one mind? Few dispute the intellectual force that Thomas Jefferson brought to the constitutional design of American government and his oceanic influence over what later became the First Amendment. But Jefferson was in Paris during the four-year period when the Constitution and the Bill of Rights were written and ratified. Moreover, in correspondence with James Madison, Jefferson, while pleased with the basic constitutional structure of the government, was disturbed at "the omission of a bill of rights," a defect he insisted must be remedied before the Constitution could be complete (as cited in Kammen, 1986, pp. 90–93). John Adams, who succeeded George Washington as president and was another monumental figure in the founding of the Republic, was in London serving the nation as an emissary to Great Britain while Jefferson was in Paris. Should the ideas of these two pivotal figures be dismissed because of their absence during the Constitutional Convention and ratification period? Originalism, despite its promises, provides no clear answer to the larger question of who framed the Constitution and whether consensus existed among those designated as Framers.

Moreover, it is important to remember that the historical materials favored by originalists were also manipulated to serve the partisan political agendas of the Framers and, later, the ratifiers. Those who would rely upon convention records should be "warn[ed] that there are problems with most of them and that some have been compromised—perhaps fatally—by the editorial interventions of hirelings and partisans . . . . To recover original intent from these records may be an impossible . . . assignment" (Hutson, 1986, p. 2). For example, James Madison's notes and commentaries on the Constitutional Convention, although reliable, are incomplete. Madison also did not permit the release of his notes in full form until after his death. Thus the American public did not have Madison's notes on the convention or his other constitutional commentaries until 1840. Problems such as these raise the question of whether an incomplete and sometimes unreliable historical record compromises the originalist enterprise beyond repair.

Second, is originalism a truly "value free" or "neutral" approach to constitutional interpretation, as its advocates suggest? Critics have charged that originalism treats the limits on government power and protections for individual rights created by the Constitution as pre-political and pre-social. In other words, such limits and protections are inalienable rights derived from the Enlightenment and so-called **natural law**, the law that dictated the nature and structure of human interaction before the establishment of formal society or government. Originalists argue that no substantive defense or theoretical justification is necessary to explain the Constitution because the Constitution explains itself. This viewpoint raises two important questions: Is it possible to interpret

Natural law

A body of principles, derived from God, that serve as the basis for human conduct and interaction.

the Constitution without taking into account the social and political context of law and litigation? Is it possible to interpret the admittedly abstract and vague provisions of the Constitution in neutral fashion?

Third, critics of originalism claim that it understates and misreads the Framers' intent. Indeed, the Constitution is quite specific in some parts—no one, for example, can dispute the constitutional requirement that one must be 35 years old to serve as president or that Congress possesses the sole power to establish the "Post Office and post Roads." However, the Constitution is also ill defined, open ended, abstract, and anything but self-evident in its meaning and application. To rely on the words only and to not "go beyond" the text assumes that the constitutional choices are self-evident in the interpretation of the president's powers during times of crisis to arrest or detain "enemy combatants;" criminal due process in light of modern, wholly unmanaged electronic and computerized surveillance and evasion techniques; and the freedom of speech guarantee in an age of instantaneous communication through the Internet. Often, there are just too many versions from too many people who could properly be considered "Framers" to provide a single vision of what some of the more abstract provisions of the Constitution mean.

LITERALISM OR TEXTUALISM

Legal formalism also finds a visible and prominent place in **literalism**, a method that is often called **textualism** as well. Literalism focuses on the plain or ordinary meaning of the text as its source of interpretation. Constitutional literalists, like originalists, argue that the Constitution, as written, settles the need to go beyond the text to understand its meaning. Literalism and originalism also share similarities in their acceptance, but fundamental distrust, of judicial review. Each approach emphasizes the need for courts to defer to the laws created by democratic majorities—especially when the Constitution is silent on a particular question or when dealing with one of its more open-ended clauses. Judges who stray from the text of the Constitution and the intent of the Framers, properly understood, have granted themselves a license to impose their own values through judicial review.

Literalism and originalism share the trait of what some scholars have called legal authoritarianism, or the belief that judicial choices are self-evident, but their similarities end there. It is far more difficult to tie literalism to a specific set of political outcomes than to do so with originalism. Another important difference between the two approaches is the role that each assigns to the Court as to how judicial review should be used to defend the clear and absolute commands of the Constitution. No individual better exemplifies the literalist approach to constitutional interpretation and its differences with originalism than former Supreme Court Justice Hugo L. Black.

Unlike most justices, Justice Black came to the Court almost fully formed in his approach to constitutional interpretation. He believed that courts should not interfere with the right of Congress and the state legislatures to regulate the

Literalism

Theory of interpretation articulating the plain meaning of the text should govern its interpretation; also known as *textualism*.

Textualism

See *literalism*.

nation's economic and business affairs unless these parties had clearly violated a citizen's right to fair treatment in the legal system.

A giant of 20th-century American law and jurisprudence, Justice Black served on the Supreme Court for 34 years (1937–1971), under five chief justices and six U.S. presidents. Prior to his appointment by President Franklin D. Roosevelt, Justice Black represented Alabama in the U.S. Senate, where he developed a justified reputation as one of the staunchest supporters of the New Deal, the name for a series of economic legislation passed by President Roosevelt to combat the economic collapse of the Great Depression.

Justice Black also adhered to a rigid conception of the separation of powers, rejecting even the slightest suggestion that one branch had the power to assume the functions of another. *Youngstown Sheet & Tube Co. v. Sawyer* (1952), which involved President Harry S. Truman's famous effort to seize the nation's steel mills, provided "the setting for the most clear-cut expression" of Justice Black's constitutional literalism outside the context of the Bill of Rights (Yarbrough, 1988, pp. 39–40). President Truman invoked his presidential authority to end a strike at the nation's steel mills and force production to ensure a steady supply of materials to the armed forces at the height of the Korean War. Black's opinion halted President Truman's action. In the following excerpt of the *Youngstown* opinion, note how Justice Black emphasizes the formal construction of the separation of powers:

> In the framework of our Constitution, the President's power to see that the laws are faithfully executed refutes the idea that he is to be a lawmaker. The Constitution limits his functions in the lawmaking process to the recommending of laws he thinks wise and the vetoing of laws he thinks bad. And the Constitution is neither silent nor equivocal about who shall make the laws which the President is to execute. The first section of [Article I] says that "All legislative Powers herein granted shall be vested in a Congress of the United States . . . ." It is said that other Presidents without congressional authority have taken possession of private business enterprises in order to settle labor disputes. But even if this is true, Congress has not thereby lost its exclusive constitutional authority to make laws necessary and proper to carry out the powers vested by the Constitution. (p. 587)

Although literalism and originalism in constitutional interpretation have their differences, each adheres to the fundamental tenets of legal formalism. Constitutional interpretation does not require one to go beyond the Constitution because its clauses and provisions define themselves. To wander in search of legal and theoretical sources "outside" the Constitution is to risk the imposition of value judgments that compromise the authority and integrity of its majestic commands. This discussion of originalism and literalism has questioned whether either approach provides a sufficient baseline from which to interpret the Constitution. But what are the alternatives, and are they any better?

INTERPRETING THE CONSTITUTION: ALTERNATIVES TO FORMALISM AND NATURAL LAW

Formalism dominated the Court's approach to constitutional interpretation from the Founding period until the early part of the 20th century, when the first serious challenge to this long-held consensus in American law and jurisprudence emerged. Parallel to the larger "progressive" movement underfoot in American politics, many scholars, jurists, and social scientists began to question the legal foundation upon which the current economic, social, and political arrangements rested.

LEGAL REALISM

In contrast to legal formalism, **legal realism** argued that law was the creation of a political process, one in which ever-changing social and economic forces competed for the control of the public interest. Existing law reflected the triumph of private interests that used the legislative process to assert their place in the social and political order, not "discoveries" of the Framers' intent or rights self-evident in the "natural" law. Legal realists believed that law developed as a result of structured social order and government; it did not reflect some natural state of affairs, and thus could not have a meaning independent of the environment in which it was created.

Legal realism

Argument that law was the creation of a political process, one in which ever-changing social and economic forces competed for the control of the public interest.

Legal realists questioned several orthodox assumptions about the organization and distribution of social, economic, and political power in American society. They argued that law not only created the status quo but also could and should be used to change it. Front and center in the legal realist movement were two of the most eminent figures in the history of American law, Oliver Wendell Holmes Jr. and Louis D. Brandeis. Their association with legal realism added luster to its strength as a counterpoint to formalism. Although scholars generally consider Holmes (1902–1932) and Brandeis (1916–1939) among the greatest justices to serve on the Supreme Court, each had left an indelible mark on American constitutional development before entering what, for each man, was the final stage of his career. In 1881, Holmes, while still in private practice, published *The Common Law*, which rejected the natural law tradition. Holmes argued in the clearest and most comprehensive terms to date that law reflected the deliberate choices made by people in response to perceived social and economic needs. Holmes's central thesis, that law embodied policy preferences and that such preferences should be allowed to stand in absence of a clear constitutional mistake by the legislature, had little influence on the Court but reverberated throughout some of the nation's most elite law schools. Holmes's often-quoted lesson that "[t]he life of the law has not been logic: it has been

Before he joined the Supreme Court, Oliver Wendell Holmes offered one of the clearest arguments on behalf of legal realism.

Library of Congress Prints and Photographs Division

experience" best summarizes his view of the law (as cited in Howe, 1963, p. 5).

Unlike Holmes, who believed that legislatures should be permitted to experiment free from judicial supervision as part of the democratic nature of American politics, Brandeis believed that judges should evaluate the reasonableness of legislation by assessing the "facts" that formed the basis of legislation. These facts, he believed, should preface legislative purpose and courts should weigh the impact that laws would have on social betterment. Brandeis also advocated a jurisprudence that enabled judges to differentiate between reform-minded legislation and laws that simply reflected the struggles between powerful private interests. Brandeis's experience in pushing public interest legislation through state legislatures had "taught him that what appeared to be a reasonable piece of legislation might be no more than a giveaway to vested interests" (as cited in Strum, 1984, p. 337). Although Holmes offered the first comprehensive argument for legal realism, Brandeis introduced "sociological jurisprudence" to American law. Holmes recognized law's dynamic qualities and insisted that they should be allowed to flourish independent of a mythical attachment to a natural order. But Brandeis believed that legislatures and courts should use their knowledge of modern social science to improve the world, an approach he first brought to the Court's attention with stunning success in *Muller v. Oregon* (1908).

Muller involved a challenge to a state law that restricted the number of hours women could work in commercial laundries. Brandeis submitted a brief of about 100 pages, only two of which dealt with questions of law. The rest consisted of evidence collected from around the country on the public health consequences for women who worked longer than 10 hours per day in such demanding conditions and their families. So impressed was the Court that it directly referred to the "very copious" body of information Brandeis provided as the basis for its decision (p. 419). The **Brandeis Brief** became a model for subsequent generations of reform-minded lawyers attacking a wide range of established government practices, from racial discrimination to public education expenditures. (Read the Brandeis Brief in its entirety here: http://www.law .louisville.edu/library/collections/brandeis/node/235).

Holmes and Brandeis are often grouped as twins in discussions of legal realism's place in American law, but other than their mutual disdain for formalism and natural law, they held very different conceptions of the law's potential to transform the conditions of American life. Holmes's skepticism of law as the protector of "natural" truths underpinned his views. Brandeis, on the other hand, believed that law and litigation could be positive forces in altering the balance of social and economic power between worker and owner, dissident and majority, and rich and poor.

Brandeis Brief

A type of appellate brief that uses empirical evidence to support legal arguments, first used by Louis D. Brandeis as an attorney in *Muller v. Oregon* (1908).

NEUTRAL PRINCIPLES

Legal realism came to dominate the Court's jurisprudence immediately after the justices embraced President Roosevelt's New Deal reforms in March 1937. Predictably, though, legal realism, like all new and bold ideas, soon came in for harsh criticism. Even constitutional theorists who acknowledged that the Court makes social and political value choices when it interprets the Constitution suggested that a more principled, less political justification was required to defend the Court's decisions. Accordingly, in the first major challenge to legal realism in the post-New Deal era, Herbert Wechsler, a prominent Harvard law professor, argued that the Court must make its decisions based on **neutral principles of law**, not on contextual or policy-based considerations.

Neutral principles of law Phrase coined by Herbert Wechsler articulating that judges should ground decisions within the law and not upon personal preference.

Wechsler's conception of neutral principles differed from the formalist model in a few crucial ways. First, Wechsler did not contest that the Constitution authorized judicial review. Second, he did not dispute the legal realists' central contention that constitutional interpretation and judicial review required the Court to make value choices. But Wechsler argued that constitutional interpretation should not be rooted in a contextual, case-specific examination of a particular set of facts. Instead, constitutional interpretation should be a neutral principle of law that applied equally to all parties. To illustrate his point, Wechsler argued that the Court's rationale was biased in the historic *Brown v. Board of Education* (1954) decision, which declared state-sponsored segregation in public schools unconstitutional. The National Association for the Advancement of Colored People (NAACP), which represented the African-American families in *Brown*, not only argued that mandated school segregation fostered unequal educational opportunities for blacks, created a racial stigma, and lessened their future economic opportunities but also introduced social science data to support these arguments.

The Court ruled that school segregation violated the Fourteenth Amendment's guarantee of equal protection under the law (the Equal Protection Clause), but Wechsler argued that the Court should have ruled that school segregation violated African Americans' freedom-of-association rights to attend the schools of their choice. Wechsler believed the Court had interpreted the Fourteenth Amendment to favor African Americans based on their disadvantaged position in public education, a decision that amounted to a partisan choice. Freedom of association was a "race neutral" principle applicable in such cases that avoided the "sociological jurisprudence" of the actual *Brown* decision. Wechsler commented that segregation laws penalized whites and African Americans to an equal degree because members of both races were denied the lawful opportunity to free association based on race.

Putting aside for the moment the unusual notion that racial segregation harmed whites and African Americans to an equal degree, are neutral principles really possible in American constitutional law? In some ways, Wechsler could not have picked a worse case to use as the basis for his neutral-principles argument. Segregation was a condition created by a political system steeped in racial prejudice, one that excluded African Americans from meaningful participation and representation until the mid-1960s. It was not a condition of nature. Segregation was precisely the sort of problem pointed out by the legal realists.

Still, Wechsler's effort to offer an alternative to legal realism was an important contribution to constitutional theory. The idea of neutral principles attempted to reconcile the consequences and subsequent changes brought about by the Court's decision to embrace the New Deal with the legal realists. The position of legal formalists, at the time, was that the Constitution should have a meaning independent of what the justices think it should mean at a given point in time. The same concerns that motivated Wechsler were also evident in the subsequent contribution of another exceptionally influential theorist, John Hart Ely. Ely, in *Democracy and Distrust* (1981), argued that courts should refrain from using their power to create rights through the "open textured" clauses of the Constitution, which he claimed they had done in the post-New Deal era. Instead, the Court should limit judicial review to laws that prevented the political process from functioning in a fair and open manner. Ely agreed with critics of legal formalism that a "clause-bound" approach to constitutional interpretation was impossible, but he was also suspicious of grandiose legal theories that granted excessive power to the courts to "discover" the Constitution's fundamental values.

Ely laid out three specific instances when the courts should strike down laws: (1) when laws violated specific substantive constitutional guarantees (e.g., free speech, criminal due-process protections); (2) when laws operated to disadvantage "discrete and insular" minorities in the political process (e.g., voting rights, political participation); and (3) when laws created procedural obstacles that erected unreasonable barriers to political and social reform through the political process. Courts should defer to the political process in disputes involving the open-ended provisions of the Constitution. Ely believed that such cases presented dangerous vehicles for the courts to impose their value choices on the general population, a practice he believed had no defense in constitutional theory.

NATURAL LAW

This discussion thus far leaves the reader with two certainties. First, the Constitution creates certain rights and freedoms that deserve protection from the exercise of "naked" majoritarian preferences. That is, majorities must have solid grounds for treating certain individuals or groups within society differently, other than for reasons of raw political power. Today, it is difficult to understand a so-called "rational basis" for practices such as slavery, Jim Crow, sex-based discrimination, zoning restrictions designed to disadvantage unpopular religious movements, or the exploitation of child labor. These practices have come to be associated with prejudice and greed, not public value. Conservatives and liberals, legal formalists and their critics, and constitutional theorists who see the Constitution and the legal culture in very different terms agree in far more cases than not that laws must, at minimum, further some rational public objective. Indeed, much of the intricate design of the Constitution is premised on the rationale that the governmental branches possess the power to veto public policies that do not serve interests beyond those of powerful, self-interested majorities. Second, and obvious by now, is that constitutional scholars cannot agree on what the Constitution means; how to enforce its substantive and procedural provisions; and who, or which branch of government, should possess the preeminent power to undertake these responsibilities.

Do certainties, then, exist in constitutional interpretation and the exercise of judicial power? If one accepts the premises of natural law and natural rights theorists, that certain rights exist independent of those established by artificial legal

While the idea of natural law can be appealing, it has also been invoked to rationalize discrimination and exploitation.

rules, then the answer is yes. Natural law theories presuppose certain unalienable truths about individuals and the rights they retain when they enter civil and political society. If the phrase "unalienable truths" sounds familiar, it should. Thomas Jefferson alluded to the natural rights tradition in the Declaration of Independence, writing that "the Laws of Nature and of Nature's God" endowed men with "certain unalienable rights," among which were "Life, Liberty and the Pursuit of Happiness." American independence owes much of its intellectual justification to the decision of the revolution's leaders "to go outside the forms and norms of English law" and claim their rights on the basis of natural law. On an abstract level, natural law has great appeal, for it posits that universal truths, absolute in their moral goodness, exist outside the relativist framework of positive law, or the legal rules that society chooses to create.

However, one must be careful when invoking natural law principles in defense of the Supreme Court's opinions. Natural law principles were prominent in three of the Court's less luminous 19th-century opinions. In all three cases, the Court rejected individual rights claims on grounds now thoroughly discredited in modern constitutional law:

- *Dred Scott v. Sandford* (1857), in which the Court ruled that African Americans were bound by the laws of nature to their status as property
- *Bradwell v. Illinois* (1872), where the Court held that state law could bar women from becoming lawyers on the grounds that

> the civil law, as well as nature herself, has always recognized a wide difference in the respective spheres and destinies of man and woman . . . . The paramount destiny and mission of women are to fulfill the noble and benign offices of wife and mother [because] this is the law of the Creator. (p. 141)

Everett Historical / Shutterstock.com

TABLE 2.4: THEORIES OF CONSTITUTIONAL INTERPRETATION		
THEORY	**DEFINITION**	**EXAMPLE**
legal realism	Constitutional interpretation is not bound by either historical intent or the literal meaning of the words. Law evolves as the social, economic, and political preferences of society change. Judges should respect these changes and allow the law to change as society changes.	Oliver Wendell Holmes summarized legal realism best: "the life of the law has not been logic; it has been experience" (as cited in Howe, 1963, p. 5). Equal rights for racial minorities, women, and gays should not depend on what the Framers intended or the literal meaning of the words in the Constitution. The law should reflect the evolution in social norms that no longer considers prejudice a value that deserves legal support.
literalism/ textualism	The Constitution (and all law) means what the words say. Historical intent or context is not relevant. The plain meaning of text should govern interpretation.	The First Amendment says that "Congress shall make no law . . . abridging the freedom of speech," so that means that judges must strike down any legal restriction on free speech, regardless of any government interest to the contrary. This prevents judges from advancing their own preferences and biases through constitutional interpretation.
originalism	The Constitution means what the Framers intended, and judges are bound to the original meaning of the law. A judge is responsible for "discovering" the intent of a particular phrase or clause and applying to the facts.	The right of citizens to own firearms and use them to hunt and defend their property was something the Framers considered fundamental. Thus, the Second Amendment should be understood to prevent government from enacting laws that restrict or prohibit the use of firearms for legal purposes.
neutral principles	A legal rule should apply equally to all parties and not reflect the personal ideologies or policy preferences of judges or non-legal considerations (e.g., social science data or public opinion).	The language of the Fourteenth Amendment states that "no state shall deny to any person . . . the equal protection of the laws." This means that affirmative action programs are inherently unconstitutional because they permit colleges and employers to consider race, ethnic origin, and sex when making decisions.

- *Plessy v. Ferguson* (1896), in which the Court upheld state-enforced racial segregation as a legitimate exercise of "the established usages, customs, and traditions of the people" (p. 552)

In modern times, natural law principles have been used to defend and attack abortion rights, affirmative action, conscientious-objector status, capital punishment, the minimum wage, gun control, gay rights, and the rights of terminally ill or comatose patients. This ambiguity leads one to ask what should be an obvious question: If natural law recognizes the existence of universal rights that can be derived from moral absolutes, why have legal scholars, philosophers, theologians, and constitutional scholars been unable to agree on what those universal rights are? One reason is that almost no one agrees on the sources of natural rights. Do natural rights have a divine origin as Jefferson's rhetoric in the Declaration of Independence suggests? Are they derived from the ancient Greek philosophers? If so, how were the Greeks able to distinguish natural rights—rights inherent in citizenship—from positive rights—rights created through deliberation and action by a political community? Another reason for the lack of agreement is that, although the constitutional founders were certainly influenced by natural rights theories, there is no indication that the founders intended a place for such theories in the Constitution.

IN SEARCH OF CONSTITUTIONAL MEANING

Do not be disappointed that this chapter ends without a clear answer to the question posed at the outset: How should Americans interpret the Constitution? The different approaches discussed here all have their intellectual roots in the law-based theories of how the courts—and the other branches of government as well—should approach constitutional interpretation. It makes little sense to dispute the notion that social and political factors—including the personal attitudes and political preferences of the justices—influence constitutional law and litigation, whether from the vantage point of the justices, elected officials, or aggrieved individuals in search of their rights and liberties. However, thinking about the Constitution in law-based terms is important. The purpose of this chapter has been twofold: to provide students the tools to understand the sources of the justices' approaches to constitutional interpretation and to encourage students to develop a theoretical rationale of their own to assist in the explanation and defense of the constitutional choices they will make. As the text moves forward, keep in mind the following questions: Does any singular, universal theory of constitutional interpretation best capture the spirit and intent of the Constitution? Is it possible to create an approach to constitutional interpretation independent of the substantive values that one believes the Constitution protects?

SUMMARY

- The Constitution establishes the legal foundation of the American political system. The powers of each branch of government are authorized by different articles of the Constitution.
- Constitutional law serves as the "connective tissue" that establishes the relationship among the branches of the national government, the national and state governments, and the rights of individuals.
- The four major components of the American political system established by the Constitution are national government, separation of powers, federalism, and individual rights.
- The American system of separation of powers is not a "pure" separation of powers. Although the officeholders in each branch are separate and distinct, their functions overlap. This overlapping of functions forms an elaborate system of checks and balances, allowing each branch to check the encroachments of the other. In this way, the separation of powers is actually maintained.
- The Bill of Rights was ratified in 1791, two years after the Constitution had received the approval of the states. Alexander Hamilton, a key force behind the ratification of the Constitution, originally argued against a Bill of Rights. James Madison and Thomas Jefferson were firm proponents of a Bill of Rights, arguing that it was necessary to contribute to the public education of the people and place a written limit on what government was allowed to do.
- The Supreme Court is primarily, but not exclusively, responsible for interpreting the meaning of the Constitution. Although each branch is expected to enact or enforce the law in a manner that is consistent with how the Court has interpreted the Constitution, conflicts inevitably arise that require the Court to settle these disputes by engaging in judicial review.
- Judicial review, which is defined as the power of the courts to review acts of Congress, the executive branch, and state and local governments whose actions have infringed upon the power of government or the rights of individuals under the federal Constitution, is intended to preserve the rule of law over the power of political majorities.
- From almost the moment the Constitution and the Bill of Rights were ratified, there have been strong disagreements over how they should be interpreted. Some advocates argue that judges are bound by what the Framers of the Constitution meant when they wrote and ratified its various provisions, whether in 1789, 1868, or 1870. Others argue that judges should be bound by the literal meaning of the words, regardless of what they think the original authors might have intended. Still others believe that the Constitution should be interpreted according

to evolving societal standards and the changes that come with a more diverse and plural nation.

- Constitutional interpretation is often tied to political outcomes. Advocates of constitutional formalism are often supportive of conservative political philosophies. Supporters of legal realism and other "progressive" approaches to constitutional interpretation often advocate liberal approaches to social and political issues.

- Whatever theory of constitutional interpretation a judge (or any individual) finds persuasive, that person must be able to offer an explanation of judicial power that is consistent with the principles and foundation of American government.

REVIEW QUESTIONS

1. How does the Constitution establish the legal foundation for the American political system?

2. What is the constitutional source of power for the Supreme Court?

3. What relationship do *The Federalist Papers* have to the Constitution?

4. What is judicial review, and what relationship does it have to constitutional interpretation?

5. What are some of the strengths and weaknesses of the various theories of constitutional interpretation discussed in this chapter? What are some of the major differences?

6. Are the justices capable of remaining "neutral" when it comes to deciding cases, or are their respective opinions the result of their own personal ideologies and policy preferences?

READINGS AND RESOURCES

LEGAL INFORMATION INSTITUTE

http://law.cornell.edu

The Legal Information Institute provides full and free access to all orders and opinions handed down by the United States Supreme Court. The site also offers materials that help people understand the law and new research technologies that make it easier for people to find legal information.

THE OYEZ PROJECT

http://www.oyez.org

The Oyez Project is a multimedia archive devoted to the Supreme Court of the United States and its work. It aims to be a complete and authoritative source for all audio recorded in the Court since the installation of a recording system in October 1955. The project also provides authoritative information on all justices and offers a virtual reality version of the Supreme Court building, including the chambers of some of the justices.

U.S. ARCHIVES: THE U.S. CONSTITUTION

http://www.archives.gov/exhibits/charters/constitution.html

Access the full transcript of the Constitution and its amendments and learn more relevant facts and history at this online exhibit.

THE FEDERALIST PAPERS

http://thomas.loc.gov/home/histdox/fedpapers.html
Read *The Federalist Papers* at the Library of Congress's THOMAS site.

THE BRANDEIS BRIEF

http://www.law.louisville.edu/library/collections/brandeis/node/235
Read Louis D. Brandeis's famous brief from *Muller v. Oregon* (1908), the Brandeis Brief, courtesy of the Louis D. Brandeis School of Law at the University of Louisville.

EXPLORING CONSTITUTIONAL CONFLICTS

http://law2.umkc.edu/faculty/projects/ftrials/conlaw/home.html
University of Missouri, Kansas City professor Doug Linder has compiled a number of resources and information relevant to topics discussed throughout this text.

FIFTEEN CURIOUS FACTS ABOUT THE FEDERALIST PAPERS

http://digitalcommons.law.uga.edu/fac_pm/2/
Learn more about the influential *Federalist Papers* by downloading this factsheet by Dan T. Coenen, University of Georgia School of Law.

YOUR BILL OF RIGHTS

http://www.time.com/time/specials/packages/0,28757,2080345,00.html
TIME Magazine features a series of videos examining the importance of Amendments 1–10 in everyday life.

IS THERE A CONSTITUTION IN THIS TEXT?

http://opinionator.blogs.nytimes.com/2012/10/08/is-there-a-constitution-in-this-text/
New York Times columnist and law professor Stanley Fish examines the implications of a literalist approach.

COURTS: THE SYSTEM

BY ROBERT ABERLE

Chapter
3

CHAPTER OVERVIEW

© Gary Blakeley, 2011. Used under license from Shutterstock, Inc.

There are two distinct court systems in the United States, the federal system and the courts of the individual states. Within this dual system, are also two primary divisions which consist of our civil courts and our criminal courts. This chapter focuses on the criminal court systems and the distinctions between them. In order to appreciate the court system in this country, you must first understand the concept of jurisdiction and be familiar with the various types of jurisdiction that individual courts may have.

The federal courts are comprised of a three tiered system with the district courts acting as the trial court, the U.S. Circuit Courts of Appeal are the intermediary appellate courts, and the U.S. Supreme Court is the highest court in the United States. The state court systems are diverse in their structure and consist of either two or three tiered systems, depending on the individual state.

*C*HAPTER LEARNING OBJECTIVES

After reading this chapter you will be able to:

1. Describe the difference between civil courts and criminal courts.
2. Understand the concept of jurisdiction as it applies to the courts.
3. Distinguish between the different types of judicial jurisdiction.
4. Explain the basic structure of the federal court system.
5. Compare the differences between the federal court system and that of the various states.
6. Describe how the United States Supreme Court selects the cases that it decides to hear.

--------------------- KEYWORDS ---------------------

Dual Court System

United States Supreme Court

Original Jurisdiction

General Jurisdiction

Federal Court System

Federal Circuit Courts of Appeal

John G. Roberts, Jr.

Writ of certiorari

Trial Courts

Preponderance of the Evidence

Jurisdiction

Limited Jurisdiction

Appellate Jurisdiction

Federal District Courts

U.S. Supreme Court

Rule of Four

State Courts

Appellate Courts

*D*EVELOPMENT OF THE AMERICAN COURT SYSTEM

Dual Court System

The United States of America has a dual court system which is comprised of the federal court system and the courts of the individual states.

The United States of America has a **dual court system** which is comprised of the federal court system and the courts of the individual states. Courts are established by statute or constitution and have the authority to make decisions on cases, controversies in law, and disputed matters of fact that are brought before it.[1]

Courts have been a part of America since settlers began coming here in the 1600s. By the time the United States became a country in 1776, each of the colonies had established their own court system. Today, all fifty states have their own court systems that operate independently and are established by the constitution and the statutes of the individual states. The federal court system was established by Article III, Section 1 of the United States Constitution which specifically set up the U.S. Supreme Court and gave congress the authority to set up and establish lower courts when it deemed necessary.

CIVIL AND CRIMINAL COURTS

The court system in the United States is divided into two primary divisions which are the civil system and the criminal system. Civil courts handle legal disputes between private parties, whether they are a person or a company or corporation. When a person brings a civil lawsuit, they are usually seeking a monetary award to reimburse actual damages inflicted (compensatory damages) or a monetary award to punish the one who was at fault for damages (punitive damages).

© Tomislav Forgo, 2011. Used under license from Shutterstock, Inc.

A person may also seek an injunction against the opposing party. An injunction is a court order that commands a person to a specific act, or to refrain from doing an act that would injure another by violating their personal or property rights. There are two ways to bring a case into civil court, which are a tort action or a breach of contract. A tort is a civil wrong that amounts to a breach of duty to an individual that results in damages to them.

In civil cases, the party that brings the suit is called the plaintiff and the party that is defending the action against them is the defendant. The level of evidence used to determine the outcome of a civil case is called the **preponderance of the evidence**. A preponderance of the evidence is much less stringent than the level of proof needed in a criminal case, which is proof beyond a reasonable doubt. In a civil case, the winner is determined by which party has the most impressive or convincing evidence.

Preponderance of the Evidence

This is the level of evidence used to determine the outcome of a civil case. The winner of a civil case is determined by which party has the most impressive or convincing evidence.

Criminal cases are brought forward by the government who is charging an individual with a criminal offense. The government is represented by a prosecutor who may be a District Attorney, an Attorney General, a Solicitor, a city or county attorney, or other government prosecutor depending on the jurisdiction of the case. The person who is charged with the crime is called the defendant, and as previously mentioned, in order to find a defendant guilty of a crime the government must prove its case beyond a reasonable doubt. This level of evidence is the highest standard of evidence that we have in this country.

© zimmytws, 2011. Used under license from Shutterstock, Inc.

*J*URISDICTION

Jurisdiction is the territory, subject matter, or persons over which a court has legal authority to hear and decide a certain type of case. State courts have jurisdiction over crimes committed within their geographic area. This is also often referred to as venue, which is the geographic area over which a court has territorial jurisdiction to decide cases. On the state level, a crime must be tried in the county in which it was committed. Federal courts have jurisdiction over federal laws.[2]

ORIGINAL JURISDICTION

Original jurisdiction is the authority of a court to hear and decide a lawsuit or criminal case that arises within a specific geographic area or territory.

LIMITED JURISDICTION

Courts of limited jurisdiction have original jurisdiction only over specific subject matter that is given to it by law. These are usually specialty courts and courts that hear and decide misdemeanor and ordinance type cases. Civil cases heard in these courts are usually limited to small claims. Municipal courts, justice courts, magistrate courts, traffic courts, and probate courts are all examples of courts of limited jurisdiction. Municipal courts, for example, are courts of limited jurisdiction because their original jurisdiction is restricted to city ordinances and violations of city laws. Traffic courts are limited to hearing traffic issues, probate courts hear issues that only deal with probate, and so on.

THE DIFFERENCES BETWEEN FEDERAL AND STATE COURTS	
STRUCTURE	
THE FEDERAL COURT SYSTEM	THE STATE COURT SYSTEM
■ Article III of the Constitution invests the judicial power of the United States in the federal court system. Article III, Section 1 specifically creates the U.S. Supreme Court and gives Congress the authority to create the lower federal courts.	■ The Constitution and laws of each state establish the state courts. A court of last resort, often known as a supreme court, is usually the highest court in a state. Some states also have an intermediate court of appeals. Below these appeals courts are the state trial courts. Some are referred to as circuit or district courts.

Continued

■ Congress has used this power to establish the 13 U.S. courts of appeals, the 94 U.S. district courts, the U.S. Court of Claims, and the U.S. Court of International Trade. U.S. bankruptcy courts handle bankruptcy cases. Magistrate judges handle some district court matters.	■ States also usually have courts that handle specific legal matters; e.g., probate court (wills and estates), juvenile court, family court, etc.
■ Parties dissatisfied with a decision of a U.S. district court, the U.S. Court of Claims, and/ or the U.S. Court of International Trade may appeal to a U.S. court of appeals.	■ Parties dissatisfied with the decision of the trial court may take their cases to the intermediate court of appeals.
■ A party may ask the U.S. Supreme Court to review a decision of the U.S. Court of Appeals, but the Supreme Court usually is under no obligation to do so. The U.S. Supreme Court is the final arbiter of federal constitutional questions.	■ Parties have the option to ask the highest state court to hear the case.
	■ Only certain state court cases are eligible for review by the U.S. Supreme Court.

GENERAL JURISDICTION

Courts of general jurisdiction have original jurisdiction over all subject matter that is not specifically assigned to a court of limited jurisdiction. These are typically the trial courts for felonies and the courts that hear and decide civil lawsuits. Courts of general jurisdiction will often also hear appeals from courts of limited jurisdiction. District courts, superior courts, and circuit courts are examples of courts with general jurisdiction.[3]

APPELLATE JURISDICTION

Courts with appellate jurisdictions can hear appeals from lower courts and review the judgments of those courts. Appeals are not trials, they are a review of the court transcripts, evidence, and legal briefs of the attorneys from both sides.

THE DIFFERENCES BETWEEN FEDERAL AND STATE COURTS—CONTINUED	
SELECTION OF JUDGES	
THE FEDERAL COURT SYSTEM	THE STATE COURT SYSTEM
(Article III, Section 1 of the Constitution) Federal judges are nominated by the President and confirmed by the Senate. They hold office during good behavior, typically, for life. Through congressional impeachment proceedings, federal judges may be removed from office for misbehavior.	**State court judges are selected in a variety of ways, including:** ■ election, ■ appointment for a given number of years, ■ appointment for life, and ■ combinations of these methods; e.g., appointment followed by election.
TYPES OF CASES HEARD	
THE FEDERAL COURT SYSTEM	THE STATE COURT SYSTEM
■ Cases that deal with the constitutionality of a law, ■ Cases involving the laws and treaties of the U.S., ■ Cases involving ambassadors and public ministers, ■ Disputes between two or more states, ■ Admiralty law, ■ Bankruptcy, and ■ Habeas corpus issues.	■ Most criminal cases ■ Probate (involving wills and estates) ■ Most contract cases ■ Tort cases (personal injuries) ■ Family law (marriages, divorces, adoptions, etc.) State courts are the final deciders of state laws and constitutions. Their interpretations of federal law or the U.S. Constitution may be appealed to the U.S. Supreme Court. The Supreme Court may choose to hear or not to hear such cases.

Source: Administrative Office of the U.S. Courts, at: http://www.uscourts.gov/FederalCourts/UnderstandingtheFederal Courts/Jurisdiction/DifferencebetweenFederalAndStateCourts.aspx.

*F*EDERAL COURT SYSTEM

Federal Court System

The federal court system is a three tiered system that was originally set up by Article III of the U.S. Constitution.

The **federal court system**, as we have seen, was originally set up by the U.S. Constitution. The federal court system is a three tiered system, which means that it has intermediate appellate courts between the trial courts and the Supreme Court. Federal courts hear cases involving:

1. The constitutionality of law
2. Laws and treaties of the United States
3. Ambassadors and public ministers
4. Disputes between two or more states
5. Admiralty law
6. Bankruptcy cases

The three tiers of the federal court system are:

1. District Courts
2. Federal Circuit Courts of Appeals
3. United States Supreme Court

THE UNITED STATES FEDERAL COURTS
SUPREME COURT
—United States Supreme Court
APPELLATE COURTS
—U.S. Court of Appeals ■ 12 Regional Circuit Courts of Appeals ■ 1 U.S. Court of Appeals for the Federal Circuit
TRIAL COURTS
—U.S. District Courts ■ 94 judicial districts ■ U.S. Bankruptcy Court —U.S. Court of International Trade —U.S. Court of Federal Claims
FEDERAL COURTS AND OTHER ENTITIES OUTSIDE THE JUDICIAL BRANCH
—Military Courts (trial and appellate) —Court of Veterans Appeals —U.S. Tax Court —Federal administrative agencies and boards

Source: http://www.uscourts.gov/FederalCourts/UnderstandingtheFederalCourts/FederalCourtsStructure.aspx

DISTRICT COURTS

Federal district courts are the trial courts of the federal government. The district courts have jurisdiction over almost every category of federal cases, including both criminal and civil cases. There are currently ninety-four federal judicial districts, which includes at least one district for every state, plus one district in each of the following: the District of Columbia, Puerto Rico, the Virgin Islands, Guam, and the Northern Mariana Islands. The federal district courts also include the U.S. Bankruptcy Courts. The U.S. Court of International Trade and the U.S. Court of Federal Claims are separate from the district courts, but are considered on the same judicial level.

Federal District Courts
Federal district courts are the trial courts of the federal government.

There were 99,835 criminal cases brought into U.S. District Courts in 2008, of which 89 percent were for felonies.[4] Most of these defendants (90 percent) were convicted and 78 percent of those were sentenced to a term of incarceration in federal prison. The average prison sentence in 2008 was sixty-one months, with the longest sentences given to those who were convicted of violent crimes (111 months), felony weapons charges (eighty-eight months), and felony drug charges (eighty-five months).[5]

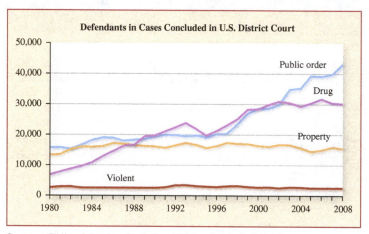

Source: Federal Justice Statistics, 2008—Statistical Tables.

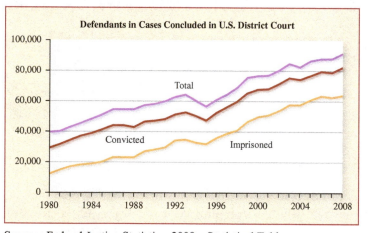

Source: Federal Justice Statistics, 2008—Statistical Tables.

Federal Circuit Courts of Appeals

The Federal Circuit Courts of Appeals consists of the ninety-four United States judicial districts which are organized into twelve regional circuits (plus the Federal Circuit), each of which has a United States court of appeals.

FEDERAL CIRCUIT COURTS OF APPEALS

The **Federal Circuit Courts of Appeals** consists of the ninety-four United States judicial districts which are organized into twelve regional circuits, each of which has a United States court of appeals. There is also one U.S. Court of Appeals for the Federal Circuit that has nationwide appellate jurisdiction to hear appeals in specialized cases such as those involving patent laws. These appellate courts hear appeals from the district courts within their circuit, as well as appeals of decisions from federal administrative agencies.

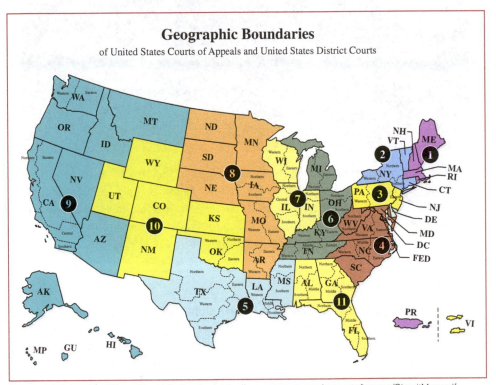

Geographic Boundaries
of United States Courts of Appeals and United States District Courts

Source: Administrative Office of the U.S. Courts at: http://www.uscourts.gov/uscourts/images/CircuitMap.pdf

THE UNITED STATES SUPREME COURT

The **United States Supreme Court** is the highest court in the federal Judiciary and in the United States. The Supreme Court consists of the Chief Justice of the United States and eight associate justices. Supreme Court justices are appointed by the president and confirmed by the U.S. Senate, and once confirmed they serve for life. The current Chief Justice of the U.S. Supreme Court is **John G. Roberts, Jr**.

While the Supreme Court has original trial jurisdiction in some very specific and limited circumstances, the primary purpose of the Court is judicial

John G. Roberts, Jr.

United States Supreme Court

The United States Supreme Court is the highest court in the federal Judiciary and in the United States.

John G. Roberts Jr.

The current Chief Justice of the United states Supreme Court.

© Associated Press

Top: Sonia Sotomayor, *Associate Justice,* Stephen G. Breyer, *Associate Justice,* Samuel Anthony Alito, Jr., *Associate Justice,* Elena Kagan, *Associate Justice.* **Bottom:** Clarence Thomas, *Associate Justice,* Antonin Scalia, *Associate Justice,* John G. Roberts, Jr., *Chief Justice of the United States,* Anthony M. Kennedy, *Associate Justice,* Ruth Bader Ginsburg, *Associate Justice.*

review of lower court decisions. It is here that the Court determines if lower court decisions, as well as laws and statutes, comply with the intent of the United States Constitution. The Court is the final interpreter of the U.S. Constitution.

Only about 5,000 cases per year qualify to be heard by the Supreme Court. These cases are reviewed and the Court selects about 150 of these cases that it will hear and rule on. The Court has complete control over what cases it will accept for review. In order for a case to be accepted for review, at least four of the Justices must agree to hear the case. This is called the "**rule of four**." Once the case is accepted for review, the Court issues a ***writ of certiorari***, which is a court order that is issued to the lower court telling them to send up the record of the proceedings of the case.

Rule of Four

In order for a case to be accepted for review, at least four of the Justices must agree to hear the case.

Writ of Certiorari

A *writ of certiorari* is a court order that is issued by an appeals court to a lower court telling them to send up the record of the proceedings of the case.

S TATE COURT SYSTEM

Each of the fifty states has its own court system. Some of these systems are similar to the structure of the federal system, in that they have a three tier system that utilizes an intermediate appellate court. Other states, those with less population, use a two tier system and eliminate the intermediate appellate court. In these states, appeals from the trial court go directly to the highest court in the state.

In 2006, over 102.4 million cases were filed in the state court systems within the United States. The majority of these cases (54 percent) were traffic cases. The remaining cases included civil cases, domestic relations, criminal, and juvenile cases.[6]

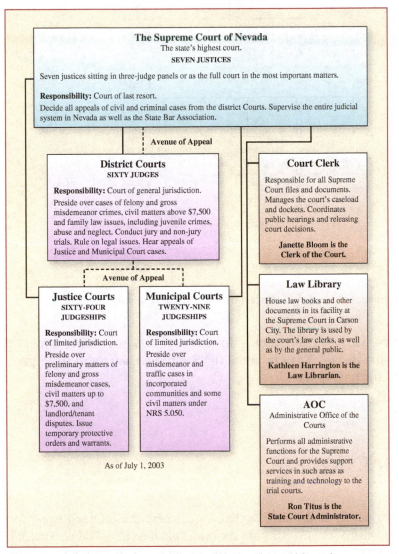

Image Source: http://lawlibrary.nevadajudiciary.us/images/chart.php

The court system of Nevada is a two tier system.

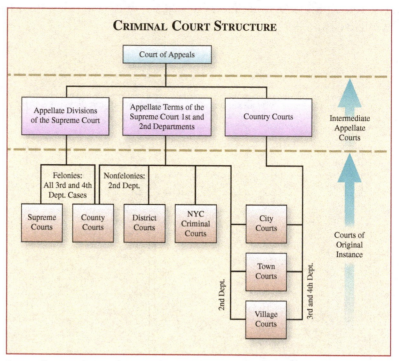

Image Source: http://www.courts.state.ny.us/courts/structure.shtml

The New York court system is three tiered. It is interesting to note that the trial court in New York is called the Supreme Court and the highest court is the Court of Appeals.

*T*RIAL COURTS

The trial courts in the state systems are where the criminal trials for felony cases are heard. These courts are the busiest in the entire United States. In 2006, an estimated 1.1 million persons were sentenced for felonies in state courts nationwide.[7]

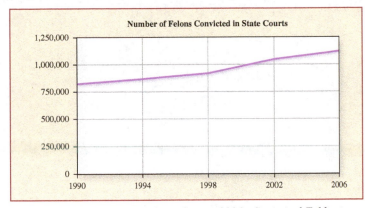

Source: *Felony Sentences in State Courts, 2006—Statistical Tables*

APPELLATE COURTS

The appellate courts in the state systems have appellate jurisdiction and review cases from the trial courts that are sent up on appeal. The state appellate courts review cases and base their rulings on the constitution of their respective states. In states with a three tier system, the initial appeal goes to the intermediate appeals court. Rulings that are appealed from these courts would then go to the state court of last resort, which is the equivalent of the Supreme Court at the state level. In states that have a two tier system, appeals from the trial courts of general jurisdiction would be sent directly to the court of last resort in the state.

REVIEW QUESTIONS:

1. The two primary divisions of the court system in the United States are the _____ and the _____ courts.

2. A _____ is a civil wrong.

3. _____ is the territory, subject matter, or persons over which a court has legal authority to hear and decide a certain type of case.

4. Article _____, Section _____ of the U.S. Constitution specifically creates the United States Supreme Court.

5. The federal court system is a _____ tier system.

6. The trial court in the federal court system is the _____ court.

7. There are _____ Regional Circuit Courts of Appeal in the federal court system.

8. _____ _____ is the current Chief Justice of the United States Supreme Court.

9. Once a case is accepted for review by the U.S. Supreme Court, the Court issues a _____ _____ _____.

10. In states that have a two tiered court system, appeals from the trial court go directly to the court of _____ _____ within that state.

CRITICAL THINKING QUESTIONS:

1. Define, in your own words, the level of evidence referred to as the preponderance of the evidence.

2. Select and explain any two of the different types of jurisdiction that are discussed in this chapter.

3. Describe some of the key differences between the federal court system and the state court systems.

4. Explain the different ways that judges are selected in the state court systems.

5. Describe how a case is selected and heard by the U.S. Supreme Court.

NOTES

CHAPTER 3

[1] Connie Estrada Ireland and George E. Rush, *The Dictionary of Criminal Justice With Summaries of Supreme Court Cases Affecting Criminal Justice,* 7th Edition (New York: McGraw-Hill Companies, Inc., 2011).

[2] Ibid.

[3] Ibid.

[4] *Federal justice Statistics, 2008—Statistical Tables,* Bureau of Justice Statistics, U.S. Department of Justice, November, 2010, accessed April, 2011 at http://bjs.ojp.usdoj.gov/index.cfm?ty=pbdetail&iid=1745.

[5] Ibid.

[6] Bureau of Justice Statistics, *State Court Caseload Statistics,* Office of Justice Programs, accessed April, 2011 at http://bjs.ojp.usdoj.gov/index.cfm?ty=tp&tid=30.

[7] Thomas H. Cohn and Tracy Kyckelhahn, *State Court Processing Statistics, 2006, Felony Defendants in Large Urban Counties, 2006* (U.S. Department of Justice, Office of Justice Programs, May, 2010).

FREEDOM OF SPEECH, ASSEMBLY, AND PRESS

By Gregg Ivers

Chapter
4

$\mathscr{C}$HAPTER OVERVIEW

Getty George Rose/Contributor

Perhaps no area within Constitutional Law has generated as much emotion or litigation as the First Amendment's protection of Freedom of Speech, Assembly, and Press. It is no co-incidence the Framers chose to address these concerns in the First Amendment. This chapter will define what is meant by "speech," and what is meant by the abridgement or regulation of it. It will do so by including in-depth analyses of actual cases and the litigants who brought them. Key concepts such as "symbolic speech" and "hate speech" will be explored and readers will learn how these concepts evolved. The chapter will also look at what is not protected by the First Amendment.

Bridgepoint Education

$\mathscr{C}$HAPTER LEARNING OBJECTIVES

After reading this chapter, you should be able to do the following:

1. Explain the Founders' views on free speech, assembly, and press.
2. Describe the effect that war and national security concerns have had on the development of the free speech and press guarantees of the First Amendment.
3. Identify what "speech" the Court protects as "symbolic speech" and when such speech is (or is not) protected by the First Amendment.
4. Identify the meaning of "hate speech" and when it is (or is not) protected by the First Amendment.
5. Describe the evolution of obscenity law.
6. Explain the impact of the Internet on First Amendment law.
7. Define the Framers' views on seditious and libelous speech.
8. Explain the principle of prior restraint and when it does or does not apply.
9. Explain the evolution of libel law and to whom it applies.

KEYWORDS

actual malice
ad hoc balancing
bad tendency test
clear and present danger test
clear and probable danger test
content neutral
criminal syndicalism
fighting words exception

hate speech
imminent lawlessness standard
libel
per curiam
prior restraint
public figure
pure speech
symbolic speech

"Congress shall make no law . . . abridging the freedom of speech, or of the press; or the right of the people peaceably to assemble, and to petition the Government for a redress of grievances."

—Free Speech, Free Press, Freedom of Assembly, and Petition Clauses,
First Amendment

Constitutional law is not immune from the social and political context in which it develops. The development of important constitutional principles, particularly in the areas of freedom of speech, press, and assembly, are often linked to important changes in American society. Accordingly, the rights of Americans to believe, say, and write what they want; to take their case to the streets; to challenge the cultural, social, and political status quo through art, music, and public expression; and to challenge some of the most fundamentally held beliefs about their nation's founding principles have undergone constant change since the First Amendment was ratified in 1791.

This chapter examines the struggles over the meaning of freedom of speech, assembly, and press. First, this chapter will discuss what the Framers were thinking when they established constitutional protection for speech, assembly, and the press. Second, this chapter will examine the origin and development of the right to free speech as it applies to political dissent. Third, this chapter will examine how the right to free speech gradually evolved to include public protests, "symbolic speech," protection for speech, and expression beyond political borders. Fourth, this chapter will discuss how the digital era and the Internet have transformed the constitutional debate over the meaning of free speech. Fifth, this chapter will discuss the guarantee of freedom of the press.

THE FRAMERS AND FREE SPEECH

Constitutional historians and other scholars of the Founding period generally agree that the Framers did support the idea that freedom of speech should receive constitutional protection. However, they diverged on the degree to which individuals were permitted to challenge the dominant social, political, and, in some cases, religious sentiments of the day free from government retribution. Contemporary discussion of freedom of speech often assumes that the protection for different points of view stems from the late 1700s, especially after the American colonies declared their independence from Great Britain, and was embodied by the ratification of the First Amendment in 1791. In truth, freedom of speech, as the term is understood now, was relatively unknown in America until the Founding period. Until then, freedom of speech was a parliamentary right allowing legislators to speak or debate in their official capacities without punishment. Freedom of speech as an individual right did not develop until later, and only after the newly established American states were secure enough to accept differences of opinion among their fellow citizens.

The First Amendment did not, however, secure an unfettered national right to freedom of speech. While Congress could not abridge the freedom of speech, it was not uncommon for states to limit political dissent, just as they limited freedom of the press and freedom of religion. Indeed, one of the distinct features of the American federal structure was that it allowed the states, free from congressional control, to tailor their laws to the culture of local communities. Although modern free speech law is dominated by a libertarian philosophy strongly protective of unpopular expression, the First Amendment initially offered greater protection to political majorities in the states than it did to individuals professing unorthodox or unpopular views. Truthful speech was certainly protected—but truth was generally understood as conformity to majority opinion.

The animosity between the Republicans and the Federalists, which prompted the unpopular Alien and Sedition Acts of 1798, came to blows in one infamous incident. As shown in this early 19th-century cartoon, Federalist Roger Griswold attacked Republican Matthew Lyon with his cane after an exchange of heated remarks.

© Getty Bettmann/Contributor

A major turning point in the meaning of free speech came in 1798, when Congress enacted the Alien and Sedition Acts. By punishing any "false, scandalous, and malicious" commentary against the national government, Congress stepped across both the structural and substantive barriers of the First Amendment by placing a content-based restriction on freedom of expression. The Sedition Act was motivated by the Federalists' desire to silence the Jeffersonian Republicans, who had become increasingly vocal in their criticism of Federalist President John Adams and his policies abroad. So unpopular was the Sedition Act in the states that voters rallied to the polls in 1800 to turn out Adams and replace him with Thomas Jefferson. Ironically, Jefferson had never opposed the law of seditious libel, which permitted state governments to punish individual citizens for political dissent. His views on freedom of speech and press were consistent with the generally accepted notion that personal liberty did not extend to "criminal acts" against the government.

The Sedition Act expired in 1801 and was not renewed. Congress never again passed a law making general criticism of the government a crime. Although Jefferson believed the Sedition Act was unconstitutional and later pardoned anyone convicted under the law, he continued to support the selective prosecution of political opponents under state seditious libel laws, in which *libel* referred to any treasonable or defamatory writing, *even if it was true* (the end of the chapter will note how this definition has changed). In an 1804 letter to Abigail Adams, the wife of President Adams, Jefferson wrote that the unconstitutionality of the Sedition Act did not

> remove all restraint from the overwhelming torrent of slander which is confounding all vice and virtue, all truth and falsehood in the U.S. The power to do that is fully possessed by the several state legislatures. . . . While we deny that Congress ha[s] a right to control the freedom of the press, we have ever asserted the right of the states, and their exclusive right to do so. (as quoted in Levy, 1985, p. 307)

Conversely, James Madison, who had been Jefferson's key political ally since the ratification period of the Constitution, was much more unnerved by the nation's experience with the Sedition Act than Jefferson was. Along with several other important writers of the early 1800s, Madison became part of a small but influential circle of thinkers advocating a more libertarian conception of freedom of speech. Granted, the states did not drop their seditious libel laws immediately, nor did they wholly discount the embedded notion that government should have some control over speech that encouraged criminal conduct or flouted societal norms of decency. Here, as elsewhere in early American constitutional theory, Madison's voice rose above the rest. For Madison, free speech became much more than just a rhetorical commitment. Free thought and exchange became essential to the health of democratic institutions and the principle of self-government. Again, Madison's early commitment to what later became known as the "marketplace model" of free speech—that government should not protect speech based on a particular point of view, but rather remain "neutral" and let ideas succeed or fail on their own—anticipated how the Supreme Court would come to define free speech by the mid-20th century.

WAR AT HOME, ENEMIES ABROAD: ESTABLISHING THE EARLY LIMITS ON POLITICAL DISSENT

In April 1917, the United States, largely in response to several attacks by German submarines on British and French luxury liners carrying American passengers, entered World War I. One month later, Congress enacted its first military conscription law since the Civil War to bolster America's standing army, which stood at approximately 110,000 soldiers. To force compliance, Congress enacted the Espionage Act of 1917, which made it illegal to

> interfere with the operation or success of the military or naval forces of the United States . . . [that] will cause or attempt to cause insubordination, disloyalty, mutiny, or refusal of duty in the military or naval forces of the United States, or shall willfully obstruct the recruiting or enlistment services of the United States. (*Abrams v. United States*, 1919, p. 617)

Congress clearly intended to quash any criticism of the government's wartime policies by drafting a law that so broadly threatened critics and potential draft resisters. Even after President Wilson presented his case for American entrance into World War I, draft-eligible men had not hurried down to local military recruiting centers, and the war's opponents had become even more vocal. Military officers were reporting that those men who reported for induction did so reluctantly, and many tried to claim health or religious exemptions. By November 1918, when World War I ended, government authorities had classified more than 330,000 American men as draft evaders, just over 10% of those who reported for duty.

Initial efforts to prosecute dissenters under the Espionage Act were not very successful. Government lawyers frequently encountered judges and juries who were unwilling to convict individuals they believed were not involved in any conspiracy, but who were simply expressing their beliefs and opinions on America's role in World War I. Congress responded by passing the Sedition Act of 1918, which made illegal "any disloyal . . . scurrilous, abusive language intended to bring the form of government of the United States. . . . into contempt, scorn . . . or disrepute" (*Abrams v. United States*, 1919, p. 617). Such was the political environment when the Court, in *Schenck v. United States* (1919), handed down its first-ever decision on the meaning of the Free Speech Clause of the First Amendment.

THE CLEAR AND PRESENT DANGER TEST

In *Schenck*, a unanimous Court ruled that the absolute phrasing of the Free Speech Clause did not mean that all speech was necessarily constitutionally protected. In upholding the conviction of Charles Schenck, a prominent member of the Socialist Party, for mailing anti-war leaflets to local draft-eligible men he identified through a Philadelphia newspaper, Justice Oliver Wendell Holmes, Jr. rejected the argument that all speech was entitled to First Amendment protection regardless of the time and context in which it took place:

> We admit that, in many places and in ordinary times, the defendants, in saying all that was said in the circular ["Do not submit to intimidation" and "Assert Your Rights!"], would have been within their constitutional rights. But the character of every act depends upon the circumstances in which it is done. The most stringent protection of free speech would not protect a man in falsely shouting fire in a theatre and causing a panic. It does not protect a man from an injunction against uttering words that may have all the effect of force. The question in every case is whether the words used are used in such circumstances and are of such a nature as to create a clear and present danger that they will bring about the substantive evils that Congress has a right to prevent. . . . When a nation is at war, many things that might be said in time of peace are such a hindrance to its effort that their utterance will not be endured so long as men fight, and that no Court could regard them as protected by any constitutional right. (*Schenck v. United States*, 1919, p. 52)

What would be the repercussions for falsely shouting "fire" at a crowded concert? In *Schenck*, the Supreme Court ruled that speech that posed a "clear and present danger" was not entitled to constitutional protection. This served as the standard in free speech cases until 1969.

© dwphotos/Shutterstock.com

Schenck remains one of Justice Holmes's most well-known opinions because of his introduction of what has become known as the **clear and present danger test**. Simply stated, the government had the right to restrict speech when it created an immediate threat to the public order.

THE BAD TENDENCY TEST

In the next major protest case decided by the Court, *Abrams v. United States* (1919), the justices upheld the conviction of several New York self-styled revolutionaries sympathetic to the ongoing revolution in Bolshevik Russia. In August 1918, Jacob Abrams and several of his comrades were arrested for dropping leaflets from downtown Manhattan buildings, printed in English and Yiddish, featuring the headline "THE HYPOCRISY OF THE UNITED STATES AND HER ALLIES" (p. 619). Another pamphlet read, "Workers— Wake Up!" and encouraged people to stop "producing bullets, bayonets, cannon, to murder not only the Germans but also your dearest, best, who are in Russia and are fighting for freedom" (pp. 620–621). The Court, 7–2, ruled that the 1918 Sedition Act made the dissenters' actions illegal. Writing for the Court, Justice John J. Clarke did not apply Holmes's clear and present danger test to assess the merits of Abrams's free speech claim. Instead, Clarke applied the **bad tendency test**, which Holmes had only hinted around in *Schenck*. Unlike the clear and present danger test established in *Schenck*, which emphasized immediacy, the bad tendency test required government to demonstrate only that speech might create unlawful action down the line.

Abrams is most noteworthy, though, for Holmes's truly great dissent, in which he introduced the "marketplace of ideas" metaphor into the lexicon of free speech thought. As First Amendment scholar Rodney Smolla has commented, "In the course of a few short months, [Holmes] underwent a spectacular conversion experience. It was if some angel of free speech had appeared to Holmes in the night" (Smolla, 1992, p. 101). Wrote Holmes,

> [W]hen men have realized that time has upset many fighting faiths, they may come to believe even more than they believe the very foundations of their own conduct that the ultimate good desired is better reached by free trade in ideas—that the best test of truth is the power of the thought to get itself accepted in the competition of the market, and that truth is the only ground upon which their wishes safely can be carried out. That, at any rate, is the theory of our Constitution. (*Abrams v. United States*, 1919, p. 635)

Six years later, in *Gitlow v. New York* (1925), the Court upheld the conviction of Socialist Party leader Benjamin Gitlow, who had been convicted under a New York **criminal syndicalism** law, a law that made it a crime to advocate, teach, or aid in any activity designed to bring about the overthrow of the government by force or violence. Such laws had become common during the 1920s, as states viewed them as powerful tools to suppress labor unrest and political

Clear and present danger test
A test established in *Schenck v. United States* (1919) permitting the government to restrict speech that posed a clear and present danger of violence or other illegal activity.

Bad tendency test
A test developed in early free speech cases that permitted the government to restrict speech if it believed the speech had a tendency to provoke illegal activity.

Criminal syndicalism
Acts of violence or terrorism, or the advocacy of such acts, as a means of promoting economic or political change.

activity by the growing number of Americans who were joining socialist and Communist parties. Justice Edward T. Sanford found that Gitlow's pamphlets calling for the overthrow of the American capitalist system posed enough of a threat to meet the bad tendency test that now guided the Court's approach to free speech claims. However, the Court handed advocates of broader free speech rights an important consolation prize by holding that

---

Socialist Party leader Benjamin Gitlow's conviction was upheld because the Court's majority believed his pamphlets could incite or cause illegal activity, thus meeting the bad tendency test.

---

for present purposes we may and do assume that freedom of speech and of the press—which are protected by the First Amendment from abridgement by Congress—are among the fundamental personal rights and "liberties" protected by the due process clause of the Fourteenth Amendment by the States. (p. 666)

Gitlow, ironically, became the constitutional baseline for incorporation—using the Due Process Clause of the Fourteenth Amendment to apply most of the provisions of the Bill of Rights to the states.

Holmes, in his dissent, argued in *Gitlow* that the Court should apply the clear and present danger test to political dissenters: To Holmes, Gitlow posed no immediate threat. Two years later, in *Whitney v. California* (1927), Justice Louis Brandeis underscored Holmes's increasingly expansive approach to free speech by suggesting that conduct, not belief, should be the threshold for triggering the clear and present danger test. Brandeis was disturbed by Charlotte Anita Whitney's conviction and subsequent lengthy jail term for simply *belonging* to the California Communist Labor Party. Absent was any evidence that Whitney had engaged in any advocacy on behalf of the organization. Brandeis and Holmes were in the minority in *Whitney*, just as they had been in *Gitlow*. But with the nation firmly immersed in the First Red Scare, free speech for political dissenters was not the Court's highest priority.

In the 1930s, the American Civil Liberties Union (ACLU) scored two important victories in the Supreme Court that broadened the rights of political dissenters. In *Stromberg v. California* (1931)—discussed later in this chapter—the Court recognized that "symbolic speech," which includes nonverbal expression, is protected under the First Amendment. In *De Jonge v. Oregon* (1937), the Court overturned the conviction of a Communist Party activist from Portland, Oregon who had been convicted under a state law prohibiting the circulation of materials that advocated the violent or forceful overthrow of the government. Dirk De Jonge had been arrested for holding a meeting of Communist Party members and other sympathizers. A unanimous Court ruled that De Jonge had not engaged in any "forceful" subversive activity, but simply held a peaceful meeting that posed no threat to anyone, suggesting that the bad tendency test might not withstand the test of time. *De Jonge* also marked the first time the Court ruled that the right to assemble applied to the states through the Fourteenth Amendment.

WORLD WAR II, THE COLD WAR, AND THE EMERGENCE OF NEW STANDARDS

After the end of World War II in August 1945, the United States and the Soviet Union settled into the Cold War, in which espionage, propaganda, and careful control of political dissent on both sides became standard fare. By 1950, Senator Joseph McCarthy was at the height of his powers as an anti-Communist warrior; that same year, the country would enter the Korean War facing an enemy that was supported by China and the Soviet Union. It was against this background that Eugene Dennis and 11 other American Communists were arrested under the Smith Act, which made it illegal to teach or advocate the overthrow of the United States by force or violence. The Department of Justice prosecuted Dennis for circulating materials that reprinted the writings of Karl Marx, Vladimir Lenin, and Joseph Stalin. Dennis and his colleagues did not circulate anything that they had said or written themselves.

But in *Dennis v. United States* (1951), the Court held that, although the defendants in Dennis did not engage in any violent behavior, they did teach what the Smith Act banned. The Court ruled that such teachings posed an "imminent and probable" danger to public order that justified their suppression, an opinion from which only Justices Black and Douglas dissented. Wrote Chief Justice Fred Vinson,

> The rule we deduce from these cases is that, where an offense is specified by a statute in non-speech or non-press terms, a conviction relying upon speech or press as evidence of violation may be sustained only when the speech or publication created a "clear and present danger" of attempting or accomplishing the prohibited crime, e.g., interference with enlistment. . . . [T]here is little doubt that subsequent opinions have inclined toward the Holmes-Brandeis rationale. . . . But . . . neither Justice Holmes nor Justice Brandeis ever envisioned that a shorthand phrase should be crystallized into a rigid rule to be applied inflexibly without regard to the circumstances of each case. (pp. 505, 507, 508)

In *Dennis*, the Court backed away from the bad tendency test but did not go so far as to adopt the clear and present danger test. What emerged from *Dennis* instead was a new standard known as the **clear and probable danger test**, a standard somewhere in the middle. Central in the clear and probable danger test was the role of the justices in weighing, on a case-by-case basis, the competing interests in an instance of free speech—for example, the government's

Clear and probable danger test

A test established in *Dennis v. United States* (1951) that is somewhat more restrictive than the clear and present danger test; limits on free speech depend on the likelihood of danger and the competing interests at play.

Clarence Brandenburg, left, and an American Nazi Party member in 1964. The Supreme Court overturned Brandenburg's conviction, ruling that speech could be limited only if it was likely to incite immediate violence or imminent lawless action. Brandenburg could not be prosecuted simply for advocating violence during the televised KKK rally.

Associated Press

interest in security versus an individual's right to peaceful political dissent. This approach is more commonly known as **ad hoc balancing**.

THE IMMINENT LAWLESS ACTION STANDARD EMERGES

By the late 1950s, the Court had begun to limit the scope of the Smith Act. In *Yates v. United States* (1957), the Court ruled that teaching "abstract doctrine" did not fall within the law's prohibition on advocacy and inciting illegal conduct. In throwing out the conviction of 14 individuals convicted of publishing and distributing Communist Party materials, the justices took a giant step away from *Dennis*. And in *First Unitarian Church of Los Angeles v. County of Los Angeles* (1958), the Court invalidated a California law that required churches to administer loyalty oaths to their members or lose their tax exemptions.

The Court continued to broaden its interpretation of the right to dissent as the nation entered the 1960s. As this and other chapters will discuss, on matters involving public protest, press freedom, religious free exercise, and assembly, the Court was no longer an ally in the Cold War campaign to suppress unpopular points of view. Major casualties in the Court's gradual campaign to broaden the constitutional rights of political and religious dissenters were laws that punished "subversive" individuals and organizations, including Communists and their various party organizations.

In 1968, the Court, in *Brandenburg v. Ohio*, ruled that an Ohio criminal syndicalism law violated the First Amendment. The law had been used to prosecute a Ku Klux Klan leader who had invited a Cincinnati television crew to film a local rally. The Court noted that recent decisions had

> fashioned the principle that the constitutional guarantees of free speech and free press do not permit a State to forbid or proscribe advocacy of the use of force or of law violation except where such advocacy is directed to inciting or producing imminent lawless action and is likely to produce such action. (p. 447)

The Court's new **imminent lawlessness standard** replaced the clear and present danger test, marginalizing *Schenck v. United States* (1919) and explicitly overruling *Whitney v. California* (1927). The ACLU, which represented Klansman Charles Brandenburg, won this important victory for political dissenters' rights using the same theory it had advocated on behalf of Charlotte Whitney.

Ad hoc balancing

An approach to judging in which the interests of the government are weighed (or "balanced") against the rights of a speaker on a case-by-case basis.

Imminent lawlessness standard

A test established in *Brandenburg v. Ohio* (1968) permitting the government to restrict speech or expressive activity that is designed to incite an imminent and violent reaction; it replaced the *clear and present danger test*.

*P*ROTESTS, PICKETS, AND DEMONSTRATIONS: SYMBOLIC SPEECH

Pure speech—communication that is only spoken—is not the only expression protected by the First Amendment. Public protests, parades, demonstrations, and even clothing all have expressive qualities. The Court has chosen to identify and, in most cases, protect such communication as **symbolic speech**. Still, the justices have also drawn firm lines between what it considers disruptive behavior and symbolic speech protected by the First Amendment. While the Court has generally held that any restrictions on symbolic speech must be **content neutral**—meaning that government may not restrict speech based on its subject matter—there are also examples of when the justices have departed from this principle to uphold restrictions on symbolic speech.

Symbolic speech

Communication expressed symbolically, rather than through *pure speech*.

Content neutral

Principle under which the government cannot restrict the time, place, or manner of individual expression based on subject matter; in other words, the government cannot forbid speech on an entire subject.

WHAT IS SYMBOLIC SPEECH?

Until 1931, the Court had never formally defined symbolic speech or ruled whether it was protected by the First Amendment. That year, in *Stromberg v. California* (1931), the Court struck down a California law making it a crime to raise a red flag that symbolized opposition to the government. Yetta Stromberg, a 19-year-old camp counselor at a summer youth camp sponsored by the Communist Party, had been convicted under the law for raising a red flag at the beginning of each day. In finding the California law overly broad and applicable to almost any form of legal, peaceful opposition to public policy, the Court, for the first time, recognized "symbolic speech" as a form of expressive conduct protected by the First Amendment.

Ole Spata/picture-alliance/dpa/AP Images

The stylized Guy Fawkes mask, popularized by the comic book series and film adaptation of *V for Vendetta*, has become a symbol worldwide for groups protesting government action (or inaction), including the Occupy Wall Street movement in the United States. Can you think of other examples of symbolic speech?

Having ruled that more than pure speech was constitutionally protected, the Court was soon confronted with another question: Do individuals have the right to refrain from speaking? Silence can be interpreted in many ways—from a quiet statement of personal conscience to outright defiance. In the early 1940s, the Court heard two important cases that involved the right of Jehovah's Witnesses not to participate in the mandatory flag salute and Pledge of Allegiance during the public school day.

THE FLAG SALUTE CONTROVERSY

In *Minersville School District v. Gobitis* (1940), the Court upheld a small Pennsylvania town's school board policy requiring all public school students to say the Pledge of Allegiance and salute the flag at the beginning of the day. Writing for the Court, Justice Felix Frankfurter concluded that the school board's interest in promoting "national cohesion" was "inferior to none" and thus did not violate the constitutional rights of students (p. 595). Frankfurter wrote that the flag salute was an important mechanism to "promote in the minds of children who attend the common schools an attachment to the institutions of their country" (p. 599). Ironically, the Minersville law required students to extend their right arm straight out, with their palm open—the signature salute of Adolf Hitler's Third Reich in Nazi Germany.

Three years later, the Court dramatically reversed its position on mandatory flag salute laws. In *West Virginia Board of Education v. Barnette* (1943), the Court ruled that the First Amendment prohibited the government from forcing an individual to affirm a repugnant belief. In *Gobitis*, the Court, much like it had been in *Schenck*, was caught up in a nationalist fervor as America prepared to go to war against the Japanese empire and Nazi Germany. *Barnette* was decided about 18 months after the United States had entered World War II. The justices, all of whom by this time had been appointed by President Franklin D. Roosevelt, were well positioned in the corridors of power in Washington, D.C. They were privy to the mounting evidence of Hitler's "Final Solution" to exterminate the Jews of Europe and anyone else undesirable to the Nazi regime, including homosexuals, "gypsies," and Jehovah's Witnesses. Thus, when Justice Robert Jackson wrote, "Those who begin coercive elimination of dissent soon find themselves exterminating dissenters. Compulsory unification of opinion achieves only the unanimity of the graveyard," the message was clear: Free nations had to tolerate dissenters, or soon they would take on the characteristics of the totalitarian regimes they had pledged to defeat (*West Virginia Board of Education v. Barnette*, 1943, p. 641). *Barnette* offers an early opportunity to see how the Court placed the principle of individual liberty above political expediency in a time of crisis.

PROTESTS, SYMBOLIC SPEECH, AND THE VIETNAM WAR

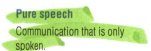

Pure speech
Communication that is only spoken.

By the late 1960s, the Court was edging toward an absolutist approach to free speech: It was increasingly willing to protect any type of speech, regardless of how controversial or potentially offensive its subject matter. *Brandenburg v. Ohio* represented the high-water mark for **pure speech** protected by the First Amendment. The key cases of this period, *United States v. O'Brien* (1968) and *Tinker v. Des Moines* (1969), demonstrated that, while the Court no longer supported the government's effort to suppress unpopular speech, there were limits on symbolic speech that did not apply to pure speech.

In *O'Brien*, the Court, 7–1, ruled that David O'Brien and three of his friends who protested the Vietnam War by burning their draft cards on the steps of a South Boston courthouse were not protected by the First Amendment from prosecution under the Selective Service Act, which prohibited any practice that interfered with the "smooth functioning" of the draft. Wrote Chief Justice Warren, "We cannot accept the view that an apparently limitless variety of conduct can be labeled 'speech' whenever the person engaging in the conduct intends thereby to express an idea" (*United States v. O'Brien*, 1968, p. 376). Furthermore, Warren established a four-part test that has remained the benchmark in symbolic speech cases:

Antiwar demonstrators burn their draft cards on the steps of the Pentagon during the Vietnam War, Washington, DC. The Supreme Court ruled that the First Amendment did not protect this action as free speech, as it interfered with the functioning of the Vietnam War draft.

© Getty Hulton Archive/Stringer

> A government regulation is sufficiently justified if it is within the constitutional power of the Government; if it furthers an important or substantial governmental interest; if the government interest is unrelated to the suppression of free expression; and if the incidental restriction on First Amendment freedoms is not greater than is essential to the furtherance of that entrance. (p. 377)

The following year, in *Tinker*, the Court ruled that a local Iowa school's decision to prohibit students from wearing black armbands to school as a form of protest against the Vietnam War violated the First Amendment (see *A Closer Look: How an Armband Became a First Amendment Symbol*). The Court found that, unlike in *O'Brien*, the students were not destroying federally issued property (the draft card) or interfering with an important government interest like the draft. They were simply expressing a dissenting opinion in a peaceful manner. Writing for the Court, Justice Abe Fortas held that

> First Amendment rights, applied in light of special characteristics of the school environment, are available to teachers and students. It can hardly be argued that either students or teachers shed their constitutional rights at the schoolhouse gate. This has been the unmistakable holding of this Court for almost fifty years. (*Tinker v. Des Moines*, 1969, p. 506)

A Closer Look: How an Armband Became a First Amendment Symbol

In November 1965, John Tinker and Christopher Eckhardt, two high school students from Des Moines, Iowa, attended a protest sponsored by several religiously affiliated groups against the Vietnam War on the Mall in Washington, D.C. On bus trip home, Tinker and Eckhardt decided they needed to express, in peaceful fashion, their opposition to the Vietnam War. About 25 high school students met at the Eckhardts' home in early December to discuss plans for a protest. A consensus soon emerged: The students would wear black armbands imprinted with a white peace sign to their classes.

Local high school administrators soon learned of the impending protest and made clear to the families and students involved that they would consider any students wearing an armband in violation of the school policies banning "disruptions" during the school day. Upon hearing the school announced its "zero tolerance" policy toward the anti-Vietnam armband, one student responded, "What a joke! Only last year we were all asked to wear black armbands to mourn the loss of school spirit at basketball games. Even a black coffin was marched through the halls" (Johnson, 1997, pp. 12–13).

On December 16 and 17, somewhere between 25 and 50 students wore black armbands adorned with the peace symbol to school. Some removed their armbands after other students threatened them, some went unreported by teachers who believed the students had a right to express their opinion, and some were sent to the principal's office and, subsequently, suspended for the remainder of the day. About a week later, the Iowa chapter of the American Civil Liberties Union approached several of the students about bringing a First Amendment challenge against the school. John and Christopher agreed to take part, and they persuaded John's 13-year-old sister, Mary Beth, who had worn an armband to her middle school and been sent home as a result, to join them. In March 1966, the ACLU filed a formal complaint on behalf of the Tinkers and Eckhardt in federal court. Three years later—by this time John and Christopher were in college and Mary Beth was a high school senior—the Supreme Court, in *Tinker v. Des Moines* (1969), ruled that the students disciplined by the Des Moines schools were entitled to wear their armbands as a form of "symbolic speech."

For Mary Beth, the decision bearing her name became a life-altering moment. She later became a registered nurse and outspoken advocate on behalf of social justice causes, including student rights. Said Mary Beth,

> I realized that kids need not only First Amendment rights, but kids have a right to clean air, clean water, a safe place to live, a *place* to live and a world that is safe and is not filled with so much violence. So, I thought if I could encourage kids to speak up for themselves and make things better for themselves in these areas, then I should do that, and I should tell them my story about the armband case and how speaking up for what you believe in can make a big difference. (Johnson, 1997, p. 198)

FLAG BURNING

The Vietnam War era also precipitated a constitutional debate over whether burning the American flag should be exempt from First Amendment protection. In *Street v. New York* (1969), the Court ruled that a New York law making it illegal to "publicly mutilate, deface, defile, or defy, trample upon, or cast contempt upon either by words or act [any flag of the United States]" had been wrongly applied to Sidney Street, a Vietnam veteran and Bronze Star recipient (p. 578). Street had burned an American flag on a New York City street corner after learning of a failed assassination attempt against civil rights activist James Meredith. The Court did not rule on the constitutionality of flag burning or laws prohibiting such an action. Instead, the Court ruled that Street had been wrongly convicted for what he said—"We don't need no damn flag"—as he set fire to the flag (p. 579).

One of the Court's most controversial decisions has been its ruling that defacing an American flag is protected symbolic speech.

Five years later, the Court, in *Spence v. Washington* (1974), overturned the conviction of a college student in Washington State who had displayed an American flag with a peace symbol in the window of his dorm room. The Court noted that, compared to the more violent demonstrations that regularly inflamed the nation's streets and college campuses, Harold Spence's protest was relatively tame and "restrained" (*Spence v. Washington*, 1974, p. 409). *Spence* put to rest, for the moment, the question of whether defacing the American flag was protected expression under the First Amendment.

In 1989, the Court, in a time of peace and prosperity, returned to a question that had been left open since *Street*: Was *burning* the American flag, as opposed to condemning or handling it inappropriately, protected symbolic speech? The question produced one of the Court's most controversial and emotionally charged opinions since *Barnette*. In August 1984, Gregory Johnson was arrested for burning an American flag outside the Dallas building that was hosting the Republican presidential nominating convention. Johnson took an American flag that had been stripped from a flagpole by another protester, placed it on the ground, and, while others chanted, "America, the red, white and blue, we spit on you," lit the flag on fire (*Texas v. Johnson*, 1989, p. 399). Johnson was charged with violating a Texas law that made it illegal to desecrate a "venerated object," defined as a public monument, a place of worship or burial, or a state or national flag.

In *Texas v. Johnson* (1989), a sharply divided 5–4 Court ruled that Johnson was convicted for "engaging in expressive conduct" protected by the First Amendment (p. 420). Justice William Brennan, who, after coming to the Court in 1956, had become a reliable vote on behalf of a broad interpretation of the First Amendment, wrote that

> [t]here is . . . no indication—either in the text of the Constitution or in our cases interpreting it—that a separate juridical category exists for the American flag alone. . . . We decline, therefore, to create for

the flag an exception to the joust of principles protected by the First Amendment. (*Texas v. Johnson*, 1989, p. 418)

Johnson elicited a predictable response from Capitol Hill. The House passed a unanimous resolution condemning the decision, and the Senate also passed a similar nonbinding measure over only three "no" votes. Senator Robert Dole (R-Kans.), a decorated World War II veteran, introduced a constitutional amendment proposing to overturn Johnson. In an interesting generational twist, opposition in the Senate to the amendment was led by Senator Bob Kerrey (D-Neb.), who earned the Medal of Honor during his service in Vietnam. Dole and Kerrey both suffered horrible and life-altering injuries—Dole lost the use of his right arm and Kerrey had his right leg removed after combat-related injuries. Ultimately, the Dole proposal fell 16 votes short of the necessary two-thirds majority required to send a constitutional amendment to the states for ratification. Congress did, however, enact legislation that attempted to satisfy the defects the Court found in the Texas law in Johnson. By the same 5 to 4 majority, the Court, in United States v. Eichman (1990), declared the Federal Flag Protection Act unconstitutional.

PROTESTS, PICKETS, AND DEMONSTRATIONS: HATE SPEECH

In April 1940, Jehovah's Witness Walter Chaplinsky had been preaching in the Rochester, New Hampshire town square when a mob, enraged by his statements, gathered and began to assault him. Chaplinsky was arrested under a state law that barred the use of "any offensive, derisive, or annoying word to any other person who is lawfully in any street" (*Chaplinsky v. New Hampshire*, 1942, p. 569). Irate, Chaplinsky demanded to know from the officer on the scene why he was being arrested and not his attackers. After the officer told him to "shut up," Chaplinsky returned the volley, calling him a "fascist" and a "goddamned racketeer" (p. 569). The Witnesses took up Chaplinsky's legal defense and succeeded in appealing his case to the Supreme Court. But the justices were no more enamored of Chaplinsky's behavior than the lower courts had been. In *Chaplinsky v. New Hampshire* (1942), a unanimous Court concluded that the First Amendment permitted a **fighting words exception**, which it defined as a "face-to-face" exchange "plainly likely to cause a breach of the peace by the addressee" (p. 573). Walter Chaplinsky then went to jail for six months.

Since *Chaplinsky*, the Court has rarely turned to the fighting words exception to justify government restraints on public speech. A splendid example of just how narrow the Court considers the fighting words exception came in *National Socialist Party of America v. Village of Skokie* (1977), in which the Court vacated a lower Illinois court's decision upholding a municipal ordinance

Fighting words exception
Spoken or written words that are intended to provoke an immediate physical or violent response from another person; not protected by the First Amendment.

banning the public display of the Nazi swastika. The Court did not decide the constitutional question, instead ordering a new trial. But the justices' short opinion made very clear that Skokie, Illinois, a small Chicago suburb then with the nation's highest per-capita population of Holocaust survivors, could not restrain the right of an American Nazi group to march in its public streets.

The Nazis-in-Skokie episode introduced a new phrase into the lexicon of American freedom of expression: **hate speech**, or offensive speech directed at racial, religious, or ethnic groups. Certainly, the Nazis' hatred of Jews, and not the desire to educate the public or criticize public policy, is what prompted them to choose Skokie as their demonstration site. The march was a carefully planned effort to select a particular audience and taunt them through peaceful means. Although the Nazis ultimately received clearance to demonstrate in Skokie after several more rounds in court, they never actually marched. Instead, the Nazis staged a small, poorly attended demonstration in downtown Chicago.

A direct outgrowth of the battle over the rights of the Nazis to march in Skokie was the subsequent introduction of "hate crimes" laws. These laws took two forms. The first involved penalty enhancement for bias-motivated crimes; the second involved specific prohibitions on particular viewpoints considered fighting words when uttered. For many people, however, hate crimes laws raised serious constitutional questions. In the case of penalty enhancement laws, they appeared to punish the thoughts that went into conduct; as for the laws based on the fighting words exception, they left unprotected particular viewpoints. These complex legal and political considerations came together in *R.A.V. v. St. Paul* (1992).

Hate speech
Offensive speech directed at racial, religious, or ethnic groups.

CROSS BURNING

R.A.V. involved a St. Paul ordinance that stated, in part, that one would be convicted of disorderly conduct for placing

> on public or private property a symbol, object, appellation, characterization or graffiti, including but not limited to, a burning cross or Nazi swastika, which one knows or has reasonable grounds to know arouses anger, alarm or resentment in others on the basis of race, color, creed, religion, or gender. (*R.A.V. v. St. Paul*, 1992, p. 380)

Robert A. Viktora, a 17-year-old high school dropout, burned an 18-inch cross in the yard of an African-American family that had moved into his neighborhood. Rather than prosecute him under a vandalism or criminal trespass statute, the St. Paul district attorney chose to charge Viktora under the new ordinance to test its constitutionality. The Court unanimously ruled that the St. Paul law violated the First Amendment. Far from falling within the fighting words exception crafted in *Chaplinsky*, the justices found the law discriminated on the basis of viewpoint by singling out particular symbols (the Nazi swastika and the burning cross) and was so sweeping in its breadth that it made almost any expressive conduct potentially illegal.

Members of the Ku Klux Klan salute a burning cross in the yard of an Indiana home. The Court has ruled that the Constitution protects cross burning except when it is done "with the intent to intimidate." Is this a double standard?

Associated Press

Just over a decade passed before the Court revisited the cross-burning issue. This time, in *Virginia v. Black* (2003), the justices again found that a prohibition against cross burning as a form of political expression was un-constitutional—but upheld the part of the Virginia law making it illegal to burn a cross "with the intent of intimidating any person or group" (p. 348). Justice Sandra Day O'Connor found the Virginia law permissible under the fighting words exception "in light of cross burning's long and pernicious history as a signal of impending violence" (p. 363).

EMOTIONAL DISTRESS

In *Snyder v. Phelps* (2011), the Court confronted a question that was a natural outgrowth of its decisions on hate speech, cross burning, and other public protests in which the expressive conduct at issue was clearly intended to offend an audience based on something far more serious than one's political beliefs. May individuals so harmed by hateful speech and expressive conduct recover civil damages from a speaker who has intentionally inflicted emotional distress?

In April 2006, Matthew Snyder, a Marine, died while serving in Iraq. The Westboro Baptist Church in Topeka, Kansas decided to picket Lance Corporal Snyder's funeral in Westminster, Maryland. Founded in 1955 by Reverend Frank W. Phelps, Sr., Westboro first drew national attention when it picketed the 1988 funeral of Matthew Shepard, a Wyoming college student who had been abducted and brutally murdered because he was gay. Phelps chose Shepard's funeral because he wanted to spread his church's message that God will continue to kill children as long as they continue to immerse themselves in sin and punish any group that accommodates homosexuals. Since then, Westboro has picketed approximately 45,000 times in more than 800 cities from coast to coast. About 600 of these pickets have taken place at military funerals, as Westboro believes that the military encourages homosexuality.

At Snyder's funeral, Westboro members held signs that read, "Fag Troops," "Priests Rape Boys," "Thank God for IEDs," "Thank You God for Dead Soldiers," and "God Hates You." But the church also complied with all local ordinances governing pickets and protests. The pickets took place 1,000 feet away from the funeral; the picketers did not approach or obstruct any mourner attending the funeral.

Shortly after his son's funeral, Matthew's father, Albert, filed a civil suit against Phelps. Snyder claimed that Phelps's picket and the ensuing publicity had been responsible for his deteriorating health. Snyder stated that he had become clinically depressed, and the mental strain had exacerbated and even led to a variety of physical ailments. A lower federal court found in favor of Snyder and awarded him $2.9 million in compensatory damages and $8 million in punitive damages. On appeal, the Fourth Circuit reversed the decision, holding that Westboro was engaged in expressive conduct protected by the First Amendment and thus could not be held liable for any damage that might occur as a result of exercising a legally protected right.

The Supreme Court, 8–1, affirmed the lower appeals court. Chief Justice John Roberts held that Westboro had engaged in constitutionally protected speech:

> Given that Westboro's speech was at a public place on a matter of public concern, that speech is entitled to "special protection" under the First Amendment. Such speech cannot be restricted simply because it is upsetting or arouses contempt. . . . As a Nation we have chosen a different course—to protect even hurtful speech on public issues to ensure that we do not stifle public debate. (*Snyder v. Phelps*, 2011, pp. 1219–1220)

*F*REE SPEECH BEYOND POLITICAL BORDERS

So far, this chapter has discussed the different levels of constitutional protection for speech based on how the Supreme Court categorizes that speech. Political speech receives the greatest protection under the First Amendment, with government infringement justified only if the speech crosses the threshold of imminent lawless action. Speech (or expressive conduct) considered offensive, hateful, profane, or defamatory is not always entitled to constitutional protection because, in the Court's analysis, it is often unrelated to the core values of the First Amendment. Some protection, however, is better than no protection, which is where speech and expression considered obscene and libelous fall in the Court's hierarchy of protected speech.

Assigning different levels of constitutional protection to speech that nonetheless has expressive value to the speaker is a curious development. Certainly, the notion that some speech is political and other speech is not is a conclusion that deserves some discussion on its own. A neo-Nazi has as much right to circulate a newsletter calling for white supremacist rule as a civil rights group has to call for racial and religious harmony. But do neo-Nazis have the right to broadcast racial epithets over the radio airwaves? Suppose a member of the Ku Klux Klan showed up in a courtroom wearing a white hood and robe to watch a trial involving an alleged racial attack against an African American by a fellow Klansman. Could the judge require the Klansman to leave the courtroom because his wardrobe was potentially disruptive? Or because it was offensive?

What establishes the constitutional dividing line—the line that protects certain speech and limits other speech by devaluing its content? Deciding what the First Amendment should mean, both in form and in substance, has been a process of constant evolution. The previous discussion of the rights of political dissenters in World War I and members of the Communist Party from the 1920s through the late 1950s offers a clear example of the importance of politics in determining the boundaries of protected speech. Over time, social and political forces have changed the meaning of abstract concepts like equality, personal freedom, and public morality. As society has changed, so has the meaning of the First Amendment, as is evident in the following cases concerning public decency and obscenity.

PUBLIC DECENCY

In Cohen v. California (1971), the Court ruled that Paul Cohen, a young man opposed to the Vietnam War, was fully within his First Amendment rights to wear a jacket in a Los Angeles county courthouse that said "Fuck the Draft." The Court noted that Cohen's behavior was in poor taste, but it emphasized that public expression could not be limited to only those words and phrases considered unobjectionable by the majority. Wrote Justice John Harlan,

> How is one to distinguish this from any other offensive word? Surely the State has no right to cleanse public debate to the point where it is grammatically palatable to the most squeamish among us. Yet no readily ascertainable general principle exists for stopping short of that result were we to affirm the judgment below. For, while the particular four-letter word being litigated here is perhaps more distasteful than others of its genre, it is nevertheless often true that one man's vulgarity is another's lyric. (p. 25)

Cohen was about more than whether government can prohibit speech it finds offensive. The message was certainly one that many people find offensive; on the other hand, Cohen was expressing an opinion about the Vietnam War and doing it in a public place. His jacket was not a pamphlet that someone could ignore or pick up and throw away. Cohen was in a public place, and many people in the courthouse were there because they had to be. The county's position was that it had an important interest in preserving public decency. To the Court, that interest was not strong enough to warrant punishing Paul Cohen. But the Court has ruled that public decency can outweigh a speaker's interest in speech or expressive conduct considered profane.

THE PUBLIC AIRWAVES

In the early afternoon of October 30, 1973, Pacifica Radio, a nonprofit radio network featuring liberal cultural, news, and political programming, aired comedian George Carlin's famous "Filthy Dirty Words" monologue. Carlin's monologue, which was featured on his Grammy Award-winning album, "Occupation Foole," included a satiric commentary on "seven words you couldn't say on the public, ah, airwaves, um, the ones you definitely wouldn't say, ever . . . shit, piss, fuck, cunt, cocksucker, motherfucker, and tits" (*FCC v. Pacifica Foundation*, 1978, p. 751). Carlin then used the words in and out of their profane context to illustrate his central point: that the words had no meaning beyond what the listener wanted to give them.

The Federal Communications Commission (FCC) received a complaint from a listener who had stumbled across Carlin's monologue on his car radio while driving with his 15-year-old son. Lawyers for the FCC concluded that Carlin's monologue was "patently offensive" and was not suitable for broadcast over the public airwaves (*FCC v. Pacifica Foundation*, 1978, p. 726). In *FCC v. Pacifica Foundation* (1978), Justice John Paul Stevens, writing for a 5–4 Court, upheld the position of the FCC. Acknowledging that the "words of the Carlin monologue are unquestionably 'speech' within the meaning of the First Amendment," Stevens held that the FCC had the power to regulate a radio broadcast that was indecent but not obscene, noting that "each medium of expression presents special First Amendment problems . . . and . . . it is broadcasting that has received the most limited First Amendment protection" (pp. 744, 748). Stevens emphasized that the Court's ruling was narrow—that the issue was not whether Carlin's words were protected in the privacy on one's home or in private conversation, but over the public airwaves. Clearly, *Pacifica* demonstrates that the medium through which speech takes place can determine whether that speech is constitutionally protected.

PUBLIC NUDITY AND PERFORMANCE

Semi-nude and erotic dancing have long graced the stages and theatres of the United States and are considered by many to be high-minded art forms. While the Court has ruled that nudity in public performances has literary qualities and is protected expression, nude dancing in bars and nightclubs is not. In *Barnes v. Glen Theatre, Inc.* (1991), a 5–4 Court held that an Indiana indecency law prohibiting public nudity applied to establishments featuring nude dancing. Chief William Rehnquist held that the Indiana indecency law was "substantially related" to protecting order and public morality (p. 567). Key in Chief Justice Rehnquist's analysis was his decision to classify nude dancing as public nudity, even though the dancers practiced their craft inside the Kitty Kat Lounge and Glen Theatre in South Bend, Indiana.

In *Erie v. Pap's A.M.* (2000), the Court confronted a slightly different but still distinct constitutional question involving nude dancing as constitutionally protected expression. In *Barnes*, the Indiana law was not written specifically to ban nude dancing. In *Pap's A.M.*, the question was whether a law specifically directed toward the suppression of nude dancing violated the First Amendment. An Erie, Pennsylvania law required dancers working in theatres and clubs to wear G-strings and pasties to cover their genitalia. Justice O'Connor, writing for the majority, applied the four-part *O'Brien* test (see previous section on protesting) to determine whether Erie had violated the First Amendment with its nude dancing ordinance. O'Connor concluded that Erie had met all four criteria of the *O'Brien* test and thus had not compromised the First Amendment rights of nude dancers working in local nightclubs. Wrote O'Connor, "The requirement that dancers wear pasties and G-strings is a minimal restriction in furtherance of the asserted government interests, and the restriction leaves ample capacity to convey the dancer's erotic message" (*Erie v. Pap's A.M.*, 2000, p. 301).

OBSCENITY

In 1864, an alarmed postmaster general of the United States reported that "great numbers" of provocative photographs and "lewd" books were being mailed to Union troops during the Civil War. Apparently, semi-nude photographs of women were among the most popular uses of this new technology. In 1865, Congress enacted legislation making the shipping of any "obscene book, pamphlet, picture, print, or other publication of vulgar and indecent character" through the United States mail a federal crime (De Grazia, 1992, p. 4). By 1873, a former dry goods clerk from New York, Anthony Comstock, had developed a national reputation as a tireless crusader against obscenity as the secretary of the New York Society for the Suppression of Vice. Leading members of Congress invited him to Washington to help draft national legislation prohibiting the sale and distribution of obscene materials through the mail. A savvy public relations man, Comstock arrived in the nation's capital with a large cloth bag stuffed with "indecent" books and articles. He was given a private office in the Capitol, where he displayed the "unsuitable" materials that he believed should not be available to the public. Comstock's tactics proved quite effective. That same year, Congress enacted a comprehensive anti-obscenity law that broadened the 1865 law's coverage and added a provision that banned sending any "article or thing, designed or intended for the prevention of conception or procuring of abortion" (p. 4). The law also enabled Comstock, who had been named a special unpaid agent of the Post Office, to walk into any post office and search any mail that he believed might contain obscene materials.

The Comstock Act's true objective, according to its author, was to protect impressionable young minds from corruption. Because the American courts had not heard any obscenity cases, lawmakers turned to the British common law system for guidance, drawing upon *Regina v. Hicklin* (1868) to justify the legal suppression of materials with sexual themes. According to *Hicklin*, any literary value a publication might have was irrelevant if the courts concluded that it might have an immoral influence on younger readers. Some courts concluded that "obscene" passages, in the hands of a skilled literary stylist, actually enhanced the power of a book to "deprave and corrupt" (Blanchard, 1992, p. 741).

Within six months, Comstock claimed to have seized almost 250,000 obscene pictures, drawings, slides, and books. He continued his moral crusade until the late 1910s, when he passed away, but his cause endured. By then, even the major New York publishing houses were intimidated by government agents and private groups determined to root out indecency. During the 1920s, books by D. H. Lawrence (*Women in Love*), Theodore Dreiser (*The Genius*), and James Joyce (*Ulysses*) were withdrawn by their publishers and future copies destroyed for fear that their "erotic" passages would result in prosecution under the Comstock Act. *Ulysses*, still considered a classic in Irish literature, was treated most harshly. In 1920, the publishers of a small literary magazine were successfully prosecuted for publishing excerpts of Joyce's novel. No American publisher went near *Ulysses* for 11 years, until Random House, a new entrant into the New York publishing world, decided to contract with a French publisher for distribution of the novel in the United States. When boxes containing French translations of *Ulysses* arrived in New York, customs officials seized them and Random House was off to court. In 1934, a federal appeals court agreed with the publisher that the material in question must be viewed as a whole, not in selected parts, when deciding if it fell under the definition of an obscenity prohibition.

THE STRUGGLE TO ESTABLISH AN OBSCENITY STANDARD: THE *ROTH* TEST

American courts did not apply the *Hicklin* rule with any real force after *Ulysses* cleared the tentacles of the Comstock Law. In 1952, the United States Supreme Court, in *Burstyn v. Wilson*, opened up a whole new debate on the boundaries of obscenity law when it struck down a New York law that banned the showing of the film "The Miracle," on the grounds that it was sacrilegious. By ruling that movies were a protected form of First Amendment expression, the Court said that moviemakers, their sponsors, and their audiences, not government boards, would now decide the content of their films. Around the same time, Congress convened hearings on the nation's growing pornographic film industry. A combination of a federal government eager to clamp down on what it believed was a social evil and the emerging "adult entertainment" industry's desire to test the limits of the First Amendment led to the Court's first major decision on obscenity, *Roth v. United States* (1957).

In *Roth*, the Court attempted to address two major goals: (1) to establish a legal definition of obscenity and (2) to develop a judicial standard to analyze whether sexually explicit material met that definition. By any reasonable measure, the Court failed to succeed on either count. Justice William Brennan concluded that "obscenity is not within the area of constitutionally protected speech" but offered no concrete definition on what that meant, other than to say that it was material "utterly without redeeming social importance" (*Roth v. United States*, 1957, pp. 485, 497). The test that emerged from Brennan's opinion was similarly imprecise. Something was obscene, wrote Brennan, if "to the average person, applying contemporary community standards, the dominant theme of the material taken as a whole appeals to a prurient interest" (p. 489). At the time, Brennan's opinion suggested that a bright line could be drawn distinguishing sexually tinged or explicit material from all other material. Certainly, in the contemporary context, many important political issues are intertwined with sexual images and themes: gay rights; abortion and contraception; the legalization of prostitution; sex education in public schools; and sexual content of movies, television, music, and, of course, the Internet. That bright line, as Justice Brennan would confess in subsequent obscenity cases, was a function of social convention and political context and did not spring from any clear principle flowing from the First Amendment.

Throughout the 1960s, the Court slogged through dozens of obscenity cases without managing to improve upon the *Roth* standard. A consensus existed among a majority of justices that hardcore pornography was not protected by the First Amendment, but the justices could not put together a majority opinion defining what that meant. Indeed, the most notable efforts to refine the *Roth* standard came from two quips by members of the Court. In *Jacobellis v. Ohio* (1964), Justice Potter Stewart admitted that he could not come up with a specific definition of obscenity other than to say, "I know it when I see it" (p. 197). Four years later, Justice Thurgood Marshall, in upholding the right of individuals to possess obscene materials in the privacy of their own homes, wrote in *Stanley v. Georgia* (1968), "If the First Amendment means anything, it means that a State has no business telling a man, sitting alone in his own house, what books he may read or what films he may watch" (p. 565).

REFINING THE OBSCENITY STANDARD: THE *MILLER* TEST

By 1971, the Court, clearly exasperated at its own efforts to find a workable legal standard for obscenity, had reversed 31 obscenity convictions, while at the same time widening the protection afforded to sexually explicit materials under the First Amendment (Strossen, 1995). In *Miller v. California* (1973), the Court finally made a comprehensive effort to rethink and revise the *Roth* standard to address the criticism it had received as being insufficiently sensitive to the needs of states and localities. Under *Roth*, the "community standards" to which sexually explicit materials were subjected were national, not state and local, in scope.

Marvin Miller, a small-time pornographer in Southern California, had sent thousands of brochures across the Los Angeles metropolitan area advertising the various sexually explicit materials he had for sale. Unfortunately for Miller, one of his brochures arrived unsolicited at a Newport Beach restaurant, where the manager opened the package in the company of his elderly mother to find sexually explicit materials. Miller was convicted under a state law that prohibited the distribution of obscene materials through the mail. Writing for a 5–4 Court, Chief Justice Warren Burger established a new standard for obscenity regulation:

It was Chief Justice Warren Burger who would clarify the standard for obscenity regulation that is still used today. Burger felt that establishing a "community standard" that could be applied nationwide would be "an exercise in futility" and that such standards should be set by the states.

The basic guidelines for the trier of fact must be: (a) whether "the average person, applying contemporary community standards" would find that the work, taken as a whole, appeals to the prurient interest; (b) whether the work depicts or describes, in a patently offensive way, sexual conduct specifically defined by the applicable *state law*; and (c) *whether the work, taken as a whole, lacks serious literary, artistic, political, or scientific value*. We do not adopt as a constitutional standard the "utterly without redeeming social value" test. (*Miller v. California*, 1973, p. 24)

In shifting the national "community standards" provision of *Roth* to the states in *Miller*, Burger commented, "To require a State to structure obscenity proceedings around evidence of a *national* 'community standard' would be an exercise in futility" (p. 30).

The Court's dissenters in *Miller* were highly critical of the majority's opinion. Justices Brennan, Douglas, Marshall, and Stewart were clearly uncomfortable with the Court acting as a national standards board for sexually expressive speech and believed that the appropriate solution was simply to let consenting adults decide for themselves what they wanted to read or watch. In *Paris Adult Theatre v. Slaton* (1973), decided the same day as *Miller*, Brennan used his dissent in that case to come out completely against any form of regulation of sexually explicit material, saying that it just could not be done without violating the First Amendment.

Forty years after these cases were decided, *Miller* remains the standard applied by the Court in cases involving alleged violations of obscenity law. Nonetheless, *Miller* has hardly curbed the wide range of sexually explicit material available to the public. Although the Court has ruled, in *New York v. Ferber* (1982) and *Osbourne v. Ohio* (1990), respectively, that neither the distribution nor possession of child pornography is entitled to constitutional protection, rapidly changing technology and, as the next section will discuss, the Internet has made it next to impossible for Congress or state legislatures to regulate access to sexually explicit material without running afoul of the First Amendment.

*T*HE NEW FRONTIER: THE INTERNET AND THE REGULATION OF DIGITAL MEDIA

The online atmosphere in the early years of the Internet represented a high-technology version of the lawless Wild West of the 1800s. Quite literally, anyone with Internet access could say or display anything he or she wanted. Such

You Be the Judge: Freedom of Expression

The Case: Pleasant Valley is a small town in a fairly rural part of the state. Every year, the town hosts an autumn apple and blueberry harvest during the second week of November, an event that attracts people from around the state. The event takes all the resources of the police and fire departments to provide direction, security, and assistance to vendors and tourists.

This year, a motorcycle gang called the "Raging Isotopes" has decided to ride through the town during the harvest celebration to, in their words, "protest the heathens and sodomites of Pleasant Valley." Last year, Pleasant Valley passed a law legalizing same-sex marriage, making it the only municipality in the state to do so. The mayor supported the legislation, and the council passed it by a unanimous vote. The Raging Isotopes were well known around the area for their opposition to gay rights. The gang's leader, Lowell Murray, contacted the Pleasant Valley mayor to inquire about a permit to conduct a rally and protest in town square. Murray informed the mayor that they would carry signs with such slogans as "One Man, One Woman = One Marriage," "Adam and Eve Were Right," and "God is Not Happy About Gay Marriage." Murray also told the mayor that the 50 bikers expected to make the trip would wear their jackets emblazoned with their insignia, which featured an elaborate sewn patch on the back of a man and woman engaged in a sexual act. Underneath the patch were the words "F———g A!"

The mayor informed Murray that he would authorize the Isotopes to stage their rally in downtown Pleasant Valley. The gang would have to pay a $1,000 permit fee to defray costs associated with the event. But the mayor informed Murray that the group could not wear their jackets because, in his view, the insignia and the slogans were "indecent" and "obscene" and inappropriate in a traditional public forum. Murray claimed the First Amendment guaranteed the right of the Isotopes to stage their rally while wearing their jackets.

The Issue: Do the Isotopes have a First Amendment right to stage their rally while wearing their jackets?

Yes or no? You be the judge! For an interactive version of this box, visit the online edition of your textbook. Otherwise, turn to the appendix to read how the Court might rule.

open and unfettered exchange and the ability to communicate with other people around the world in real time were certainly exciting. But it also meant that individuals navigating the web could encounter sexually explicit, racist, or other offensive materials just by entering seemingly benign keywords into a search engine. Naturally, questions soon arose over whether government regulation was necessary to police the Internet.

To forestall such regulation, many Internet providers of sexually explicit images agreed to warn users of their sites' contents. For purveyors of sexually explicit material, gratuitous references to the First Amendment, the Constitution, and the importance of free speech in a democracy usually prefaced the graphic images to follow. In the 1980s, the VCR revolutionized the adult film industry by allowing individuals to rent movies and view them in the privacy of their own homes. But the Internet went one step further: It allowed individuals to watch anything they wanted without having to leave their homes, making the Court's early decisions in *Miller* and *Paris Adult Theatre* largely irrelevant to questions involving sexually explicit material viewed or acquired through the Internet. Concern that such self-policing would not work prompted Congress to enact the Communications Decency Act (CDA) of 1996. The battle over Internet regulation had just begun.

In *Reno v. American Civil Liberties Union* (1997), the Court took up the challenge of defining the constitutional status of the Internet and, accordingly, the power of government to regulate it. The most pressing question before the Court was whether the Internet should be considered a form of broadcast media, and thus within federal regulatory power, or more akin to print journalism, and thus entitled to broad First Amendment protection.

The Court has often overruled legislative attempts to protect children from certain Internet content, noting that such efforts often end up limiting the free speech rights of adults.

In *Reno*, the Court ruled that the provisions of the CDA banning "indecent" or "patently offensive" material transmitted through the Internet were unconstitutional. Justice John Paul Stevens acknowledged that Congress had a strong interest in protecting minors from harmful materials—the stated goal of the CDA—but held that "interest does not justify an unnecessarily broad suppression of speech addressed to adults. As we have explained, the Government may not reduce the adult population . . . to . . . only what is fit for children" (*Reno v. American Civil Liberties Union*, 1997, p. 875). Justice Stevens also found the law unconstitutionally vague, overly broad, and lacking "the precision that the First Amendment requires when a statute regulates the content of speech" (p. 846). Finally, Justice Stevens found that the Internet was analogous to the print media, not the broadcast media, and thus entitled to be left alone to foster the free exchange of ideas. "[F]reedom of expression in a democratic society," Stevens wrote, "outweighs any theoretical but unproven benefit of censorship" (p. 885).

Reno did not deter Congress from making additional efforts to regulate sexually explicit material on the Internet. Those efforts, however, were not successful. In *Ashcroft v. Free Speech Coalition* (2002), the Court struck down the Child Pornography Prevention Act (CPPA) of 1996, ruling that the law's provision prohibiting the distribution of images on the Internet that "appeared to be" or "conveyed the impression" of minors engaging in sexual activity was overly broad and thus unconstitutional. Two years later, in *Ashcroft v. American Civil Liberties Union* (2004), the Court narrowly held that the Child Online Protection Act (COPA) of 1998 was unconstitutional because it included a provision prohibiting the display of any material that was harmful to minors. Five justices believed that this language was too broad and risked banning material that was constitutionally protected by the First Amendment. The law never went into effect. Most recently, the Court ruled, in *United States v. Stevens* (2010), that a 1999 federal law barring displays of "animal cruelty" on the Internet was unconstitutional. *Stevens* involved the prosecution of a man for putting images of dog fighting on the Internet, but the real target of the law was a web phenomenon known as "crush videos." These videos depicted women in high heels stomping on small animals until they died. Chief Justice John Roberts, writing for an 8–1 Court, invalidated the law on the grounds that it was overly broad and noted that videos depicting animal cruelty were not categorically unprotected by the First Amendment.

THE FRAMERS AND FREEDOM OF THE PRESS

Prior restraint

Government action that prohibits the publication or broadcast of any material prior to its release.

Libel

To publish in print an untruth about another that will defame that person or his or her reputation. A public official or public figure must demonstrate *actual malice* to win a libel judgment.

The next few sections focus on the development of the freedom of press guarantee of the First Amendment. The focus here is on the two major areas involving the Press Clause: (1) **prior restraint**, in which the government prohibits the publication, broadcast, or dissemination of any material prior to its distribution, and (2) **libel**, a legal doctrine that establishes the boundaries of protected expression after its publication and whether individuals are entitled to monetary damages for injuries to their reputation based on false or defamatory statements.

The notion that colonial America was a bastion of freedom where anyone could voice an opinion on anything or practice religion free from government persecution or community antagonism is, as historian Leonard Levy has commented, "a sentimental hallucination that ignores history" (Levy, 1986, p. 72). Each settlement tended to harbor orthodox views on religion, politics, and just about any other matter of social significance. Dissenters were not tolerated; indeed, their expulsion from communities where their opinions were considered heretical or dangerous was quite common.

The legal instrument used to enforce the conformity of opinion was the law of seditious libel, which had been adopted from the English common law tradition (see framers and free speech section). Sedition laws in the colonies punished persons for publishing or writing material that was considered dangerous, offensive, or otherwise improper. These prohibitions were so broad that

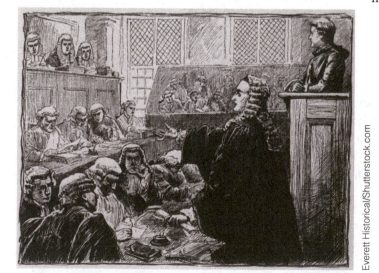

The trial of journalist Peter Zenger, seated in the upper right corner, is one illustration of the consequences under the colonial seditious libel laws. Zenger had been imprisoned and put on trial for publishing critical opinions of the colonial governor. In the Zenger trial, truth was used as a successful defense against a libel accusation, but this distinction would be phased out in the 19th century.

Everett Historical/Shutterstock.com

just about any undesirable opinion could fall within their limitations. By the early 1700s, the American colonies had lifted nearly all prior restraints on the press, a development that followed the decision of the British Parliament in 1694 not to renew its system of requiring publishers to obtain a government license to operate. The licensing system in England allowed government officials to control the content of material that circulated to the public, thus making the free exchange of opinion or criticism of the government impossible. Indeed, John Milton's *Areopagitica—A Speech for the Liberty of Unlicensed Printing*, published in 1644 and considered one of the great defenses of modern free speech principles, emerged out of the long and bitter battle between writers, editors, and publishers and the British government.

But Milton never questioned the right of the government to punish anyone who published material that was considered libelous, nor did most opponents of prior restraint in 17th- and 18th-century England and colonial America. And because seditious libel was a common law crime, the power rested with judges to define the alleged offense, giving the state a powerful weapon with which to intimidate potential dissidents. Truth served as no defense, because the harm prohibited by seditious libel laws was simply whether people had their feelings hurt or their self-esteem lowered by the offending material.

Even after the ratification of the First Amendment, the United States continued to embrace the British common law definition of freedom of press offered by William Blackstone, the great British legal scholar whose *Commentaries on the Laws of England* (1765–1769) were enormously influential among the judges, lawyers, and statesmen of the early American Republic. Wrote Blackstone,

> The liberty of the press is indeed essential to the nature of a free state; but this consists in laying no previous restraints upon publications, and not in freedom from censure from criminal matter when published. Every freeman has an undoubted right to lay what sentiments he pleases before the public: to forbid this is to destroy the freedom of the press: but if he publishes what is improper, mischievous or illegal, he must take the consequences of his own temerity. (1979, pp. 151–152)

Unfortunately for libel defendants, Blackstone believed that judges, not juries, should decide sedition charges, and truth was not considered an admissible defense. By denying truth as a defense and permitting only judges to determine guilt or innocence, state sedition laws discouraged newspapers and pamphleteers from circulating material critical of the government. Not even James Madison, the primary architect of the First Amendment, saw a contradiction between the absolute language of the free press guarantee and the Blackstonian principles that guided its understanding. By 1791, the Press Clause had come to mean that Congress was barred from passing any law placing a prior restraint on the right of the press to publish. The Supreme Court would not rule until 1931 on what the prior restraint principle behind the First Amendment meant. And it would take just more than 30 more years after that for the Court to decide the protection, if any, afforded to the news media to criticize public officials and private citizens without fear of retribution.

FREEDOM OF THE PRESS AND PRIOR RESTRAINT

Prior restraint is not a concept unique to the rights of the news media or the crusading freelance reporter to publish controversial material. As discussed at the beginning of the chapter, seditious libel laws during the colonial period prohibited anyone, including the press, from uttering or publishing any "false, scandalous, and malicious" statements against the government. After World War I, the Court upheld various pieces of legislation that made it illegal to say or publish anything intended to cause contempt and scorn for the United States or interfere with defense production (these include the earlier discussions of *Schenck v. United States* [1919] and *Abrams v. United States* [1919]). Again, these laws applied to all persons and not just the press. But they still amounted to a prior restraint because they made criminal the publication or utterance of ideas the government believed threatened public order.

THE NEWSPAPER THAT REFUSED TO STAY GAGGED

In *Near v. Minnesota* (1931), the Court handed down its first major decision on the constitutionality of prior restraint laws outside the context of national security. Jay Near, who edited the Minneapolis newspaper *Saturday Press*, had been convicted under a state law for publishing overtly anti-Jewish, anti-Catholic, and racist articles and editorials. The Minnesota law said that anyone who "engaged in the business of regularly or customarily producing, publishing or circulating, having in possession, selling or giving away" an obscene, lewd, or lascivious periodical or "malicious, scandalous and defamatory newspaper" was guilty of being a public nuisance (p. 702). Chief Justice Charles Evans Hughes, writing for a 5–4 Court, held that the law violated the First Amendment. The Court also ruled that the Free Press Clause applied to the states through the Due Process Clause of the Fourteenth Amendment, continuing the process of incorporation of the First Amendment that began in *Gitlow v. United States* (1925) (see "war at home" section). Near's victory established an important precedent for newsrooms and publishing houses everywhere by writing the no-prior-restraint rule into American constitutional law. However, Chief Justice Hughes did not embrace an absolute prohibition on prior restraint, noting that the "location of troops" or "the sailing dates of transports" were sufficiently compelling national security concerns to justify a ban on the publication of such information by the news media (*Near v. Minnesota*, 1931, p. 716).

Still, after *Near*, the Court struck down several types of laws imposing either direct or indirect prior restraints on the press. From the 1930s until the late 1960s, the Court ruled that state laws imposing taxes on newspapers were unconstitutional when their impact was to limit circulation; found local ordinances controlling or prohibiting outright the distribution of handbills and pamphlets an unconstitutional form of censorship; and made clear that the Press Clause, as much as the Free Exercise Clause, protected the rights of religious groups to distribute materials in public places. These cases, though, did not require the Court to return to the constitutionality of prior restraint on information that might compromise national security—an exception that Chief Justice Hughes hinted was permissible in *Near*.

THE PENTAGON PAPERS CASE

In June 1967, Secretary of Defense Robert McNamara commissioned the Rand Corporation, a prominent non-governmental research group, to collect top-secret government materials as part of an effort to produce a comprehensive analysis of America's involvement in the Vietnam War. McNamara had his own private doubts about the war, but he believed that the report would vindicate the government's position. The 47-volume report, however, proved so critical of America's war effort that plans for its publication were immediately cancelled. Only 15 copies of the "Pentagon Papers" were distributed, to McNamara and other high-level officials involved with the Vietnam War. Embarrassed by their contents, Pentagon officials gave the Pentagon Papers a top-secret classification to ensure that no one within the government would be able to make them public. This strategy enabled the Pentagon Papers to remain secret for almost four years.

In March 1971, after months of careful negotiation, Daniel Ellsberg, one of the lead authors on the project, agreed to provide copies of the Pentagon Papers to *New York Times* reporter Neil Sheehan, who had once served as the paper's Vietnam correspondent. Ellsberg had once been an enthusiastic supporter of the Vietnam War. He was a former Marine officer who was honorably discharged in 1957 and later served in Vietnam as a civilian advisor to the State Department and the military high-command. By the late 1960s, Ellsberg's opposition to the war had intensified to the point where he viewed his decision to leak all but the final four volumes of the report as a way to help stop the "bombing and killing" (Ungar, 1972, pp. 83–84).

After months of internal discussion and negotiation, *The New York Times* began running excerpts of the Pentagon Papers on June 13, 1971. Two days later, President Richard Nixon asked for and obtained a federal court order to enjoin the *Times* from publishing the Pentagon Papers on national security grounds. In the meantime, Ellsberg had provided copies of the Pentagon Papers to 18 other newspapers, including the *Washington Post*. Although no recipient of the Pentagon Papers disclosed Ellsberg's name publicly, Ellsberg feared for his safety and went into hiding while the *Times* and *Post* appealed the lower court's decision to the Supreme Court.

On June 30, the Court, 6–3, ruled that the president possessed no inherent power to order the prior restraint of the Pentagon Papers from publication by either the *Times* or the *Post*. So divided was the Court that the justices were left to issue an unsigned, **per curiam** opinion, with each individual justice in the majority writing a concurring opinion explaining his position. Only two justices, Hugo Black and William Douglas, believed that any government-imposed prior restraint was always unconstitutional. The four remaining justices in the majority, William Brennan, Thurgood Marshall, Potter Stewart, and Byron White, agreed that the government had not met the "heavy" burden required to justify a prior restraint. In varying degrees, these four justices believed that the government could order a prior restraint when information could cause irreparable damage to national security. Congressional authorization and the individual merits of the government's claim, however, bolstered the constitutionality of such an action. The *Times* and *Post* resumed publication of the Papers the next day.

Per curiam

Latin for "by the court"; describes an opinion attributed to the Court collectively, rather than to an individual justice.

PRIOR RESTRAINT AFTER THE PENTAGON PAPERS

Although the justices in *New York Times* did not declare prior restraints on the news media unconstitutional per se, their ruling has prevented any similar showdowns since then. But the Court has dealt with the issue of prior restraint on the press in other contexts. In *Hazelwood v. Kuhlmeier* (1988), the Court upheld the right of a suburban St. Louis high school principal to pull several pages of material discussing teen pregnancy, divorce, and other sensitive family issues from the school newspaper over the objection of its student editors. The principal explained his decision was motivated by the privacy of the students and families, who, in his own words, "were described in such a way that the readers could tell who they were" (Uhlig, 1987, p. 102). The Court rejected the argument that the principal's action was the equivalent of prior restraint, instead holding that the principal's decision involved "special circumstances" unique to the public school environment. In fact, the Court did not even broach the prior restraint issues raised in *New York Times*. *Hazelwood* was, for the Court, a case in which a public school's interest in the privacy rights of its students and their families justified what it referred to as "editorial control" by school administrators. Although it generated a considerable amount of attention at the time, *Hazelwood* has had no impact beyond the public schools, where it continues to have an important bearing.

FREEDOM OF THE PRESS AND LIBEL

After the American Revolution, state libel laws distinguished between "truth" and "facts," which were permissible defenses, and "falsehoods," which were punishable under criminal law. Similar distinctions in libel law were also drawn between statements made with "good motives" and those motivated by "criminal intent." These distinctions were gradually phased out during the 19th century, as they were perceived to be unhelpful to juries with determining the guilt or innocence of persons charged with libel.

Libel law did not follow the libertarian model that James Madison and other advocates of broad free speech and press rights preferred. By the early 1960s, most states still followed the common law of libel that had developed after the demise of the Sedition Act of 1798. Three principles formed the basis of libel law during this period. First, a statement considered defamatory was presumed false. This placed the burden of proof in libel trials on the publisher, and truth was—and remains—difficult to prove. Second, it did not matter whether a falsehood was published intentionally or negligently. All that mattered was whether the information was false. Finally, the injured party did not have to demonstrate *actual* harm to his or her reputation. Harm was presumed to exist from publication. Combined, the force of these three rules meant that libel defendants had to prove the absolute accuracy of what they said or they would lose.

THE "ACTUAL MALICE" STANDARD

New York Times v. Sullivan (1964) completely revolutionized libel law. For the first time, the Court forged a constitutional definition of libel by drawing upon the common law rules that had sought to balance freedom of the press with the right of individuals against defamation. Before Sullivan, the Court had only briefly encountered libel law, upholding in *Beauharnais v. Illinois* (1952) a state law mandating penalties for words or photos depicting the "depravity, criminality, unchastity, or lack of virtue of a class of citizens, or any race, color or creed" (p. 251). Justice William Douglas, dissenting, noted the implications the Court's decision might have for individuals who chose to denounce public officials, the very basis of the civil libel action in *Sullivan*. Wrote Douglas,

> Today, a white man stands convicted for protesting in unseemly language against our decisions invalidating restrictive covenants. Tomorrow a Negro will be hauled before a court for denouncing lynch law in heated terms. . . . Intemperate speech is a distinctive characteristic of man. Hot-heads blow off and release destructive energy in the process. (*Beauharnais v. Illinois*, 1952, pp. 286–287)

Sullivan resulted from the ongoing confrontation between Alabama law enforcement and civil rights demonstrators during the early 1960s. After Martin Luther King, Jr. had been jailed on trumped-up charges by Alabama officials in March 1960, civil rights organizations set up a committee in New York City to raise funds to fight the legal battles that lay ahead. Just a few weeks after King's arrest, the committee put together an advertisement entitled "Heed Their Rising Voices," which described Southern hostility toward the civil rights movement.

The ad was signed by more than 50 people, including professional entertainers, athletes, political activists, and clergy from numerous religious faiths.

L. B. Sullivan, an elected city commissioner, believed the ad wrongly implicated him and the Montgomery, Alabama police in "grave misconduct." Sullivan sent a letter to the *Times* demanding a "full and fair retraction of the entire false and defamatory matter" (Lewis, 1991, p. 11). Lawyers for the *Times* asked Sullivan to identify how the ad defamed him, because it never mentioned him by name. Sullivan did not reply to the *Times*. Instead, he filed a libel suit against the paper in Alabama state court, where a jury awarded him $500,000. Separately, Alabama Governor John Patterson filed a libel action asking for $2.5 million against four local black ministers and the *Times*.

In a unanimous opinion, the Court ruled on behalf of the *Times*. Justice William Brennan swept away centuries of libel law that had long favored public officials. To collect a damage award in a libel action, Brennan held, it was not enough for a public official to demonstrate merely that a newspaper had published a false statement or factual error. Rather, a public official had to demonstrate **actual malice** against critics of their official conduct, defined as a statement made (1) with the knowledge that it was false and (2) with reckless disregard of the truth. Absent a showing of actual malice, a public official had no right to a damage award. *Sullivan* is rightly considered one of the most important decisions the Court has handed down on the First Amendment.

Actual malice

The legal standard developed in *New York Times v. Sullivan* (1964) for public officials to win a libel judgment. An individual must demonstrate that written material is "knowingly false" or created with "reckless disregard for the truth" to prove libel.

The Heed Their Rising Voices ad that appeared in The New York Times. *Read the transcript of the ad at a National Archives exhibit: http://www.archives.gov/exhibits/documented-rights/exhibit/section4/detail/heed-rising-voices.html*

LIMITS OF ACTUAL MALICE: PUBLIC AND PRIVATE FIGURES

Three years later, the Court addressed one of the major questions left unanswered in *Sullivan*: Did the virtual immunity the Court created for the news media against libel suits by public officials extend to **public figures**—those who operate in the public arena but do not hold public office? In two cases, *Associated Press v. Walker* (1967) and *Curtis Publishing Co. v. Butts* (1967), a divided Court ruled that libel actions brought by public figures were subject to the actual malice standard.

Associated Press involved a lawsuit brought by a retired Army general who claimed that the news service falsely reported that he encouraged white students at the University of Mississippi to attack federal prosecutors assigned to protect James Meredith, the first African-American student admitted to the university. Walker claimed the eyewitness's statements published by the Associated Press were libelous. Writing for a 5–4 majority, Justice John Harlan ruled that Walker

Public figure

In a libel or slander case, a person of great public interest, such as a professional athlete, celebrity, actor, or person who willingly engages the public. A public figure must also demonstrate *actual malice* to win a libel judgment.

was a public figure who had sufficient access to the news media to counter any statements made about him considered erroneous. Thus, he was bound by the actual malice standard.

In *Butts*, Harlan, again writing for a 5–4 majority, upheld a libel award against the *Saturday Evening Post*, a then-prominent weekly general interest magazine. The *Post* had run an article accusing a college athletic director, Wally Butts, of conspiring to throw a football game against an opponent. A jury determined the *Post* had not met the standards of professional reporting before running the story and awarded Butts $480,000. Harlan agreed with the *Post* that Butts was a public figure and thus bound by the *Sullivan* standard, but he agreed with Butts that the magazine had been guilty of "highly unreasonable conduct constituting an extreme departure from the standards of investigative reporting" (Butts, 1967, p. 158).

The upshot of these two cases was that public figures were now considered no different under libel law than public officials. However, what did that mean for private figures who found themselves thrust into the public eye by no action of their own? In *Gertz v. Welch* (1974), the Court ruled that private figures who find themselves the object of public discussion are not required to meet the *Sullivan* standard to collect damages for damage to their reputation. Two years later, in *Time, Inc. v. Firestone* (1976), the Court ruled that the ex-wife of the heir to the tire company fortune, Mary Alice Firestone, was not a public figure, even though she had been the subject of intense media coverage for months over her very public divorce proceedings. *Time*, the weekly news magazine, had said that Firestone's extramarital relationships were among the reasons the couple was divorcing. Firestone demanded a published retraction. After *Time* refused, Firestone successfully sued the news magazine, claiming she did not become a public figure simply because the news media chose to publish a story about her.

Justice William Rehnquist held that public figures are persons who are connected to a story or behavior of public concern. Divorce proceedings between two private parties were not, Rehnquist said, a public interest.

But in 1988, Rehnquist again authored an important decision on libel law, this time handing the press a victory. In *Hustler Magazine v. Falwell*, a unanimous Court held that public figures were not entitled to recover damages for the intentional infliction of emotional distress by the news media if no reasonable person had reason to believe the material or statement in question was true. Chief Justice Rehnquist affirmed the belief that "on issues of public concern, the match between the First Amendment and [a law banning] the . . . intentional

Hustler magazine publisher Larry Flynt holds a copy of the ad parody that portrayed Rev. Jerry Falwell as an incestuous drunk and prompted Falwell to take Flynt to court for "emotional distress." However, in *Hustler Magazine v. Falwell*, the Court ruled that, under the First Amendment, public figures are not entitled to damages simply because the published material hurt their feelings.

infliction of emotional distress is no contest; the First Amendment always wins" (quoted in Smolla, 1992, p. 148). Emotional distress has nothing to do with whether published material is true or false, but whether it has any bearing on the public interest.

SUMMARY

- Despite the guarantee of freedom of speech and press in the First Amendment, Congress and the states regularly passed laws that limited political dissent during the late 1700s and early 1800s. These laws, such as the Alien and Sedition Acts of 1798, were very broad in their application and permitted government to punish speech considered threatening to the United States.
- In *Schenck v. United States* (1919), the Supreme Court ruled that the Free Speech Clause did not guarantee absolute protection to all speech. The case introduced the "clear and present danger test," which remained in place until 1968, when it was overruled in *Brandenburg v. Ohio*.
- By the early 1930s, the Court, using the Due Process Clause of the Fourteenth Amendment, had incorporated the Free Speech Clause and made it applicable to the states.
- Although the Court began to expand the guarantee of freedom of expression after World War II, it continued to create numerous exceptions to what it considered protected speech. Exceptions to speech fully protected by the First Amendment include "fighting words," libel, slander, and obscenity. Speech that threatens national security and leads to imminent lawlessness is not protected either.
- In *West Virginia Board of Education v. Barnette* (1943), the Court held that the Free Speech Clause also protected the right of individuals not to speak or express an opinion with which they disagreed. Justice Robert Jackson's opinion noted that a nation that refuses to protect the right of its citizens to hold and express unpopular ideas was a nation destined to become like its enemies.
- In such cases as *Tinker v. Des Moines* (1968) and *United States v. O'Brien* (1949), the Court ruled that "symbolic speech" was protected by the First Amendment. In *O'Brien*, the Court established a four-part test that is still used today in deciding symbolic speech cases: government regulation is sufficiently justified if (1) it is within the constitutional power of the government, (2) it furthers an important or substantial governmental interest, (3) it is unrelated to the suppression of free expression, (4) and its restriction on First Amendment freedoms is not greater than is essential to further that interest.

- The Court has ruled that the First Amendment protects more than just political speech. Speech having literary, artistic, and scientific value is also fully protected by the First Amendment.

- In 1996, the Court, in *American Civil Liberties Union v. Reno*, ruled that the material communicated on and through the Internet is entitled to the same protection as all other forms of written speech. Since then, Congress has been relatively unsuccessful in attempting to regulate sexually explicit and other materials available on the Internet.

- The Court has largely rejected efforts to regulate what is commonly called "hate speech," ruling that laws prohibiting the display of such symbols as a burning cross or Nazi swastika are unconstitutional. On a similar note, the Court has also declared laws prohibiting flag burning unconstitutional as well.

- The fundamental principle behind the Free Press Clause is that the government may not engage in prior restraint of material it finds objectionable. Although the Court has never declared that the right of newspapers and other news media to publish is absolute, it has ruled that the government must demonstrate that any questionable material compromises national security, such as the location of troops or plans for military operations.

- Public officials and public figures must demonstrate that the news media engaged in "actual malice" to win a libel judgment. Private figures are not required to meet this burden.

REVIEW QUESTIONS

1. Does the absolute language of the First Amendment mean that all speech is protected?

2. What factors make it more likely that the Supreme Court will uphold restrictions on speech or press?

3. When is government regulation of speech justified?

4. What is "symbolic speech"? Does it deserve the same protection as "pure speech"?

5. Is the Internet more like a newspaper or the broadcast media?

6. Should government have more or less authority to regulate sexually explicit materials than other forms of speech?

7. Should the "actual malice" standard apply to private figures as well as public figures and public officials?

READINGS AND RESOURCES

LIBRARY OF CONGRESS: ALIEN AND SEDITION ACTS

http://www.loc.gov/rr/program/bib/ourdocs/Alien.html
Visit the Library of Congress to read about responses to the Alien and Sedition Acts and copies of the acts themselves, among other resources.

NATIONAL SECURITY ARCHIVE

http://www.gwu.edu/~nsarchiv/
The National Security Archive, maintained by George Washington University, combines a unique range of functions: investigative journalism center, research institute on international affairs, library and archive of declassified U.S. documents, leading nonprofit user of the U.S. Freedom of Information Act, and public interest law firm defending and expanding public access to government information.

THE FIRST AMENDMENT CENTER

http://www.firstamendmentcenter.org/
Visit the First Amendment Center online, sponsored by the Newseum and Vanderbilt University, to learn more about the freedoms of the press and to

assemble, among others, and learn journalists' take on the speech freedoms they exercise every day at work.

ACTUAL MALICE: KELLY/WARNER LAW PRACTICE

http://kellywarnerlaw.com/what-is-actual-malice/
The attorneys at Arizona law practice Kelly/Warner explain what actual malice is in defamation cases, with examples and without the legalese.

"LARRY FLYNT: MY FRIEND, JERRY FALWELL"

http://www.latimes.com/news/opinion/commentary/la-op-flynt
20may20,0,2751741.story
In this 2007 op-ed, *Hustler* magazine publisher Larry Flynt recounts the facts leading up to the Supreme Court case *Hustler Magazine v. Falwell* and how he found himself becoming friends with the reverend who sued him.

The Law of Search and Seizure

By Craig D. Harter

Chapter Overview

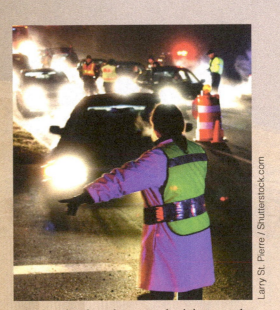

Larry St. Pierre / Shutterstock.com

The Fourth Amendment is to criminal justice what a baseball is to the game of baseball. It is absolutely essential. Understanding that, this chapter covers all the basics from defining what a search or seizure is for Constitutional purposes to describing how those concepts have been changed over the years by new technologies. Key concepts such as "expectation of privacy," "exclusionary rule," and "fruit of the poisonous tree" are explored while key terms such as "inevitable discovery" and "good faith exception" are defined. As in other chapters, these concepts and terms are discussed by analyzing landmark court decisions and real-life situations. Students and criminal justice practitioners will find the material in this chapter invaluable and ready to be applied.

𝒞HAPTER LEARNING OBJECTIVES

After reading this chapter, you will be able to:

1. Define what is considered a search under the Fourth Amendment
2. Define what is considered a seizure under the Fourth Amendment
3. Describe the difference between probable cause and reasonable suspicion
4. Discuss the requirements for issuance of a valid warrant
5. Describe exceptions to the probable cause and warrant requirements
6. Describe what is meant by the "exclusionary rule"

𝒫OLICE AND THE COURTS

FOURTH AMENDMENT (U.S. CONSTITUTION)

The right of the people to be secure in their persons, houses, papers, and effects, against unreasonable searches and seizures, shall not be violated, and no Warrants shall issue, but upon probable cause, supported by Oath or affirmation, and particularly describing the place to be searched, and the person or things to be seized.

IS THERE A REASONABLE EXPECTATION OF PRIVACY?

In order to determine whether or not one's constitutional rights have been violated, it must first be determined whether or not a reasonable expectation of privacy may properly be invoked in the places to be searched and the items to be seized. According to the Fourth Amendment, a reasonable expectation of privacy can be found in the search of the following areas: store, dwelling house, phone booths, business and commercial premises, and private areas in public places (i.e., bathroom stalls)(*Kamisar*).

Over the years, there has been a great deal of discussion of which areas deserve a reasonable expectation of privacy and which areas do not. In fact, the list is so numerous that it is impossible to define each and every area individually. However, for purposes of this chapter, there will be many areas defined to give the reader a good understanding of which areas extend to Fourth Amendment protection and which do not. For instance, in the case of *Hudson v. Palmer* (1984), an inmate asserted that he had a reasonable expectation of privacy in his prison cell in order to prevent administrative searches for contraband. The U.S. Supreme Court found that the Fourth Amendment has no applicability to a prison cell because it is "fundamentally incompatible" with the close and continual surveillance of inmates, and their cells required to ensure security and internal order (*Kamisar*).

ADMINISTRATIVE INSPECTIONS AND REGULATORY SEARCHES

Similarly, there is no reasonable expectation of privacy in administrative inspection and regulatory searches. The reasoning behind this rationale is that administrative searches are generally issued upon a lesser showing of *probable cause*, a reasonable belief that a party has committed a crime, or that a specific place contains evidence of that crime. Administrative searches are searches that do not even rise to the level of probable cause and may be determined by a lesser showing of probable cause. For instance, post 911, there are terrorist checkpoints set up in airports (TSA) in order to protect passengers from weapons and explosives prior to boarding a commercial airline.

Another type of regulatory search is border searches. Here, routine warrantless searches are performed of individuals in order to prevent any illegal activity from entering into a country. Border patrols may lawfully search and deprive private persons of their personal effects without violating their Fourth Amendment rights. While the exercise of discretion by border patrol allows many to pass through without being subject to a search, a vehicle may be subject to search without a showing of probable cause. This discretion to search is given to agents working at the border or its functional equivalent such as international airports, and post offices where foreign mail enters (*Kamisar*).

Vehicle checkpoints are permissible and may be performed without a warrant, but probable cause is needed in order to search the interior of the vehicle and its contents (*Kamisar*).

SEARCH OF STUDENTS

In order for a school official to search a student, it must first be determined that a student does not have a Fourth Amendment reasonable expectation of privacy if (1) the student is an active student who is under their authority; (2) there are reasonable grounds to believe that the search will turn up evidence and that the student has either broken the law or is violating the rules of the school; and (3) the search is reasonably related and not excessively intrusive (*Kamisar*). Here, if there were grounds for a school official to search a student, a search of their school locker would be a search that would be practical in scope and not rise to the level of a search that is "excessively intrusive."

DRUG TESTING

Employers may lawfully employ a practice of random drug testing of their employees without violating any of their Fourth Amendment rights. Drug testing is a practice that is widely used in employer/employee relationships and are often necessary for promotions for positions that may involve a job of interdiction of illegal drugs, or even positions that require employees to use a weapon.

On the other hand, there is a limited expectation of privacy applicable to the random drug testing policy that applies to both middle- and high-school students who are participating in any extracurricular activities.

GARBAGE

In the case of *California v. Greenwood,* 486 U.S. 35 (1988), local police officers believed that a suspect was involved in dealing illegal narcotics and aided the help of the local garbage collector in providing them with a suspect's garbage bags on two separate occasions. On both occasions, when the trash was searched, there was evidence of narcotics found, which served as a basis for the police officers to obtain a warrant and search the suspect's home which revealed the discovery of narcotics. The question that the U.S. Supreme Court answered was "is there a reasonable expectation of privacy in one's garbage?" Ultimately, the final decision by the U.S. Supreme Court was that there is not a reasonable expectation of privacy in one's garbage once it is left for collection (i.e., on the street corner). However, while it is located in or about the residence a reasonable expectation of privacy still exists until the trash is left for collection outside the *curtilage* of a home.

NETWORK SURVEILLANCE

Today, electronic communication has become much more widely utilized by consumers. In fact, when individuals communicate over communication networks they often both send and receive various types of communication to and from other users. Is there a reasonable expectation of privacy enjoyed by communications sent and received from other users? In order to determine whether or not the Fourth Amendment reasonable expectation of privacy extends to these types communications there must be two questions asked? First, is there a Fourth Amendment right in the communication sent over the network? Second, do the network users have a Fourth Amendment right in information used by the network?

EMAILS

A subscriber enjoys a reasonable expectation of privacy in the contents of emails that are stored with, or sent or received through, a commercial ISP, and the government may not compel a commercial ISP to turn over the contents of a subscriber's emails without first obtaining a warrant based on probable cause (U.S. v. Warshak, 2011).

ELECTRONIC SURVEILLANCE (PEN REGISTERS)

Smith v. Maryland, 442 U.S. 735 (1979) involved a case where the police installed a pen register at a telephone company's offices that was used to determine what numbers were being dialed by a party suspected of criminal conduct. At trial, the defendant asserted that his Fourth Amendment rights were violated because he believed that he had a reasonable expectation of privacy in the numbers that he dialed over the phone. This case was later reviewed by the U.S. Supreme Court who determined that an individual does not have a reasonable expectation of privacy in numbers that were dialed on a telephone. The rationale behind this finding was a party voluntarily conveys those numbers to the telephone when a phone call is placed.

PAROLEES

A California prisoner challenged a statute that required every prisoner who was eligible for parole to sign a consent form permitting a parole/peace officer to search their residence and personal effects without a warrant without contravening their Fourth Amendment reasonable expectations of privacy. On one such occasion, a search was conducted and revealed that the parolee was in possession of methamphetamines (*Samson v. California*, 2006). The parolee in this instance challenged this finding and the U.S. Supreme Court later confirmed that "any evidence that is seized in a suspicionless search of parolee is admissible under the Fourth Amendment" (*Samson*). The reasoning behind this finding was that "Parolees are on the 'continuum' of state-imposed punishments and have fewer expectations of privacy than probationers because parole is more akin to imprisonment than probation is to imprisonment" (*Kamisar*).

GPS TRACKING DEVICES

In the case of *United States v. Jones*, the Government obtained a search warrant permitting it to install a Global-Positioning-System (GPS) tracking device on a vehicle registered to respondent Jones's wife. The warrant authorized installation in the District of Columbia and within 10 days, but agents installed the device on the 11th day and in Maryland. The Government then tracked the vehicle's movements for 28 days. It subsequently secured an indictment of Jones and others on drug trafficking conspiracy charges (*United States v. Jones*).

The District Court suppressed the GPS data obtained while the vehicle was parked at Jones's residence but held the remaining data admissible because Jones had no reasonable expectation of privacy when the vehicle was on public streets (*United States v. Jones*). Jones was convicted. The D. C. Circuit reversed, concluding that admission of the evidence obtained by warrantless use of the GPS device violated the Fourth Amendment (*United States v. Jones*). The Government's attachment of the GPS device to the vehicle, and its use of that device to monitor the vehicle's movements, constitutes a search under the Fourth Amendment.

ABANDONED PROPERTY

There is no reasonable expectation of privacy in abandoned property because once the owner relinquishes interest in the property there is also a relinquishment of the owner/occupancy interest therein, and a warrant will not need to issue upon further expectation of the abandoned property in order to determine if there is criminal activity. However, if the abandoned property reveals evidence of a crime that may be traced back to the defendant it may be properly admitted into court as evidence against him.

PRIVATE PARTY SEARCHES

A private citizen is not limited by the requirements set forth in the Fourth Amendment. Information obtained by a private citizen in a search may be lawfully used by the police so long as no law enforcement officer took part, or encouraged, the intrusion upon the suspect's seclusion and solitude. A citizen's intrusion may be inspected by a law enforcement officer, but it must not intrude any deeper than the initial search by private citizen who initially performed the search. The police officer's search is limited in scope by what the private citizen revealed (*Law Officer's Pocket Manual, 2013 Edition Bloomberg BNA*).

CANINE SNIFFS

The federal courts and many of the state courts have held that an "alert" by a drug detection canine can provide probable cause to believe that area which the dog alerted contains narcotics (*Law Officer's Pocket Manual, 2013 Edition Bloomberg BNA*). A canine sniff is not a search that violates one's Fourth Amendment rights. It can be enough to establish probable cause in order to obtain a warrant (*Law Officer's Pocket Manual, 2013 Edition Bloomberg BNA*).

KNOCK AND ANNOUNCE

While the police may extend the courtesy of knocking and announcing their presence immediately prior to executing a search warrant, they may readily dispense with this announcement if they reasonably believe that doing so may provide harm to the police officers or the destruction of evidence (Hudson v. Michigan 2006). Police officers do not have to abide by a time requirement prior to entry after announcing their presence in entering the dwelling to search. This would allow the suspects inside to destroy the evidence or grab weapons that could put the officers executing the search warrant in danger. Further, the exclusionary rule won't apply because evidence obtained after a knock-and-announce violation cannot be linked with the seizure of evidence.

SEARCH AND SEIZURE

There are many laws that speak to the execution of search and seizure of a private party. However, in this chapter, we discuss more of the procedural issues

revolve around whether there is a reasonable expectation of privacy that exists or a valid warrant exception to that rule. Police officers that execute the search and seizure must adhere to the proper ethical behavior in the manner in which they are performing the search. For instance, they should keep property damage to a minimum in order to avoid any civil complaints by the party who is being searched. They should also use appropriate force that requires a proper balance in the need for officer safety, and the need to keep the party content while the search is being performed. Officers executing the search warrant must pay attention to the time constraints within the search and avoid the possibility of any pre-trial publicity associated with the crime by preventing the filming of the search.

*W*ARRANT REQUIREMENTS

In order to obtain a validly procured search warrant, there are three requirements that need to be met. First, the warrant needs to be issued by a neutral and detached magistrate who is able to review evidence that is submitted by police officers and determine whether probable cause to issue the warrant exists. Second, the warrant application must be supported by a sworn statement (oral or written) to the judge or magistrate who can reasonably determine whether probable cause to issue a warrant exists. Third, the specific language set forth within the warrant must describe with particularity the places to be searched and items to be seized. Once given, the scope of the search extends only to search the named places or persons.

GENERAL LANGUAGE IN THE WARRANT

General warrants are prohibited by the Fourth Amendment because they prevent the seizure of evidence if found outside of the places to be searched and the items to be seized (*Andresen v. Maryland* 1976). This means that a warrant cannot generally name a three story residence with vague language that would permit them to search the entire house. This type of conduct in search warrant applications has been frowned upon because if an application cannot claim with specificity the "places to be searched, and the items to be seized," the chances are that the police officers do not have sufficient information to establish probable cause. For example, the language in the search warrant application must plead with particularity the areas where there is probable cause to believe that the illegal evidence is being kept. In a search warrant application for a three story dwelling (two story home with a basement), the language should read that there is probable cause to believe evidence of illegal drugs being kept in the master bedroom closet. This will help establish that the officers are acting on more than a reasonable suspicion that somewhere in the residence contains evidence of drugs.

GOOD-FAITH EXCEPTION

What if the warrant is defective? For instance, what if police officers effectively effectuate a search that turn up illegal contraband? Should the exclusionary rule be used to prevent this evidence from coming into court against the defendant if the arresting officers reasonably believed in good-faith that the warrant complied with the Fourth Amendment? The U.S. Supreme Court ultimately determined that if the police officers knew that the warrant was defective prior to effectuating the search then the evidence will be suppressed against the defendant. The reasoning behind this rationale is that the police officers can still go back and validate the defective search warrant by fixing the errors necessary to search the premises. If the police officers effectuate the search not knowing that it is defective the evidence will not likely be suppressed because of the good-faith reasonable reliance by the arresting officers in effectuate what they thought to be a valid search warrant (*U.S. v. Leon*). The U.S. Supreme Court elaborated on this school of thought by explaining that only "when a warrant is grounded upon an affidavit knowingly or recklessly false has the court suppressed the introduction of evidence at trial" (*U.S. v. Leon; Kamisar*).

Justice White delivered the opinion of the court by saying (1) the exclusionary rule is designed to deter police misconduct rather than to punish the errors of judge or magistrates; (2) no evidence suggests that the judges and magistrates are inclined to ignore or subvert the Fourth Amendment; and (3) excluding evidence-seized pursuant to the warrant will not have a significant deterrent effect on the judge or magistrate because they have no stake in the outcome of the particular criminal prosecutions. Suppression was found to be an appropriate remedy only if the officers were dishonest or reckless in preparing their affidavit or could not have harbored an objectively reasonable belief in the existence of probable cause.

If evidence is consistently excluded, police departments will be prompted to instruct their officers to devote greater care and attention to providing sufficient information to establish probable cause when applying for a warrant and to review w/some attention the form of the warrant that they have been issued, rather than automatically assuming that whatever document the magistrate has signed will necessarily comport w/Fourth Amendment requirements (U.S. v. Leon, Justice White).

ADMINISTRATIVE ERRORS

A defendant drove to a neighboring county to ask about an impounded vehicle. A routine check for outstanding warrants revealed that the defendant had a warrant for his arrest. Deputies arrived and performed a routine search of defendant's vehicle and found methamphetamines and firearms. Within minutes of reporting, the outstanding warrant county officials reported that they had made a clerical error, and there were no warrants for defendant (*U.S. v. Herring, 2009*). The Exclusionary Rule will not be applied to police errors that lead to an unlawful search if the arresting officers are innocent of any wrongdoing (*U.S. v. Herring, 2009*).

PROBABLE CAUSE

Search warrants that fail to meet the necessary requirements are invalid, and the evidence may not be used in court against the defendant. The element of probable cause in order to obtain a warrant can be established by a reliable and anonymous informant. Police officers must be aware not to take such information at face value but must do some independent investigation to establish the credibility of the information in which they have received. Probable cause generally requires a reasonably particularized belief of defendant's guilt (*Maryland v. Pringle, 2003*).

INFORMANTS

Information gathered from an anonymous informant is sufficient to establish probable cause for a search warrant if (1) there is evidence showing that the informant was reliable; and (2) there are facts showing a "basis of knowledge" of information. This test was originally established by the *Spinelli v. United States* case and the *Texas v. Aguilar* case. This test was originally established in order to give rise to probable cause on an informant's tip by indicating a sufficient statement underlying circumstances from which the informant gained his knowledge or information supporting the applying officer's belief that the informant is in fact reliable and credible. The *Aguilar/Spinelli* case was replaced with a *totality of the circumstances* test in *Illinois v. Gates (1983)*, where the U.S. Supreme Court said that a neutral and detached magistrate can determine the existence of probable cause based on a totality of the circumstances that a search is justified and may properly issue a warrant if fair probability can be determined that contraband or evidence is likely to be found in the place to be searched.

UNDERCOVER LAW ENFORCEMENT OFFICERS AND CONFIDENTIAL INFORMANTS

There are two categories of law enforcement officers (*Kamisar*). First, undercover law enforcement officers are police officers who are disguised in order to gather criminal information. Second, a confidential informant, which is a private citizen who has agreed to work for the cops for (1) money or (2) to persuade the government to either drop or lower the pending charges against them. A confidential informant becomes a Fourth Amendment state actor just like an undercover police officer because they are acting under the direction of law enforcement and can in limited circumstances be considered an extension of a government actor. The use of undercover agents and recording devices are valid if they do not violate a defendant's reasonable expectation of privacy (*Kamisar*). The use of criminal informants in undercover operations is not a widely accepted practice. Chief Justice Warren criticized the use of criminal informants because he believed that would lie about other in exchange for getting a break in their own case.

ENTRAPMENT

While *entrapment* is commonly known as a criminal law defense, it also limits the use of undercover agents to encourage a target to engage in criminal activity (*Kamisar*). A law-enforcement officer's inducement of a person to commit a crime for the purposes of bringing criminal prosecution against that person will act as a defense to any charges against the defendant. In order to claim a defense of entrapment, the defendant must show that the criminal plan originated with the police officers and that defendant is not predisposed to committing the crime (*Sherman v. United States,* 1958). Further, in order to successfully convict a defendant of any wrongdoing, the prosecution must bring evidence showing that the defendant was predisposed beyond a reasonable doubt to violate the law (*Jacobsen v. United States,* 1992).

*W*ARRANTLESS SEARCHES AND ARRESTS

The question is often asked "When can a police officer dispense with the search warrant requirement?" This question is asked of both search warrants and arrest warrants. In reference to the arrest warrant requirement, an officer may arrest without a warrant whenever a crime or breach of the peace has been committed in the police officer's presence. Additionally, an officer may arrest a person without an arrest warrant if probable cause exists (*United States v. Watson 1976*). Arrest warrants are seldom used and are not constitutionally required like search warrants.

When discussing the warrant exceptions to the warrant requirement, there are multiple exceptions to the requirement, but the most common search warrant exceptions are found in the following exceptions:

- Search incident to a lawful arrest
- Automobile exception
- Plain view
- Consent
- Stop and frisk
- Hot pursuit/evanescent evidence

SEARCH INCIDENT TO A LAWFUL ARREST

In the case of *Chimel v. California*, police officers went to defendant's home with an arrest warrant for burglary but did not have a search warrant. Upon arrival, defendant's wife let the police officers into the residence. When the defendant returned home, he was served with the warrant and specifically denied police officers the ability to search the residence. The police officers conducted a search of the entire house based on the foregoing exception to the warrant requirement and seized evidence that was later admitted at trial against the defendant (Chimel v. California, 1969). At trial, the courts held that the search was justified as a warrant exception based the search incident to a lawful arrest exception. When this matter was reviewed before for the U.S. Supreme Court, it was held that "a warrantless search incident to arrest may extend only to the person of the arrestee and area within the immediate control" (*Chimel v. California,* 1969). Based on the fact that the home is a broad extension of an area within that would qualify as an area within the defendant's immediate control, the U.S. Supreme Court reasoned that "a warrantless search of an arrestees entire residence cannot be constitutionally justified as incident to the arrest itself" (*Chimel v. California,* 1969).

Similarly, in the case of *United States v. Robinson*, a defendant was lawfully arrested for driving on a revoked license. During a routine pat-down incident to the arrest, the officer removed a cigarette pack from his front pocket. Upon removal, the officer looked in the crumpled cigarette pack and found heroin (*United States v. Robinson,* 1973). The defendant moved to suppress the evidence of the heroin at trial to no avail. When this matter was brought before for U.S. Supreme Court, it was found that a lawful custodial arrest justifies a full search of the arrestee's person (*United States v. Robinson,* 1973). A search incident to a lawful arrest is a traditional exception to the warrant requirement of the Fourth Amendment. The U.S. Supreme Court found that "it is reasonable for the arresting officer to search the person arrested in order to remove any weapons that the latter might seek to use in order to resist arrest or effect his escape" (*United States v. Robinson, USSC cited Chimel v. California in reaching this decision*).

INVENTORIES OF ARRESTEES

A police officer may conduct a warrantless inventory search at the police station, of any personal property that is in the possession of an arrestee at the time of the arrest. This allows police officers to open any containers, such as purses, and that you do not have to use less intrusive measures. Additionally, a visual strip of an arrestee who is going to be placed in "general population" may be performed in order to verify that they are not in possession of any weapons or other contraband hidden underneath their clothing. Inventory searches also help to prevent any allegations by the defendant against the police for fraud, theft, or destruction of personal property.

AUTOMOBILE SEARCHES

A search of the interior of a vehicle does not need a warrant if probable cause to search can be established by the police officers effectuating the search. However, there are a number of exceptions to this rule, that police officers need to be aware of prior to executing the search. For instance, in the case of *Cardwell v. Lewis,* police officers seized an automobile from a public parking lot and took a small paint sample from the car to match it with tire tracks found at the scene of the crime. The U.S. Supreme Court found that the "search" was limited in scope to the examination of the tire on the wheel, and the paint scraping from the exterior of the vehicle left in a public parking lot, there was no Fourth Amendment violation which occurred in this instance. Similarly, in the case of *New York v. Class*, it was found that there was no reasonable expectation of privacy in the VIN numbers of an automobile to amount to a search because it is readily accessible to any passerby who can view this information.

MOTOR HOMES

In the matter of *California v. Carney,* police officers who were able to establish probable cause that the defendant (Carney) was dealing narcotics searched his motor home without a warrant and obtained evidence of the same. The question that was specifically brought before the court was whether the defendant's motor home was more like a residence, requiring a valid warrant, or whether it was more like an automobile, needing only probable cause to search the interior? It was held that any vehicle that is readily mobile may be searched without a search warrant so long as there was probable cause to support the search (*California v. Carney*). Further, law enforcement agents are not found to violate one's Fourth Amendment rights in conducting a search of a motor home because it more like a vehicle than it is a residence, so the *automobile exception* to the warrant requirement is readily available. When asked how to differentiate the difference between a "readily mobile vehicle" as opposed to one that is not, a two-prong test was established. First, the vehicle must be readily mobile by the turn of a key. Second, it must be a licensed motor vehicle in a setting that may indicate that the vehicle is actively being used for transportation. Other modes of transportation that have been found to be exceptions to the Fourth Amendment expectation of privacy are ships, motorboats, and wagons (*Kamisar*).

AUTOMOBILE TRUNKS

It should be noted that "closed repository areas warrant an application to the exception *(i.e., trunk)*." In the case of *California v. Acevedo,* police officers established probable cause to search a bag located in the trunk of defendant (Acevedo's) car which allegedly contained narcotics. The police officers executing the search without a warrant opened the trunk and looked in the bag which contained marijuana (*California v. Acevedo*). Police officers may search a closed contained located in an automobile without a warrant if they have probable cause to search the container because it is reasonable for police officers to examine packages and container without a showing of individualized probable cause for each and every one (*California v. Acevedo*). Passengers possess a reduced expectation of privacy with regard to property they transport in automobiles (*California v. Acevedo*).

PRETEXT STOPS/ROADBLOCK SEARCHES

While there are many law enforcement officers who will try and dispel the myth of profiling as a means to stop a vehicle and investigate further, there are many other law enforcement officers who will admit that certain types of vehicles, ages of drivers, national origin, and license plates may all bear on a suspicion of whether or not illegal activity is afoot. The ongoing problem is that when a vehicle is stopped an occupant of a vehicle may allege that their civil rights have been violated if they are able to determine that they were stopped on any one of the foregoing profiling indicators. As a result, there are often pretext stops and roadblock searches that are permissible for police officers to pull you over and perform a search of the interior of the vehicle for public safety. An example of such a stop would be DUI checkpoints to help eliminate the danger that drugs and alcohol pose to other motorists. However, police officers cannot establish any particularized pattern of suspicion when pulling over vehicles. For instance, if police officers who are setting up a roadblock search with the impression that they are being proactive on DUI motorists but are pulling over every white vehicle because there is a high probability that out of state white SUV vehicles yield a high rate of drug couriers, it is not permissible. In order to avoid any particularized patterns of suspicion, it would be less problematic for police officers if they established a number, such as making it a practice to pull over every 25th vehicle passing through in order to check for sobriety.

BUS SWEEPS (COMMON CARRIER/PASSENGER)

When traveling on a common carrier, such as a commercial bus, the passengers should realize that they have a reasonable expectation of privacy on their personal effects located inside of the vehicle (*Bond v. U.S.,* 529 U.S. 334 2000). The rationale behind this doctrine is that when a bus passenger places a bag in an overhead bin there is a reasonable expectation that it will be moved by either other passengers, or bus employees, but not inspected in an "exploratory manner."

AUTOMOBILE INVENTORIES

A police officer may conduct a routine warrantless inventory search of the vehicle of any lawfully impounded vehicle. Automobile inventory searches are used as a justifiable way to protect the owner's property. Additionally, automobile searches are an effective way to safeguard against any claims of lost or stolen property and ensure that no dangerous weapons or other instrumentalities fall in the wrong hands of criminals. If the initial arrest is unlawful, any evidence of a crime that is discovered through a routine inventory search will be prevented from coming in at trial against the defendant.

PLAIN VIEW

If a police officer who is lawfully on the premises, witnesses evidence of crime or illegal activity he does not need to effectuate a validly procured warrant prior to taking possession of it. An example of this would be an officer who has a validly procured warrant to search the upstairs master bedroom closet for narcotics.

Here, the police officer is lawfully on the premises to execute the search and enters into the dwelling for the purposes of doing so. In this particular home, one must pass through the kitchen in order to get to the stairs leading into the upstairs bedroom. While entering through the kitchen on his way up to the master bedroom, he sees child pornography on the kitchen table. Here, the police officer will be able to obtain the child pornography which was in plain view en route to execute the search warrant for narcotics.

OPEN FIELDS DOCTRINES

One should realize that some areas immediately surrounding the dwelling are protected by the Fourth Amendment, and areas that are not sufficiently annexed to the realty, or located within a close proximity are not. For instance, the *open fields* doctrine allows a police officer to lawfully view an area immediately behind the dwelling house without a warrant. The U.S. Supreme Court held that Fourth Amendment protections do not extend to open fields or areas that are not immediately surrounding a home (*Oliver v. United States,* 466 U.S. 170).

SURVEILLANCE

Surveillance of a residence is a permissible police practice that does not violate one's Fourth Amendment reasonable expectation of privacy so long as it is not physically intrusive (*Kyllo v. United States,* 2001). In the matter of *Kyllo v. United States,* police officers believed that a townhome annexed directly in between two other townhomes was utilizing heat lamps for the purposes of indoor marijuana growth. Police officers then obtained a thermal imaging device as a means to show that a significant amount of heat was emanating through the home which was consistent with indoor marijuana growth which was used to establish probable cause for a warrant. When the search was executed, the police officer's suspicions were validated when they were able to obtain a significant amount of marijuana plants that had been nurtured by the use of indoor heat lamps. This matter was later brought before the U.S. Supreme Court on appeal based on the defendant's assertion that the use of a thermal imaging device was "physically intrusive" and consistent with a search of the residence in violation of the Fourth Amendment reasonable expectation of privacy. The U.S Supreme Court held that when the government uses a device that is not in general public use to monitor the radiation of heat from a person's home it is a search and requires a warrant. The reasoning was that exploring the details of a private home that would otherwise have been unknowable is unreasonable without a warrant.

ENHANCING THE SENSES

Generally speaking, it is not a search for an officer who is lawfully present at a certain place to detect something by one of his natural senses (*United States v. Mankani,* 738 F.2d 538). Typically, the result is ordinarily the same when common means of enhancing the senses, such as a flashlight or binoculars, are used. An example of this would be the case of *Florida v. Riley,* where a police officer observed marijuana growing with binoculars through a small missing panel on the roof of a greenhouse behind a mobile home from a helicopter flying at 400 feet.

CONSENT SEARCHES

In order for consent to be valid, it must be voluntary (*Schneckloth v. Bustamonte*). Voluntariness is a question of fact that should be determined by all of the circumstances. However, while a party's right to refuse is a factor to be considered, it is not required as a prerequisite to determining whether consent is voluntary. For a consent search to be valid, it must only be proved that consent was voluntarily given and not the result of duress or coercion. The consent give does not need to know of his right to refuse consent, but it may be established as one factor in determining whether consent was voluntary (*Schneckloth v. Bustamonte*).

THIRD-PARTY CONSENT

A warrantless entry based on consent of a third party is reasonable and does not violate the Fourth Amendment so long as it is reasonable for the law enforcement to believe that the third party had authority to give consent (*Illinois v. Rodriguez, 1990*). In the case of *Illinois v. Rodriguez,* the defendant (Rodriguez) had a former girlfriend with whom he shared a residence prior to the demise of their relationship. However, the former girlfriend used her key to defendant's apartment to let police in to arrest him. While defendant was outside the police officers discovered evidence of narcotics and subsequently challenged the entry by the police officers as a Fourth Amendment violation. The U.S. Supreme Court found that a warrantless entry based on the consent of third party whom the police reasonably believed had common authority to give consent is valid, even if they do not. The U.S. Supreme Court reasoned that since she used a key to open the door prior to giving the police officers consent to enter and search the premises that it was objectively reasonable to assume that she was living at the residence and had authority to enter.

UNDERCOVER AGENTS AND THE SCOPE OF CONSENT

An undercover agent does not violate the Fourth Amendment if they are invited into a target's home and observes illegally activity (*Kamisar*). However, the scope of consent is exceeded if the initial entrance is gained by the use of fraud, force, illegal threat, or show of force. An example of this might be an undercover agent posing as cable service repairman, and knocking on the door to gain entry into the residence. Once inside, the undercover agent sees evidence of illegal activity and immediately arrests the target. This evidence will likely be suppressed under the foregoing exception.

STOP AND FRISK

"Where a`has *reasonable* and *articulable* suspicion that a suspect is armed and dangerous he may without PC perform a pat-down for concealed weapons" (*Terry v. Ohio,* 1968). In the case of *Terry v. Ohio,* a police officer observed defendant (Terry) and two other individuals casing the front of a store. Their behavior gave the police officer the reasonable belief that they were planning on robbing it. When the officer approached the three men, they acted extremely suspicious, so the officer frisked them and discovered that defendant and another were armed (*Terry v. Ohio*). When this matter was presented before the U.S. Supreme Court, it was held that "where an officer observes conduct that in light of experience and all other circumstances, would lead to an objectively reasonable belief that a suspect is armed and dangerous he may perform a frisk, limited in scope, to searching for weapons" (*Terry v. Ohio, Kamisar*).

Limitations:

Weapons Only-Terry is limited in scope to a pat-down of outer clothing for the purpose of finding concealed weapons.

- The evidence must reasonably be believed to be a possible weapon before the frisk is made.
- Pat-downs yielding soft-plastic bags are unconstitutional.

Failure to Produce Identification
- A Police Officer may not perform a Stop and Frisk if an individual fails to produce identification upon request.

Tip from unnamed informant
- An anonymous tip alone seldom demonstrates the informant's basis of knowledge or veracity.
- If the anonymous tip is suitably corroborated elicits sufficient indicia of reliability to provide reasonable suspicion to make the investigatory stop.

Reasonable Belief
- A police officer should demonstrate that he bears a reasonable belief that criminal activity is afoot and that the suspect committed the crime.

HOT PURSUIT/EXIGENT CIRCUMSTANCES

Police officers may forego the warrant requirement if they are in *hot pursuit* of a suspect that has committed a crime, or if they reasonably believe that *exigent circumstances* exist that may result in the destruction of evidence associated with a crime. Additionally, other examples may include the danger of escape or even the threat to others. If exigent circumstances do not exist, police are required to have an arrest warrant before entering a suspect's home to make an arrest, otherwise any evidence seized therein is inadmissible against the suspect (*Payton v. New York,* 1980). Police officers must not "create" or "manufacture" a exigency that justifies a warrantless search (*Kentucky v. King,* 2011).

In the case of *Payton v. New York*, police officers were entering homes without a search warrant to effectuate a felony arrest. Police officers entered the dwelling under the belief that a New York statute permitted them to enter into the residence without a warrant. The threshold requirement in the *Payton case* was that the Fourth Amendment draws a line at the entrance of the house. If exigent circumstances do not exist to cross the threshold, it cannot be crossed without a warrant (*Payton v. New York*). However, when this case reached the U.S. Supreme Court, it was held that "for Fourth Amendment purposes as arrest warrant founded on probable cause implicitly carries with it the limited authority to enter a dwelling in which the suspect lives where there is reason to believe that the suspect is located inside."

THE EXCLUSIONARY RULE

Evidence of all materials seized in violation of the Fourth Amendment is inadmissible in a criminal proceeding. A procedural rule of federal constitutional law used to deter unlawful police conduct. There has been some clarification over the years discussing what the primary role of the exclusionary was, and who it was applied to? The U.S. Supreme Court in the case of *Weeks v. United States*, stated that purpose of the exclusionary rule was to disallow illegally seized evidence from being admitted at trial (*United States v. Weeks,* 232 U.S. 383 (1914; *Kamisar*). However, the exclusionary rule argues against the *Weeks Doctrine*, saying that there are no such powers of exclusion in the Fourth Amendment, rather it is a judicially created law that was created to serve as a sanction against police misconduct.

Initially, the exclusionary rule only applied to the exclusion of illegally seized evidence in federal court (*Wolf v. Colorado,* 1949). The court in *Wolf* determined that it is the decision of the individual states to determine what sanctions to use. In his opinion, Justice Frankfurter stated that "the Fourth Amendment applied to the states but declined to ban the use of illegally seized evidence in the states" (*Wolf v. Colorado; Kamisar*). In 1961, the case of *Mapp v. Ohio*, 1961, was brought before the U.S. Supreme Court the case involving a possession of obscene materials resulted from an illegal search of Dollree Mapp's home for a fugitive. Mapp appealed her conviction on the basis of freedom of expression. When brought before the U.S. Supreme Court, the issue of whether the obscene materials should have been excluded based on the alleged government misconduct, the final decision was six votes in favor of Mapp, and three votes against. The holding in *Mapp v. Ohio*, *overruled* the previous decision in *Wolf v. Colorado,* making the exclusionary rule applicable to state courts and federal courts alike. This placed the requirement of excluding illegally seized evidence on all levels of government. Justice Brandeis was referred to in the *Mapp v. Ohio* decision citing words from his dissent in the *Olmstead v. United States* as saying *"Our government is the potent, the omnipresent teacher. For good or for ill, it teaches the whole people by its example. . . If the government becomes a lawbreaker, it breeds contempt for law; it invites every man to become a law unto himself; it invites anarchy."*

Freedom from unreasonable searches and seizures is substantive protection available to all inhabitants of the U.S. whether or not they are charged w/a crime *(Kamisar)*. "Failure to teach and enforce constitutional requirements exposes municipalities to financial liability" (Justice White).

PROS AND CONS OF THE EXCLUSIONARY RULE

Pros:

- The Fifth and Sixth Amendments specifically refer to persons charged w/a crime or the accused.
- Respondents believe that officers care about convictions and experience adverse personal reactions when they lose evidence.
- Police change their behavior in response to the suppression of evidence.
- Suppression effectively educates officers in the law of search and seizure.
- The law of search and seizure is not too complicated for police officers to perform effectively.
- The exclusionary rules deterrent effect is greater when officers are working on big or important cases.
- Exclusionary rule has a greater deterrent effect on officers in specialized units like Narcotics section.
- Fosters a closer working relationship between police officers and prosecutors (*Prosecutors help police officer's conduct proper searches and understand why evidence is suppressed*).

Cons:

- Police officers often perjure themselves to avoid requirements of the Fourth Amendment.
- Dishonesty in both the investigative process and the courtroom.
- Police reports are often fabricated.
- Affidavits for search warrants are fabricated creating artificial P/C (probable cause) which forms the basis for later perjured testimony.
- Exculpatory evidence in street files may be edited from the official record.

- Police officers commit perjury between 20% and 50% of the time when they testify on Fourth Amendment issues.
- Perjury is often encouraged/tolerated or even encouraged by prosecutors at each step in the process in both direct/indirect ways.
- Judges may purposefully ignore the law to prevent evidence from being suppressed.
- Judges may knowingly accept police perjury as "truthful."
- When the crime is serious, judicial cheating is likely to occur for three (3) reasons:

  1. Judge's sense that it is unjust to suppress the evidence under the circumstances.
  2. Judge's fear of adverse publicity.
  3. Fear that suppression will hurt their chances in judicial elections.

ILLEGALLY SEIZED EVIDENCE BY PAROLE OFFICERS

In the case of *Pennsylvania Board v. Probation and Parole v. Scott,* parole officers made an illegal search of the parolee's residence and found weapons there which were later admitted at his parole revocation hearing resulting in a recommendation that the parolee (Scott) being recommitted for a time period of 36 months. When this matter was brought before the court, it was ultimately held that the exclusionary rule is inapplicable to parole revocation hearings.

EVIDENCE OBTAINED BY PRIVATE PERSONS, AND USED IN CRIMINAL PROCEEDINGS

Courts have declined to exclude evidence in criminal cases when obtained by private persons. However, the Fourth Amendment is applicable "to private individuals who are acting as instrumentalities or agents of the government" (*Burdeau v. McDowell,* 256 U.S. 465 (1921)).

When determining whether or not a private party is acting as an agent for the government, there will be a determination by a *totality-of-the-circumstances test.* First, what is the motive of the private actor? Is he/she acting on their own initiative or have they been directed otherwise? Second, is there compensation being received, or another benefit conferred upon the private by the government? Third, did the private actor receive any advice, direction, and what is the level of participation by the government?

PRIVATE POLICE

Have traditionally been treated as private persons, a conclusion recently questioned because today "private police participate in much of the police work that their public counterparts do." (*Elizabeth E. Joh, The Paradox of Private Policing,* 95 J. Crim.L. & Criminology 49, 51 (2004)).

FRUIT OF THE POISONOUS TREE

The exclusionary rule will exclude primary evidence obtained in violation of one's Fourth Amendment reasonable expectation of privacy. The fruit of the poisonous tree will exclude secondary evidence that was found as a result of the illegal search and seizure. This secondary evidence will not be used because it is often referred to as "tainted," meaning that it was derived from evidence obtained illegally, or in a manner in which was not admissible. For instance, if a police officer suspects a party of possessing narcotics with the intention of distributing them and fails to secure a search warrant before obtaining the narcotics as evidence against the suspect. Additionally, let's consider that when the police officer found evidence of the narcotics he was seeking he found evidence from a burglary that happened just two days prior but does not collect the evidence when he arrests the suspect rather he goes back and gets a validly procured warrant for the stolen items from the burglary. The exclusionary rule will exclude any evidence of the narcotics being admitted against the suspect at trial because it was obtained in violation of his Fourth Amendment rights when the police officer failed to secure either a warrant, or a warrant exception. The argument will be made that while the narcotics will be excluded, evidence of the burglaries should come in against him because subsequently, a validly procured warrant was obtained and the second entry into the dwelling house of the suspect was valid. Here, the evidence of the burglaries will also be excluded even though it is arguably a separate and unrelated crime, but the philosophy behind this doctrine is that it is *derivative* of the illegal entry and it never would have been discovered if the police officer had not violated the suspect's Fourth Amendment rights. Therefore, it is fruit of the poisonous tree (i.e., the illegal entry) and will be excluded at trial.

INEVITABLE DISCOVERY

Historically, the inevitable discovery rule has applied to involuntary statements made in violation of one's Fifth Amendment rights, more specifically, the privilege against self-incrimination. The exclusionary rule applies to illegally gathered evidence and coerced statements. The philosophy behind this doctrine is that if a defendant tells an officer where a murder weapon is located before being apprised of their Miranda Warnings, the defendant will likely try and suppress the statement and the murder weapon from coming in against him at trial under the exclusionary rule. However, the court may still allow the murder weapon with the defendant's DNA all over it under the inevitable discovery rule because it arguably would have been discovered regardless of the defendant's statement. Here, police must show that they would have found the murder weapon without the defendant's statement.

《

THE LAW OF SEARCH AND SEIZURE   **135**

WORKS CITED

Kamisar, Yale; LaFave, Wayne; Israel, Jerold; King, Nancy; Kerr, Orin; Primus, Eve.
   Basic Criminal Procedure. Minnesota: West Publishing (2012)

California *v. Greenwood*, 486 U.S. 35 (1988)

U.S. v. Warshak, 631 F.3d 266 (2011)

Smith v. Maryland, 442 U.S. 735 (1979)

Samson v. California, 547 U.S. 842 (2006)

United States v. Jones, 109 U.S. 513 (1883)

Law Officer's Pocket Manual, 2013 Edition Bloomberg BNA

Hudson v. Michigan, 547 U.S. 586 (2006)

Andresen v. Maryland, 427 U.S. 463 (1976)

U.S. v. Leon, 468 U.S. 897 (1984)

U.S. v. Herring, 555 U.S. 135 (2009)

Maryland v. Pringle, 540 U.S. 366 (2003)

Spinelli v. United States, 393 U.S. 410 (1969)

Texas v. Aguilar, 378 U.S 108 (1964)

Illinois v. Gates, 462 U.S. 213 (1983)

Jacobsen v. United States, 503 U.S. 540 (1992)

United States v. Watson, 423 U.S. 411 (1976)

Chimel v. California, 395 U.S. 752 (1969)

United States v. Robinson, 414 U.S. 218 (1973)

California v. Acevedo, 500 U.S. 565 (1991)

Bond v. U.S., 529 U.S. 334 (2000)

Oliver v. United States, 466 U.S. 170 (1984)

Kyllo v.United States, 533 U.S. 27 (2001)

United States v. Mankani, 738 F.2d 538 (1984)

Florida v. Riley, 488 U.S. 445 (1989)

Schneckloth v. Bustamonte, 412 U.S. 218 (1973)

Illinois v. Rodriguez, 497 U.S. 177 (1990)

Terry v. Ohio, 392 U.S. 1 (1968)

Payton v. New York, 445 U.S. 573 (1980)

Kentucky v. King, 131 S.Ct. (2011)

United States v. *Weeks*, 232 U.S. 383 (1914)

Wolf v. Colorado, 338 U.S. 25 (1949)

Mapp v. Ohio, 367 U.S. 643 (1961)

Olmstead v. United States, 277 U.S. 438 (1928)

Pennsylvania Board v. Probation and Parole v. Scott, 524 U.S. 357 (1998)

Burdeau v. McDowell, 256 U.S. 465 (1921)

*Elizabeth E. Joh, The Paradox of Private Policing, 95 J. Crim.L. & Criminology 49, 51
   (2004)*

POLICE PROCEDURES

By Robert Aberle

CHAPTER OVERVIEW

© Dani Simmonds. 2011. Used under license from Shutterstock, Inc.

Police procedures are the accumulation of United States Supreme Court decisions that have dealt with the way that police must conduct themselves while performing their duties. This chapter will examine many of the important procedures that every law enforcement officer must have a working knowledge of in order to comply with the law and with the constitutional requirements as interpreted by the courts. The chapter will also examine many of the landmark U.S. Supreme Court cases that have had tremendous impact on the way police must now conduct themselves in a lawful manner.

The laws of arrest and the laws of search and seizure are derived from the Fourth Amendment and will be examined in detail. The concept of probable cause must be understood by all police officers and students of criminal justice because it is a requirement of all arrests and searches that are conducted in this country. The courts have also allowed police to detain suspects without arresting them in certain limited situations. These detentions require a level of evidence known as reasonable suspicion which is less stringent than that of probable cause.

There are many exceptions to the requirement that a search warrant must be obtained by the police prior to conducting any type of search in the United States. This chapter will discuss and explain some of the more common exceptions that have been allowed by the courts and are encountered by police on a regular basis. A discussion of when the police may conduct a lawful interrogation of a suspect and the implications of the infamous Miranda decision will conclude the chapter.

CHAPTER LEARNING OBJECTIVES

After reading this chapter you will be able to:

1. Explain the requirements necessary for the police to conduct a lawful arrest.
2. Understand the legal concept of probable cause.
3. Understand the legal concept of reasonable suspicion.
4. Distinguish between a lawful arrest and a lawful detention.
5. Explain what the exclusionary rule is and when it is applied.
6. Identify and explain the exceptions to the exclusionary rule.
7. List and explain at least five of the exceptions to the search warrant requirement.
8. Understand the requirements of the *Miranda* decision and know when the rights granted by that decision must be given to a suspect.

KEYWORDS

Arrest
Probable Cause
Terry v. Ohio
Pat Down Search
Search with a Warrant
Mapp v. Ohio
Inevitable Discovery Exception
Search Warrant Exceptions
Plain View Doctrine
Exigent Circumstances
Miranda v. Arizona

Warrant
Stop & Frisk
Reasonable Suspicion
Search
Exclusionary Rule
Good Faith Exception
Poison Tree Doctrine
Search incident to a Lawful Arrest
Consent Searches
Carroll Doctrine

U.S. SUPREME COURT HANDS-OFF POLICY PRIOR TO THE 1960S

Prior to the 1960s, the United States Supreme Court decided very few cases that dealt with police procedures on the state level. Although there were exceptions, the Supreme Court limited itself to cases that dealt primarily to federal law enforcement in the area of police procedures. Beginning in the 1960s, the Warren Court[1] began deciding a host of cases that directly impacted police procedures at the state level. In particular, the Court has made numerous interpretations of the Fourth, Fifth, and Sixth Amendments to the U.S. Constitution that have directly affected the way that police must conduct themselves procedurally.

*A*RREST

An **arrest** is the legal detention of a person to answer for criminal charges. An arrest must be based on probable cause, and depending on the circumstances may be made with or without a **warrant**. An arrest is the 'seizure' of a person; therefore an arrest, just like the laws and procedures dealing with searches, is based upon the Fourth Amendment to the U.S. Constitution.

Arrest

An arrest is the legal detention of a person to answer for criminal charges. An arrest must be based on probable cause.

Warrant

A warrant is a court order issued by a judge that authorizes a police officer to make an arrest or conduct a search.

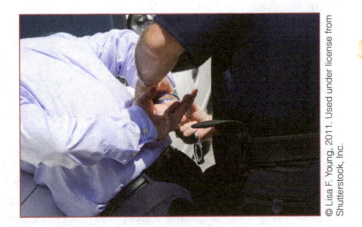

© Lisa F. Young, 2011. Used under license from Shutterstock, Inc.

There are two ways to make a lawful arrest, with a warrant and without a warrant. An arrest with a warrant is accomplished when an investigation has been conducted and probable cause has been developed which is then presented to a judge who reviews the probable cause and then issues the warrant. Any police officer can then serve the warrant and arrest the suspect. There are times when a judge will issue a warrant from the bench during a court session. These warrants are called bench warrants and can be issued for a variety of reasons, but are normally issued when a defendant does not appear in court for a scheduled hearing or trial.

The majority of arrests that are made by police officers are made without a warrant. A police officer may arrest a suspect without a warrant when any of the following has taken place[2]:

1. The person to be arrested has committed a felony or misdemeanor in the officer's presence.
2. The person to be arrested has committed a felony not in the officer's presence.
3. A felony has been committed and the officer has probable cause to believe that the person to be arrested has committed it.
4. The officer has reasonable grounds to believe that a felony has been or is being committed and has probable cause to believe that the person to be arrested has committed it or is committing it.

In summary, a police officer can usually make an arrest without a warrant for felonies that have or have not taken place in their presence, provided that they have probable cause. Most jurisdictions in the United States do not allow a police office to arrest a person for a misdemeanor crime unless that crime has taken place in the officer's presence. There are several ways that a crime can take place in an officer's 'presence':

1. Seeing the crime
2. Smelling the crime
3. Hearing the crime

Obviously if the officer sees the crime, he can make an arrest. There are times that an officer can 'smell' a crime. The most common way is when an officer smells drugs that are being smoked even though they are not being smoked directly in his presence. An officer may also hear a misdemeanor crime take place. The officer may hear a fight taking place but when he arrives the combatants are just standing next to each other.

Some jurisdictions have enacted laws that mandate police officers to make an arrest for domestic battery, a misdemeanor, even if the crime took place up to twenty-four hours prior to the arrival of the police officer. If there is physical evidence that the battery took place, the officer must arrest the suspect under these laws.

PROBABLE CAUSE

Probable Cause

A simplified working definition (not a legal definition) of probable cause for an arrest is: *It is more likely than not that the person being arrested committed the crime that they are being arrested for.*

The Fourth Amendment to the U.S. Constitution states that "no warrants shall issue, but upon probable cause." The U.S. Supreme Court has equated **probable cause** to the concept of reasonableness.[3] The Court has further stated that the facts and circumstances that lead to an arrest or a seizure must be sufficient to persuade a reasonable person that an illegal act has been or is being committed. Probable cause is an issue of law and therefore the final determiner of whether probable cause exists is a judge, not the police officer.

© Mark R, 2011. Used under license from Shutterstock, Inc.

*S*TOP AND FRISK

We have seen that the police may stop and arrest a suspect when they have probable cause to believe that the suspect has committed a crime. There are times when the police need to stop individuals in order to question them about possible criminal activity even though they do not have probable cause to arrest them. Prior to 1968, police officers were very limited in their ability to do this. While a police officer could always ask a suspicious person questions, they did not have the power or authority to actually detain them while investigating criminal activity.

TERRY V. OHIO

In 1968 the United States Supreme Court ruled on the case of **Terry v. Ohio**.[4] This landmark case established a new level of evidence that allows police officers to detain suspicious individuals, for a limited amount of time, while investigating criminal activity. This new level of evidence is reasonable suspicion. Reasonable suspicion also allows the police to pat-down a person while being lawfully detained.

    The following is the summary of the facts as reflected in the Supreme Court decision that took place leading up to the decision in the *Terry* case. The court looked at all of the facts in this case in order to come up with their decision. The Court concluded that police officers are in a distinctive position to be able to draw "rational inferences" based upon "specific and articulable facts" because of their training and experience. In 1989, in the case of *United States v. Sokolow,*[5] the Court clarified and

Terry v. Ohio
The landmark U.S. Supreme Court case that established the level of evidence of reasonable suspicion.

refined these criteria to include the "totality of the circumstances" when considering if reasonable suspicion is present in any particular case.

--- TERRY V. OHIO ---

Officer McFadden testified that, while he was patrolling in plain clothes in downtown Cleveland at approximately 2:30 in the afternoon of October 31, 1963, his attention was attracted by two men, Chilton and Terry, standing on the corner of Huron Road and Euclid Avenue. He had never seen the two men before, and he was unable to say precisely what first drew his eye to them. However, he testified that he had been a policeman for 39 years and a detective for 35, and that he had been assigned to patrol this vicinity of downtown Cleveland for shoplifters and pickpockets for 30 years. He explained that he had developed routine habits of observation over the years, and that he would "stand and watch people or walk and watch people at many intervals of the day." He added: "Now, in this case, when I looked over, they didn't look right to me at the time."

His interest aroused, Officer McFadden took up a post of observation in the entrance to a store 300 to 400 feet away from the two men. "I get more purpose to watch them when I seen their movements," he testified. He saw one of the men leave the other one and walk southwest on Huron Road, past some stores. The man paused for a moment and looked in a store window, then walked on a short distance, turned around and walked back toward the corner, pausing once again to look in the same store window. He rejoined his companion at the corner, and the two conferred briefly. Then the second man went through the same series of motions, strolling down Huron Road, looking in the same window, walking on a short distance, turning back, peering in the store window again, and returning to confer with the first man at the corner. The two men repeated this ritual alternately between five and six times apiece—in all, roughly a dozen trips. At one point, while the two were standing together on the corner, a third man approached them and engaged them briefly in conversation. This man then left the two others and walked west on Euclid Avenue. Chilton and Terry resumed their measured pacing, peering, and conferring. After this had gone on for 10 to 12 minutes, the two men walked off together, heading west on Euclid Avenue, following the path taken earlier by the third man.

By this time, Officer McFadden had become thoroughly suspicious. He testified that, after observing their elaborately casual and oft-repeated reconnaissance of the store window on Huron Road, he suspected the two men of "casing a job, a stick-up," and that he considered it his duty as a police officer to investigate further. He added that he feared "they may have a gun." Thus, Officer McFadden followed Chilton and Terry and saw them stop in front of Zucker's store to talk to the same man who had conferred with them earlier on the street corner. Deciding that the situation was ripe for direct action, Officer McFadden approached the three men, identified [p7] himself as a police officer and asked for their names. At this point, his knowledge was confined to what he had observed. He was not acquainted with any of the three men by name or by sight, and he had received no information concerning them from any other source. When the men "mumbled something" in response to his inquiries, Officer McFadden grabbed petitioner Terry, spun him around so that they were facing the other two, with Terry between McFadden and the others, and patted down the outside of his clothing. In the left breast pocket of Terry's overcoat, Officer McFadden felt a pistol. He reached inside the overcoat pocket, but was unable to remove the gun. At this point, keeping Terry between himself and the others, the officer ordered all three men to enter Zucker's store. As they went in, he removed Terry's overcoat completely, removed a .38 caliber revolver from the pocket and ordered all three men to face the wall with their hands raised. Officer McFadden proceeded to pat down the outer clothing of Chilton and the third man, Katz. He discovered another revolver in the outer pocket of Chilton's overcoat, but no weapons were found on Katz. The officer testified that he only patted the men down to see whether they had weapons, and that he did not put his hands beneath the outer garments of either Terry or Chilton until he felt their guns. So far as appears from the record, he never placed his hands beneath Katz' outer garments. Officer McFadden seized Chilton's gun, asked the proprietor of the store to call a police wagon, and took all three men to the station, where Chilton and Terry were formally charged with carrying concealed weapons.[6]

REASONABLE SUSPICION

Reasonable suspicion can be defined as the level of evidence that a police officer needs in order to justify the detention of an individual who is suspected of engaging in criminal activity. The officer must be able to articulate that the suspicion was reasonable and may do so based upon their training and experience. The criminal activity being investigated may be past, present, or future activity. A mere hunch is not sufficient; they must be able to articulable their suspicion.

The amount of time that a person may be detained under a reasonable suspicion stop has not been ruled on by the courts; however, the person may not be detained for an "unreasonable" amount of time. There must be an active investigation to determine if the detained person has in fact been involved in criminal activity. Some jurisdictions have limited investigative detentions to a maximum of sixty minutes.

The Supreme Court, in the 2004 case of *Hiibel v. Sixth Judicial District Court of Nevada, Humbult County, et al.,*[7] ruled that police officers can require persons who are detained under a *Terry* stop to identify themselves to the officer.

Reasonable Suspicion

Reasonable suspicion can be defined as the level of evidence that a police officer needs in order to justify the detention of an individual who is suspected of engaging in criminal activity.

PAT-DOWN SEARCH

The ruling under the *Terry* stop allows officers, in some circumstances, to 'pat-down' persons who are being detained. A **pat-down search** is a cursory search of the outer clothing for the purpose of determining if the suspect has a weapon. There are certain conditions that must be met in order for the police to be able to conduct a pat-down; it is not automatically allowed just because there is reasonable suspicion to detain the suspect. In order to justify a pat-down the officer must be able to articulate that there was reason to believe that the suspect may have a weapon. The search may than be conducted for the safety of the officer or other citizens. The search cannot be a "fishing expedition" to look for other illegal substances; it must be for weapons only.[8] If illegal substances are found during a lawful pat-down, that evidence may be used against the suspect.

Pat-down Search

A pat-down search is a cursory search of the outer clothing for the purpose of determining if the suspect has a weapon.

Lisa F. Young/Shutterstock.com

SEARCH

One of the fundamental freedoms that Americans enjoy is the right to privacy. The Fourth Amendment to the U.S. Constitution states: "The right of the people to be secure in their persons, houses, paper, and effects, against unreasonable searches and seizures, shall not be violated …" In order for the police to intrude on the privacy of a person, they must have a lawful reason and, with very limited exceptions, they must have probable cause.

SEARCH WITH A WARRANT

The Fourth Amendment specifically states that "… no warrant shall issue, but upon probable cause, supported by oath or affirmation, and particularly describing the place to searched, and the persons or things to be seized." This protection insures that a neutral party, a judge or magistrate, reviews the police officers probable cause before a search warrant is issued and the actual search is conducted. Even though it was written over two hundred years ago, the procedures set forth in the Fourth Amendment for obtaining a warrant are still the process used today.

EXCLUSIONARY RULE

The **exclusionary rule** states that any evidence that is illegally seized by the police will be inadmissible in a criminal trial. The exclusionary rule was first introduced by the U.S. Supreme Court in the 1914 case of *Weeks v. U.S.*[9] This case established the exclusionary rule for federal agents and the federal court system. State and local police were still allowed to enter illegally seized evidence into court, and were able to do so until 1961, except in those states that wrote their own exclusionary rule statutes. During the interim period of time, federal officers often exploited a loophole in the wording of the *Weeks* case that said "evidence illegally seized by federal officers is inadmissible." The federal officers would often simply ask state or local officers to make illegal seizures on their behalf and then use the evidence in federal court.[10] This practice was referred to as the "silver platter" doctrine because it appeared that state and local police were handing over illegally seized evidence to the federal officers on a "silver platter."

The Supreme Court applied the exclusionary rule to the states in 1961 in the case of *Mapp v. Ohio*.[11]

Exclusionary Rule

The exclusionary rule states that any evidence that is illegally seized by the police will be inadmissible in a criminal trial.

Mapp v. Ohio

This is the 1961 landmark U.S. Supreme Court case that applied the exclusionary rule to the states.

— MAPP V. OHIO —

On May 23, 1957, three Cleveland police officers arrived at appellant's residence in that city pursuant to information that a person [was] hiding out in the home, who was wanted for questioning in connection with a recent bombing, and that there was a large amount of policy paraphernalia being hidden in the home.

Miss Mapp and her daughter by a former marriage lived on the top floor of the two-family dwelling. Upon their arrival at that house, the officers knocked on the door and demanded entrance, but appellant, after telephoning her attorney, refused to admit them without a search warrant. They advised their headquarters of the situation and undertook a surveillance of the house.

The officers again sought entrance some three hours later when four or more additional officers arrived on the scene. When Miss Mapp did not come to the door immediately, at least one of the several doors to the house was forcibly opened and the policemen gained admittance. Meanwhile Miss Mapp's attorney arrived, but the officers, having secured their own entry, and continuing in their defiance of the law, would permit him neither to see Miss Mapp nor to enter the house. It appears that Miss Mapp was halfway down the stairs from the upper floor to the front door when the officers, in this highhanded manner, broke into the hall. She demanded to see the search warrant. A paper, claimed to be a warrant, was held up by one of the officers. She grabbed the "warrant" and placed it in her bosom. A struggle ensued in which the officers recovered the piece of paper and as a result of which they handcuffed appellant because she had been "belligerent" in resisting their official rescue of the "warrant" from her person. Running roughshod over appellant, a policeman "grabbed" her, "twisted [her] hand," and she "yelled [and] pleaded with him" because "it was hurting." Appellant, in handcuffs, was then forcibly taken upstairs to her bedroom where the officers searched a dresser, a chest of drawers, a closet and some suitcases. They also looked into a photo album and through personal papers belonging to the appellant. The search spread to the rest of the second floor including the child's bedroom, the living room, the kitchen and a dinette. The basement of the building and a trunk found therein were also searched. The obscene materials for possession of which she was ultimately convicted were discovered in the course of that widespread search.[12]

At the trial, the police were unable to produce a search warrant and the Court ruled that the exclusionary rule now applied to all police officers throughout the country.

FRUIT OF THE POISONOUS TREE DOCTRINE

The fruit of the poisonous tree doctrine was established in the 1920 Supreme Court case of *Silverthorne Lumber Co. v. U.S.*[13] The Court ruled that if evidence that is seized is inadmissible in court, any other evidence that was obtained as a result of the illegally seized evidence would also be inadmissible. The Court ruled that if the tree is poisoned (the original illegally seized evidence), then the fruit (evidence seized that is based on the original) would also be poisoned.

EXCEPTIONS TO THE EXCLUSIONARY RULE

The U.S. Supreme Court has established several exceptions to the exclusionary rule. Two of the most significant exceptions are the good faith exception and the inevitable discovery exception.

GOOD FAITH EXCEPTION

The Supreme Court has ruled that there are times that even when evidence is seized pursuant to a defective search warrant it can still be admitted into court. The 1984 case of *United States v. Leon* established what is now known as the **good faith exception** to the exclusionary rule.[14] In this case, an officer from the Burbank, California police department applied for a search warrant that was reviewed by several Deputy District Attorneys and signed by a state-court judge. Large quantities of drugs and other evidence were seized. The case was appealed and the appellant court found that the probable cause in the affidavit was insufficient and the evidence was ruled inadmissible under the exclusionary rule. The Supreme Court disagreed and said that even though the affidavit was defective, the officer acted in good faith when he executed the search warrant, and therefore the evidence was admissible. The Court did point out that if the officer had known that the warrant was defective prior to executing it, any evidence seized would be excluded.

Good Faith Exception

In the 1984 U.S. Supreme Court case of *United States v. Leon* the court allowed for the admission of evidence that would normally not be admissible under the exclusionary rule, if the officers acted in good faith.

INEVITABLE DISCOVERY EXCEPTION

Inevitable Discovery Exception

In the 1984 case of *Nix v. Leon*, the court established an exception to the exclusionary rule stating that if illegally seized evidence would have been found legally in the normal course of an investigation (it would have been inevitably discovered), it can be admitted into court.

In the Supreme Court case of *Nix v. Williams,* that was decided the same year as the *Leon* case in 1984, the Court established another exception to the exclusionary rule that is known as the **inevitable discovery exception.**[15] In this case police officers from Davenport, Iowa, were driving an arrested suspect back to Des Moines. The suspect had been arrested for the murder of a ten-year-old girl, but the body had not been found yet. On the way back to Des Moines, the officers engaged the suspect in a conversation saying that he should tell the officers where the body of the girl was, because if he didn't, the body may never be found and would not be able to have a Christian burial. The suspect then led the officers to where the body was. In court, the defense argued that the suspect had been given his rights and therefore the evidence of the body should not be allowed into court as evidence based on the exclusionary rule. On appeal, the Supreme Court ruled that the body would have been discovered independently since there were large search parties looking for it. The Court ruled that the body was admissible because it would inevitably have been discovered.

EXCEPTIONS TO THE SEARCH WARRANT REQUIREMENTS

The Fourth Amendment specifically states that before they may conduct a search, they are required to obtain a search warrant. Over the years, the U.S. Supreme Court has established several exceptions to the warrant rule. These exceptions allow officers to conduct searches without a prior determination of probable cause by a judge and conduct the search without a warrant. Some of the more common exceptions are:

1. Search incident to a lawful arrest
2. Plain view
3. Consent
4. Exigent circumstances
5. Vehicle searches

Search Incident to a Lawful Arrest

When the police make a lawful arrest, they are allowed to conduct a complete search of the person arrested as well as the area within the immediate control of the arrestee.

SEARCH INCIDENT TO A LAWFUL ARREST

When the police make a lawful arrest, they are allowed to conduct a complete search of the person arrested as well as the area within the immediate control of the arrestee. This type of search is called a '**search incident to a lawful arrest.**' The Supreme Court in the case of *United States v. Robinson* (1973) stated that there are two reasons that the police may conduct this type of search[16]:

1. Officer safety—officers may search for and confiscate any weapons that the suspect has.
2. Prevent the destruction of evidence.

The Supreme Court further refined the area that may be searched without a warrant when a suspect is arrested in a home. In the case of *Chimel v. California* (1969) the Court held that a search incident to an arrest in a home is limited to "the area into which an arrestee might reach in order to grab a weapon or other evidentiary items."[17] This established "area of immediate control" has been referred to as the arms reach doctrine.

PLAIN VIEW

The "**plain view doctrine**" was established in the 1968 Supreme Court case of *Harris v. United States.*[18] The "plain view doctrine" states that if a police officer is lawfully at a location and he sees contraband within his view, he may seize it without a warrant. Contraband is anything that is illegal on its face; that is, the officer does not have to move it or inspect it to determine that it is illegal. Contraband includes such things as illegal drugs, drug paraphernalia, and certain illegal weapons. If the officer has to move the item to read a serial number to determine if it is stolen, it is probably not contraband.

If an officer is invited into a home to take a police report and sees illegal drugs on the kitchen counter, the officer may legally seize the drugs and charge the owner. The officer was legally in the home and in a position where he could see the contraband.

Plain View Doctrine

The "plain view doctrine" states that if a police officer is lawfully at a location and he sees contraband within his view, he may seize it without a warrant.

CONSENT SEARCHES

A person may waive their Fourth Amendment rights and voluntarily allow the police to search their property (or themselves) without a warrant by giving their **consent** to do so. The person who is giving consent must have "standing" to do so. Standing means that the person who gives the permission has the legal right to do so. The owner of a house may give consent for the police to search the home, but a guest of the homeowner may not give consent because they do not have standing to do so. The guest has no legal right to allow the search because they have no ownership.

A roommate who lives in one bedroom of a two bedroom apartment and pays half of the rent, could give the police consent to search only the common areas of the apartment as well as their own room, but could not give permission to search the roommate's room. A landlord could not give consent to search a tenants apartment and a hotel cannot give consent to search a paying customers room.

In order to give consent, it must be given voluntarily and knowingly. The police cannot coerce or threaten a person in order to obtain consent to search.

Consent

A person may waive their Fourth Amendment rights and voluntarily allow the police to search their property (or themselves) without a warrant by giving their consent to do so.

Once consent is given, it may be withdrawn at any time. The person can also put limitations on the search. The person could tell the police that they have permission to search particular rooms of a house but not others. They could also put a time limit on the search by telling the police that they only have a specified amount of time to conduct the search and then they must leave.

EXIGENT CIRCUMSTANCES

Exigent (emergency) Circumstances

Exigent (emergency) circumstances necessitate that police officers enter a home or other building, or extend the parameters of a search, without obtaining a warrant.

There are times when **exigent (emergency) circumstances** necessitate that police officers enter a home or other building, or extend the parameters of a search, without obtaining a warrant. If a police officer sees a fire in a home they may enter to look for or warn the occupants. If an officer on patrol hears gunshots or screams coming from a home they could enter to investigate. If the police are chasing a suspect who is known to be armed and poses an immediate threat, and that suspect enters a home, they could follow him without first obtaining a warrant.

The Supreme Court has also said that if police are executing an arrest warrant in a home, they may search the premises for other people who may be hiding and could potentially cause a danger to the officers.[19]

© Wade H. Massie, 2011. Used under license from Shutterstock, Inc

VEHICLE SEARCHES

Motor vehicles are a major exception to the warrant requirement of the Fourth Amendment. The Supreme Court as early as 1925 in the case of *Carroll v. U.S.* recognized that vehicles are highly mobile and police officers often do not have time to obtain search warrants.[20] The *Carroll* case established what is known as the "**Carroll doctrine**" or the "mobility doctrine." The "Carroll doctrine" states that because vehicles are mobile, police cannot routinely obtain search warrants for them and therefore, if the officer has probable cause that a crime has been committed, they may search without a warrant.

Carroll Doctrine

The Supreme Court as early as 1925 in the case of *Carroll v. U.S.* recognized that vehicles are highly mobile and police officers often do not have time to obtain search warrants.

© Lisa F. Young, 2011. Used under license from Shutterstock, Inc.

If the police stop a vehicle and arrest the driver, they may conduct a search of the entire front and rear compartments as well as any unlocked containers within that area of the vehicle. This extended area of search was made permissible in the 1981 Supreme Court case of *New York v. Belton.*[21] The *Belton* case expanded *Chimel* limits of a search when vehicles are involved. Areas officers may search under the *Belton* ruling include: under the front seat, under the dashboard, the entire back seat (including being able to move items to look under them), over the visors, and any unlocked interior compartments.

In 2009, the Supreme Court of the United States further clarified and restricted the *Belton* ruling in the case of *Arizona v. Gant.*[22] The court ruled that the police may search the passenger compartment of a vehicle incident to a recent occupant's arrest only if it is reasonable to believe that the arrestee might access the vehicle at the time of the search or that the vehicle contains evidence of the offense that the occupant is being arrested for. If the arrestee is in handcuffs or otherwise restrained so that they cannot access the vehicle, the police are restricted in their warrantless search.

A police officer may search an entire vehicle, including locked compartments and the trunk, if the officer has probable cause. The Court in the case of the *United States v. Ross* (1982) ruled that "Police officers who have legitimately stopped an automobile and who have probable cause to believe that contraband is concealed somewhere within it may conduct a warrantless search of the vehicle that is as thorough as a magistrate could authorize by warrant."[23]

*I*NTERROGATION

Miranda v. Arizona
This 1966 United States Supreme Court case established the rights that must be given to a suspect who is in custody and being questioned by the police.

Without a doubt, the most famous U.S. Supreme Court case dealing with police procedures would have to be the 1966 case of **Miranda v. Arizona.**[24] This case established the rights that must be given to a suspect who is in custody and being questioned by the police. The basis for this decision comes from the Fifth Amendment protection that we all have against self-incrimination. This right dictates that no one can be forced to testify, or give any statements to authorities, that could implicate them in any criminal act.

Prior to the 1936 Supreme Court case of *Brown v. Mississippi,* police would routinely coerce, and at times even physically abuse suspects, in order to obtain confessions.[25] In 1964, the U.S. Supreme

Bettmann/Contributor

Court again addressed how confessions could be obtained from suspects in the case of *Escobedo v. Illinois.*[26] In this case the Court recognized for the first time that suspects need to be advised that they are entitled to have an attorney present whenever they are a suspect and are being questioned by the police. The ruling in *Escobedo* left some questions unanswered concerning exactly what rights needed to be given to suspects prior to questioning, other than the right to an attorney, and also left several other issues unanswered. The Court clarified their decision in the *Escobedo* case when they decided the *Miranda* case two years later in 1966.

MIRANDA V. ARIZONA

To summarize, we hold that, when an individual is taken into custody or otherwise deprived of his freedom by the authorities in any significant way and is subjected to questioning, the privilege against self-incrimination is jeopardized. Procedural safeguards must be employed to protect the privilege, and unless other fully effective means are adopted to notify the person of his right of silence and to assure that the exercise of the right will be scrupulously honored, the following measures are required. **He must be warned prior to any questioning that he has the right to remain silent, that anything he says can be used against him in a court of law, that he has the right to the presence of an attorney, and that, if he cannot afford an attorney one will be appointed for him prior to any questioning if he so desires.** *Opportunity to exercise these rights must be afforded to him throughout the interrogation. After such warnings have been given, and such opportunity afforded him, the individual may knowingly and intelligently waive these rights and agree to answer questions or make a statement. But unless and until such warnings and waiver are demonstrated by the prosecution at trial, no evidence obtained as a result of interrogation can be used against him.*[27]

WHEN IS MIRANDA REQUIRED?

The Miranda Rights are required to be given to a suspect prior to any questioning when the suspect is going to be questioned in a custodial setting. A custodial setting would be anytime the suspect is under arrest or is otherwise being deprived of the freedom to leave.

WHEN IS MIRANDA NOT REQUIRED?

There are many situations that involve contact with the police that do NOT require the issuing of the Miranda Rights. Miranda is not required when:

1. The suspect makes a statement to the police before they ask a question.
2. The suspect gives a confession to a third party who is not the police. In these cases the third party may testify to what they were told.

3. The suspect is booked into a jail and is asked routine "booking questions" that include asking the suspect their name, address, date of birth, etc.
4. The suspect is stopped for a routine traffic violation.
5. The suspect is temporarily detained during a *Terry* stop.
6. The suspect is in the custody of the police but is not being asked any questions that would be "testimonial" in nature.
7. The suspect is intoxicated or does not understand English.

It is important to note that failing to give Miranda Rights to an arrested subject DOES NOT negate or make an arrest illegal. Miranda has nothing to do with the actual arrest; it only has to do with the questioning of a suspect in a custodial setting.

REVIEW QUESTIONS:

1. Prior to the 1960s, the United States Supreme Court maintained a _____ policy when it came to interfering with the procedures used by state and local police.

2. All arrests and search and seizures are based on the _____ Amendment to the U.S. Constitution.

3. All arrests must be based upon _____ _____.

4. In the 1968 case of _____, the U.S. Supreme Court ruled that a police officer may, under certain conditions, lawfully detain a suspect without arresting them.

5. _____ _____ is the level of evidence that a police officer needs in order to conduct a "stop and frisk."

6. The exclusionary rule was originally established in the U.S. Supreme Court case of

   _____.

7. _____ was the 1961 Supreme Court case that made the exclusionary rule applicable to all police officers in the United States.

8. The good faith exception and the inevitable discovery exception are both exceptions to the

   _____ _____.

9. _____ _____ _____ _____ _____ _____ allows an officer to conduct a complete search of an arrested person as well the area within their immediate control.

10. The _____ _____ doctrine states that if a police officer is lawfully at a location and he sees contraband within his view, he may seize it without a warrant.

11. In the 1925 Supreme Court case of _____, the Court first recognized that vehicles are highly mobile and police do not usually have time to obtain a search warrant.

12. It wasn't until _____ in the case of *Brown v. Mississippi* that the Supreme Court recognized that police could not coerce or physically abuse suspects in order to obtain a confession.

13. The Miranda Rights are required to be given to a suspect prior to any questioning, when the suspect is going to be questioned in a _____ setting.

CRITICAL THINKING QUESTIONS:

1. Explain the circumstances under which a police officer may make a lawful misdemeanor arrest without a warrant.

2. Discuss the differences between probable cause and reasonable suspicion and what each of these levels of evidence allow a police officer to do.

3. How does the fruit of the poisonous tree doctrine expand the exclusionary rule?

4. Select and explain two of the exceptions to the search warrant requirements that are discussed in this chapter.

5. Discuss at least three of the circumstances when a police officer does not have to advise an arrested suspect of his Miranda Rights.

NOTES

CHAPTER 6

[1] U.S. Supreme Courts are named for the Chief Justice who presides over the Court. Earl Warren served as Chief Justice of the United States Supreme Court from 1953 until 1969.

[2] Connie Estrada Ireland and George E. Rush, *The Dictionary of Criminal Justice With Summaries of Supreme Court Cases Affecting Criminal Justice*, 7th Edition, (New York: McGraw Hill Companies, Inc., 2011).

[3] Brinegar v. United States, 338 U.S. 160 (1949).

[4] Terry v. Ohio, 392 U.S. 1 (1968).

[5] United States v. Sokolow, 490 U.S. 1 (1989).

[6] Ibid.

[7] Hiibel v. Sixth Judicial Court of Nevada, Humbult County, et al., 542 U.S. 177 (2004).

[8] Minnesota v. Dickerson, 508 U.S. 366 (1993).

[9] Weeks v. U.S. 232 U.S. 383 (1914).

[10] Ireland, *Dictionary of Criminal Justice,* pg 420.

[11] Mapp v. Ohio, 367 U.S 643 (1961).

[12] Ibid.

[13] Siverthorne Lumber Co. v. U.S., 251 U.S. 385 (1920).

[14] United States v. Leon, 468 U.S. 897 (1984).

[15] Nix v. Williams, 467 U.S. 431 (1984).

[16] Robinson v. United States, 414 U.S. 234 (1973).

[17] Chimel v. California, 395 U.S. 752 (1969).

[18] Harris v. United States, 390 U.S. 234 (1968).

[19] Maryland v. Buie, 494 U.S. 325 (1990).

[20] Carroll v. U.S., 267 U.S. 132 (1925).

[21] New York v. Belton, 453 U.S. 454 (1981).

[22] Arizona v. Gant, 556 U.S. 332 (2009).

[23] United States v. Ross, 456 U.S. 798 (1982).

[24] Miranda v. Arizona, 384 U.S. 436 (1966).

[25] Brown v. Mississippi, 297 U.S. 278 (1936).

[26] Escobedo v. Illinois, 378 U.S. 478 (1964).

[27] Miranda v. Arizona, 384 U.S. 436 (1966).

CUSTODIAL INTERROGATIONS

By Craig D. Harter

Chapter 7

CHAPTER OVERVIEW

Fisun Ivan / Shutterstock.com

Beginning with a description of the history of interrogation law, Chapter Seven goes on to discuss the relationship between the Fifth Amendment and confessions; the right to counsel and confessions; and, the rules pertaining to access to incriminating information on computers, pen registers, etc. Numerous case studies are used to show how the law of interrogation has been applied in various real life situations, thus facilitating understanding. And because the landmark case of *Miranda v. Arizona* has had such profound impact on conducting interrogations, considerable attention has been paid to (a) when and how *Miranda* warnings should be given (b) who has to give them, and (c) circumstances that will alleviate the police from having to give the warnings. The chapter ends with a discussion of the Fifth Amendment's protection against double jeopardy.

𝒞HAPTER LEARNING OBJECTIVES

After reading this chapter, you will be able to:

1. Describe the history of interrogation law
2. Define custodial interrogation
3. Discuss when and how Miranda Warnings must be given and who must give them
4. Discuss exceptions to the Miranda warning requirements
5. Describe the Sixth Amendment right to counsel and when it's applicable
6. Describe a reasonable expectation of privacy in the context of computers
7. Discuss the law of double jeopardy

𝒯HE HISTORY OF INTERROGATION

THE THIRD DEGREE

In the early days of common law, a confession was admissible in court against a defendant even it was obtained by the use of torture *(Scheb)*. One of these methods of early interrogation is referred to as *the third degree,* which is an interrogation tactic that used the infliction of physical pain or mental suffering in order to obtain information about a crime. The terminology "third degree" is derived from police folklore, which came to be known as the third stage of the criminal process, following arrest and confinement. One of the most common forms of interrogation was *incommunicado questioning* where suspects were secluded and psychologically pressured into confessing and/or communicating about important details of a purported crime. One of the major differences between incommunicado questioning and different types of questioning was the importance of hiding suspects from attorneys, courts, friends, and family for the purposes of extracting the relevant information before they may have otherwise been counseled to refrain from. One of the frequent practices during "incommunicado" questioning was to "sweat" or "grill" suspects into long bouts of questioning consisting of verbally bullying the suspect by the following methods: shining a bright blinding light continuously on a suspect's face, slapping or jolting a suspect when he started to fall asleep, consistently turning on and off the light, and requiring a suspect to remain standing for a prolonged period of time.

Another common practice was referred to as "losing" the suspect. This occurred by failing to record the arrest so that an attorney could not locate the suspect. Additionally, police officers would also mislead both friends and defense counsel as to the whereabouts of the party by charging the suspect with a different felony every 48 hours or booking them on either "open charges" or "vagrancy charges."

PHYSICALLY ABUSING THE SUSPECT

Police officers suspected that "invisible" marks left on the suspect during a physically abusive interrogation session would gather the sympathies of both judges and juries, so they started utilizing forms of physical punishment that failed to leave any marks on the suspect such as local phone book, rubber hose, and blackjack (soaked in water before being wrapped in a handkerchief). During the third degree era, police officers often used interrogation tactic similar to those that were used during the CIA after 9/11. For instance, the *water cure* was a torture that was similar to waterboarding in that a suspect was strapped to a board while his face was covered with a cloth, and water was poured over the cloth in order to provide the suspect with the feeling that he was drowning. The distinct difference between *water cure* and *waterboarding* was that a suspect's head was held in water until he almost drowned, or involved putting a water hose into his mouth or down his throat. In almost every instance of complaints against the detectives who used the third degree, there were rarely, if ever, any instances where they were reprimanded or disciplined for their actions.

POLICE PROFESSIONALISM AND THE RISE OF THE INTERROGATION MANUAL

In 1940, the end of the *"third degree"* brought forth the publication of the first American Interrogation Manual in 1940 by former police lieutenant W.R. Kidd. Kidd who urged police to never use the "third degree" because it did not produce the truth since under severe enough torture a suspect may tell you everything you want to know in order to build your case. In fact, if a case is built upon a confession there is a possibility that the man did not even commit the crime. Defendant attorneys started to quickly develop facts around how the statement was secured and would often make the allegations that the third degree was used even if it was not. Kidd explained that "public confidence in the police is shattered if knowledge of such methods is publicized. Unless the suspect dies, it is difficult to prevent such publicity. If he dies, a terrific public protest is inevitable" *(Police Interrogation and American Justice,* Richard A. Leo*)*.

One of the greatest harms that a police department may suffer from use of the third degree is the reputation and destroyed public confidence that may occur. If the public becomes aware that such methods are resorted, it becomes difficult for police to convict if guilty even in the event that it is a good solid case. Judges or juries will likely to believe the allegations by the defense attorney that a confession was obtained by use of the third degree even if it had not. According to *Kidd,* there were three things that could happen to the suspect when the third degree was used. First, he will tell you anything you want, second he will go insane if the torture is severe enough, and third, he will die.

EVOLUTION OF COERCION

As the common law progressed, many judges began to notice that the use of confession resulting from interrogation was extremely flawed unless the confession was voluntary *(Scheb)*. In fact, the case of *Bram v. United States* was brought before the U.S. Supreme Court in 1897 and dealt specifically with the issue of *coerced confessions (Scheb)*. The U.S. Supreme Court decision in *Bram* held that if a defendant provided a coerced confession then it would be inapplicable as a violation of the defendant's due process rights inherently found within the 14th Amendment of the United States *(Scheb)*. However, it was not until the year 1964 that the *self-incrimination clause* was made applicable to the state courts as well as to the federal courts *(Malloy v. Hogan,* 378 U.S. 1, 84 S.Ct. 1489, 12 L.Ed.2d 653, 1964*)*. In the case of *Malloy v. Hogan,* the U.S. Supreme Court expressly forbid the use of a confession if obtained by improper influence *(Scheb)*. In *United States v. Carnignan,* a confession was deemed to be voluntary if "it was made with knowledge of its nature and consequences and without duress or inducement" *(United States v. Carnignan,* 342 U.S. 36, 72 S.Ct. 97, 96 L.Ed. 48, 1951*)*.

MODERN TACTICS USED IN INTERROGATION

Professor Inabu (former Director of Scientific Crime Detection for Chicago, and Professor of Law at Northwestern University) improved interrogation by focusing upon psychological methods such as

1. deceiving the suspect,
2. cajoling the suspect,
3. manipulating the suspect, and
4. pressuring the suspects to stop denying crimes the police "knew" they had committed and start confessing.

Note: In 1966, the Miranda Court quoted extensively from Inabu's manual referring to it as "The most enlightening and effective means presently used to obtain statements through a custodial interrogation."

"The art of criminal investigation has not developed to a point where the search for and the examination of physical evidence will always, or even in most cases, reveal a clue to the identity of the perpetrator or provide the necessary proof of his guilt" *(Police Interrogation-A practical necessity-Fred E. Inabu)*. Professor Inabu's philosophy was that in many criminal investigations, there was an absence of physical evidence, and the only approach to possible solutions of crime is to interrogate the criminal suspect, as well as others who may possess such information *(Police Interrogation)*. Tactics such as "trickery" and "deceit" were effective methods of securing information from guilty parties or leads from uncooperative informants and witnesses *(Police Interrogation)*.

The general purpose of the police interrogation is to aid police officers in obtaining a confession from a guilty suspect *(Nolo)*. This is an image that has been re-enacted on numerous crime scene dramas where a "quivering suspect" is placed in a room and questioned relentlessly until he gives the detectives the information in which they need to move forward. Although this image is often being referred to as a "thing of the past," there are a number of individuals who are questioned in a variety of different ways *(Nolo)*. When police officers ask questions many are unwilling to give any information because they believe that it will be used to prosecute them. However, what needs to be realized is that police officers may be investigating a crime where in fact they have no leads, no physical evidence, and a duty to solve the crime. In these instances, police officers will usually refer to investigative questions in order to get a general idea as to where they need to focus their attention or even where to start their investigation. If a suspect has a suspicion that they may be charged with a crime they should never talk to a police officer prior to talking to their lawyer *(Nolo)*.

When a police officer attempts to question a civilian when they have not been placed into custody, you will often see them resort to the following types of communication: On-the-street questioning, in-your-face questioning, traffic violations, visits to homes, visits to offices/places of business, and telephone conversations *(Nolo)*. A police officer may stop a civilian on the street and question them without even suspecting of being involved in a crime. This is where a police officer will approach a civilian and ask them questions. However, the person is generally not required to answer a police officer's questions. In fact, unless a police officer has "probable cause" to arrest a person they have the legal right to walk away from the police officer *(Nolo)*. If a person begins to answer a police officer's questions prior to the questions mounting to a custodial interrogation, they may stop the officer's questioning at any time and indicate that they do not have a desire to talk any further.

If a police officer asks a citizen about a crime that a friend or relative committed, there is always that temptation to try and protect the ones you love. However, this can become extremely problematic as the citizen giving the false information may be charged as "accessories after the fact," or even with obstruction of justice *(Nolo)*. One of the most common types of psychological intimidation that is used by police officers during a custodial interrogation is police deception *(Scheb)*. A misstatement of fact by the police may affect whether or not the confession is deemed to be voluntary. However, the effect of the misstatements may properly be considered in light of the totality of the circumstances. For example, in the case of *Frazier v. Cupp*, U.S. 731, 89 S.Ct. 1420, 22 L.Ed.2d 684 (1969), the U.S. Supreme Court reversed a lower court decision where the police obtained a confession by informing the suspect that his codefendant had confessed. The decision in *Frazier v. Cupp* indicated that the misstatement did speak to the fact of whether the statement had been given voluntarily, it did not make the confession inadmissible.

One of the questions that is often asked in regards to police interrogation is "how far is too far?" Police officers have resorted to countless tactics that have been both used and upheld in considering whether or not a confession should come into court, but the deceit and trickery can have its' limitations too. For instance, a Florida appellate court upheld a lower trial judge's order that rendered a confession involuntary when police officers presented fabricated lab reports in order to gain a defendant's confession *(Scheb)*. One of the reasons that the courts rendered the use of such fabricated documentation is because of the high likelihood that it would be deemed to be genuine and find their way into police files or in the alternative into the court files *(State v. Cayward,* 552 So.2d 971, Fla. App. 1989).

More recently, the court in *State v. Patton* heard a matter where a police officer posed as an eyewitness to the crime and gave a detailed accounting on an audio tape, which was subsequently played to the suspect *(State v. Patton,* 826 A.2d 783, N.J. Super 2005*)*. The detailed accounting ultimately resulted in his confession to the murder, which was sought to be excluded at trial. The confession was ultimately admitted at trial, and the defendant was found guilty of the murder in that he confessed to earlier. The New Jersey court ultimately found that the evidence that was offered against to the defendant at trial was fabricated and should not have been admitted. As a result, the defendant's conviction was reversed *(Scheb)*.

JUDICIAL DISCRETION IN EVALUATING CONFESSIONS

It is often overlooked by many the role that judges play in either deciding to admit or exclude evidence into court against a defendant. For example, if a judge determines that the deceit and trickery by the police officers in obtaining an initial confession was too egregious then it will not be used in court against him. The problem with this is that it may be the only piece of evidence linking the suspect/defendant to the crime. If it is excluded, the case may typically fall by the wayside and the criminal may arguably walk free. When determining whether or not the confession was voluntary in the first place, there should be consideration placed upon multiple variables. First, the duration and methods of interrogation used in obtaining a confession. Second, the length of the delay between arrest and appearance before a magistrate. Third, the conditions of detention. Fourth, the attitudes of the police toward the defendant. Fifth, the defendant's physical and psychological state. Sixth, anything else that might bear on the defendant's resistance *(Commonwealth v. Kichline,* 361 A.3d 292, 290, Pa. 1976*)*.

*F*IFTH AMENDMENT OF THE CONSTITUTION

A person shall be held to answer for a capital, or otherwise infamous crime, unless on a presentment or indictment of a Grand Jury, except in cases arising in the land or naval forces, or in the Militia, when in actual service in time of War of Public danger; nor shall any person be subject for the same offense to be twice put in jeopardy of life or limb; nor shall be compelled in any criminal case to be a witness against himself, nor be deprived of life, liberty, or property, without due process of law; nor shall private property be taken for public use without just compensation.

THE MIRANDA WARNINGS

In 1966, the case of *Miranda v. Arizona* was involved a rapist who allegedly confessed during an investigation that was deemed to be custodial in nature, and defendant was not apprised of right to counsel or his right to remain silent. The U.S. Supreme Court ultimately held that confessions by custodial interrogation are inadmissible unless the suspect was informed of (1) his right to silence, (2) the consequences of waiving that right, (3) the right to retain appointed counsel, and (4) waived those rights knowingly and intelligently.

"If adequate *Miranda* warnings are not given prior to a custodial interrogation, incriminating statements (even though voluntary) made by the accused are ordinarily inadmissible on the prosecution's case-in-chief. A voluntary confession obtained in violation of an accused rights to adequate *Miranda* warnings may, however, be used to *impeach* him if he testifies at trial" *(Harris v. New York)*. Any inquiry, statement, or conduct exerted by a police officer which likely to elicit an incriminating response amount to an *interrogation* for purposes of the Miranda rule. An interrogation should be differentiated from a mere investigative inquiry in order to determine whether the Miranda rule was violated. In order for the Miranda rule to apply it should be determined that there is a custodial interrogation.

CUSTODIAL INTERROGATIONS

When is an interrogation considered custodial? When considering whether or not a suspect is in custody under *Miranda*, it is determined objectively. More specifically, would a reasonably prudent person in the suspect's situation believe that he had the ability to terminate questioning and leave? *(Yarborough v. Alvarado)*. One of the biggest oversights made by citizens and law enforcement alike is looking to the properties of the structure when determining whether or not an interrogation is custodial in nature. The properties of the structure are irrelevant. In fact, an interrogation can be custodial in nature in a wide open space such as a field. If a police officer does anything to discourage your right to leave then the interrogation is custodial in nature. Take for instance the example where a citizen accepts an invitation by the police to be questioned down at the stationhouse. Upon arrival he is ushered back to a room with a desk and two chairs. After the citizen sits on one side of the desk, the detective sits on the other side of the desk and explains that there is no need to give you any Miranda warnings because you are free to terminate the interview and leave at any time. In fact, to make good on this promise he keeps the door wide open in order to make the citizen feel more comfortable. However, there is a police officer standing at the door preventing anyone from either entering into the room or exiting. This would be an example of a *custodial interrogation* because the regardless of the words that the detective is telling you, that you can terminate the interview at any time and leave, the placement of the police officer at the door blocking your exit is telling you otherwise.

The Fifth Amendment serves to protects writings and statements.

PUBLIC SAFETY EXCEPTION

Evidence that is obtained from a custodial interrogation is admissible without prior *Miranda* warnings, if (1) it was voluntarily given and (2) a risk to the public's safety existed at the time of the questioning *(New York v. Quarles)*. If the Miranda rights are invoked by the suspect being interrogated *(i.e., they indicate that they don't want to communicate any further)*, all interrogations must cease. If the suspect either initiates further discussions with police after invoking his right to silence the earlier "invocation" of Miranda rights are waived. Generally, police provide *Miranda Warnings* immediately following arrest, or when it is deemed to be practical *(Scheb)*.

WHEN MUST AN INTERROGATION CEASE?

An interrogation must cease when a defendant either requests an attorney or states that he wants to remain silent. An interrogation can resume where there has been a significant amount of time that has lapsed, and the questioning is about an unrelated crime.

INTERROGATION OF MINORS

If a law enforcement officer is faced with interrogating a minor child, there is a slightly different standard that needs to be considered. In the case of *J.D.B. v. North Carolina,* a uniformed police officer removed a 13 year-old seventh grade student from his class and brought him to a conference room with the door shut. The student was questioned by the police officer for approximately 30 minutes concerning home break-ins. Immediately prior to the questioning, the student was not apprised of his Miranda warnings, and ultimately confessed to the crime. At trial, the state would not take into consideration the age of the student that was questioned by the police officer. This matter appealed to the U.S. Supreme Court where a determination was rendered that a child's age may be considered during an interrogation because (1) a reasonable child subjected to police questioning will sometimes feel pressured to submit when a reasonable adult would feel free to leave and (2) it bears no responsibility on an officer's objectivity.

QUESTIONS CONCERNING PUBLIC SAFETY

In the case of *New York v. Quarles,* a woman who claimed that she had been raped identified the suspect to a police officer while inside a supermarket. When the officers frisked the suspect for weapons, he found an empty shoulder holster and asked where the gun was located. The suspect responded that "the gun is over there," and the police officer retrieved the weapon and then returned to give the suspect his Miranda warnings. When this matter was brought before the U.S. Supreme Court, the issue was heard as to whether there was an exception to the requirement that a suspect be read their Miranda right prior to their answers being admitted into evidence when the police officer's motivation in asking the question was to insure that no danger to the public results from concealment of a weapon. Ultimately, the U.S. Supreme Court found that there was no violation of the Miranda warnings where the police officers asked for the location of a weapon in order to prevent injury to another party.

CONVERSATIONS LIKELY TO ILLICIT AN INCRIMINATING RESPONSE

After a murder suspect in police custody requested counsel, one officer remarked that the lost murder weapon might injure nearby children, which induced the suspect to locate the weapon *(Rhode Island v. Innis, 1980)*. At trial, the murder suspect (defendant) sought to suppress the statement locating the whereabouts of the weapon used in the murder because he believed the conversation violated the Miranda warnings because the police officer allegedly started the conversation with the other police officer for the purpose of getting the suspect to confess.

Even if a suspect is in police custody, police officers' statements are not deemed "interrogation" unless they express either questions or equivalent statements that are reasonably likely to elicit an incriminating response, and in fact elicit such a response *(Rhode Island v. Innis* 1990*)*.

RECORDED CONVERSATIONS

In the case of *U.S. v. Turk*, police officers pulled over Kabbaby and gathered two cassette tapes from the vehicle. When the cassette tapes were listened to, they revealed conversations between Kabbaby and Turk (defendant). Turk was subpoenaed to appear before the grand jury and based on the testimony, Turk was subsequently charged with perjury. When the matter was brought before the trial court, he filed a motion to suppress the recordings based upon the fact that the officers' listening to the recordings constituted a violation of the Omnibus Crime Control and Safe Streets Act (U.S. v. Turk 1976). The U.S. Supreme Court held that the replaying of legally recorded conversations does not constitute an illegal interception.

INTERCEPTIONS OF ELECTRONIC COMMUNICATIONS

Sibbie Deal worked at an establishment named "White Oak Package Store," which was owned and operated by both Newell and Juanita Spears. The Spears lived next to the package store and had only one phone for their residential and business calls. Deal had a history of making personal calls during her shift, and she was admonished by the Spears that they would be monitoring her phone calls, which was an attempt to keep her from making them. The package store was burglarized and the Spears suspected that Deal may be involved so they recorded 24 hours of telephone calls in an attempt to find the perpetrator. Newell Spears listened to most of the recordings even though a majority of it had nothing to do with the suspected burglary. In fact, most of the conversations were sexually explicit phone conversations between Deal and her lover with whom she was having an extramarital affair at the time. The Spears never told Deal that they were monitoring her calls. When Deal became aware of the circumstances she brought a civil suit based on the Omnibus Crime Control and Safe Streets Act, prohibiting the interception of oral and wire communications. The trial court found for Deal, but the Spears appealed on the grounds that Deal gave implied consent to the recordings and that the recordings fell under the business exception to the Act. When the U.S. Supreme Court decided on this matter, it was held that the Omnibus Crime Control and Safe Streets Act of 1968 prohibits the interception of electronic communications without a court order unless one party to the conversations consents *(Deal v. Spears)*.

FRUIT OF THE POISONOUS TREE DOCTRINE

The *Miranda* decision relied upon the exclusionary rule was applicable to statements that were made by suspects during custodial interrogations. Additionally, under the fruit of the poisonous tree standard, the evidence that may be derived from inadmissible evidence is also inadmissible *(Wong Sun v. United States, 371 U.S. 471, 83 S.Ct. 407, 9 L.Ed.2d 441, 1963)*. An example of this would be police officers who were to be made aware of a weapon that was used in the commission of a crime by interrogating a suspect who is in custody, the weapon would be considered derivative evidence. However, if the physical evidence was located independently and lawfully, it may be applicable under the independent source exception *(Segura v. United States, 468 U.S. 796, 104 S.Ct. 3380, 82 L.Ed.2d 599, 1984)*.

*R*IGHT TO COUNSEL

When a party is being interrogated and he invokes his right to an attorney, all questioning must cease. While there is no specific language that needs to be spoken verbatim if the party being interrogated communicates that he wants a lawyer present or that he would like to talk to an attorney before he answers any questions, then the interrogation must cease. However, the interrogation can resume when the attorney is present. In the case of *Minnick v. Mississippi*, a suspect invoked his right to an attorney, and the police allowed him to consult with his attorney, but then began to interrogate him without his attorney present.

RE-INITIATION OF INTERROGATION AFTER RIGHT TO COUNSEL IS INVOKED

In 2003, a police detective tried to question the inmate, who was incarcerated at a Maryland prison pursuant to a prior conviction, about allegations that he had sexually abused his son. The inmate invoked his Miranda right to have counsel present during interrogation, so the interview was terminated. The inmate was released back into the general prison population, and the investigation was closed. Another detective reopened the investigation in 2006 and attempted to interrogate the inmate, who was still incarcerated. The inmate waived his Miranda rights and made incriminating statements. The Court held that if more than a 14-day break-in-custody between the first and second attempts at interrogation occurs it does not mandate suppression of statements *(Maryland v. Shatzer, 2010)*.

WAIVER OF FIFTH AMENDMENT RIGHTS

Petitioner waived his rights to silence and was found guilty of first degree murder when he answered a detective's question about "whether he prayed to God for forgiveness for shooting the victim" was a course of conduct indicating waiver of the right to remain silent. The court found a waiver "has two distinct dimensions": (1) waiver must be voluntarily given and the product of a free and deliberate choice rather than intimidation, coercion, and (2) made with a full awareness of both the nature of the right being abandoned and the consequences of the decision to abandon it" *(Berghius v. Thompkins, 2010)*.

WRITTEN STATEMENTS TO THIRD PARTIES

Montejo, a murder suspect, waived his Miranda rights and was interrogated at the sheriff's office on 9/6 and on 9/7. While he was in the process of accompanying detectives to show the whereabouts of the murder weapon, he wrote a letter of apology to the victim's widow before meeting with his attorney. The letter was introduced as a statement at trial against him. A defendant who does not want to speak to police without counsel present need only say as much when he is first approached and given the Miranda warnings. At that point, not only must immediate contact end, but badgering by later requests are prohibited *(Montejo v. Louisiana 2009)*.

FAILURE TO NOTIFY A SUSPECT THAT AN ATTORNEY HAS BEEN RETAINED ON HIS BEHALF

After the police failed to tell a suspect that a lawyer had been appointed for him and falsely told the lawyer the suspect would not be interrogated, the suspect moved to suppress his confession.

A confession is not rendered inadmissible merely because the police failed to inform the suspect that a lawyer tried to contact him, or because the police did not grant the lawyer access, although egregious police misconduct may violate constitutional due process *(Moran v. Burbine)*.

*R*EASONABLE EXPECTATIONS OF PRIVACY IN PERSONAL COMPUTERS ON A UNIVERSITY NETWORK

In the last chapter, we looked to unreasonable searches and seizures where there was a reasonable expectation of privacy. In this chapter, we focus on incriminating statements and whether or not they can be admitted at trial against them. But the question often arises "When is there a reasonable expectation of privacy in verbal, oral, or written statements?" *"When can it be searched, gathered, and used as evidence?"* In the following, we will address the issue on when a private citizen can enjoy a reasonable expectation of privacy in the foregoing communication.

UNIVERSITY COMPUTER NETWORKS

When dealing with computers, there is often a lot of sensitive information that is stored and placed on the hard drive for safekeeping. When does law enforcement have access to it and when does a warrant need to be secured in order to access that information? For instance, on a university network, there is a reasonable expectation of privacy exists in a computer if (1) it has a protected screen saver password, (2) it is located in a place where you have a reasonable expectation of privacy (i.e., dorm room), and (3) the institution has a policy where they actively monitor or audit computer usage.

WORLD WIDE WEB POSTINGS

There is no reasonable expectation of privacy for postings (i.e., pictures) posted on the World Wide Web.

*R*IGHTS IN CONTENT INFORMATION

The purpose of any network is to send and receive the contents of communications, whether they are *written messages* or *physical objects*.

POSTAL MAIL PRIVACY

When a package is being sent through the mail, there is the expectation that your mail and its contents are protected. Additionally, when a package is sent, there is an expectation of privacy that exists that the package will not be opened, and the contents left unexamined unless until it reaches its destination. The contents of sealed packages are protected by the Fourth Amendment during transmission. However, postal regulation stated that the mailing of sealed parcels of fourth class rates of postage is considered to be *consent* by the sender to postal inspections of the contents. In short, there is no Fourth Amendment reasonable expectation of privacy that exists in a fourth class package, and the contents can be readily examined without a warrant, or even probable cause.

HISTORY OF TELEPHONE PRIVACY

Technology around telephone usage has evolved over the course of the last century, and so has the law dictating what is and what is not considered to be a search. In 1928, there were not any rules concerning whether or not a warrant had to be secured in order to monitor telephone communication because the U.S. Supreme Court ruled that wiretapping did not amount to a Fourth Amendment search requiring a warrant. This case was subsequently overruled by *U.S. v. Katz* and *Berger v. N.Y.*

When technology changed again and cordless telephones became available to the public, the issue had to be addressed once again as to whether or not a warrant or warrant exception had to exist in order to monitor the telephone communication between parties? In this instance, the courts held that cordless calls that are broadcast over *FM radio waves do not violate the Fourth Amendment rights of cordless users, or the party with whom the user is conversing with.* Additionally, interception is much less likely to occur in this manner for two reasons: (1) Congress amended the Statutory Wiretap Act of '94 to include cell phones and (2) modern cell phones and cordless phones are encrypted making interception much more difficult.

PAGER COMMUNICATIONS AND TEXT MESSAGE PRIVACY

The appeal revolves around a string of bank robberies McCreary committed in 2002 with several coconspirators to the crime. The group communicated via text pagers that were able to send and receive messages in several different ways. First, a party was permitted to enter the pin number of the pager from a remote pager and communicate a message. Second, communication could be sent via website, enter a pin number, and then send a message over the website. Third, a party could send an e-mail to the pin number of the text pager domain. At this time, MCI/Skytel was a company who kept records of all messaging correspondence sent, so the records were subpoenaed and used against them in court.

The question brought before the court was whether the government violated the defendants' Fourth Amendment rights by resorting to a subpoena rather than a search warrant? The decision from the district court in this case said that pager messages that were subpoenaed were inadmissible to be used in court against them.

𝓡IGHTS IN NONCONTENT INFORMATION

Noncontent information consists of information such as destination address, phone numbers, stored wire and electronic communications held by third-party internet service providers (ISP). While the Fourth Amendment applies specifically to right of privacy for people "to be secure in their persons, houses, and papers, and effects, against unreasonable searches and seizures," it generally has no application to information that is stored online. This means that a subpoena and prior notice are needed to compel an ISP to disclose files. However, there is an exception to the rules concerning the reasonable expectation of privacy of emails. A subscriber enjoys a reasonable expectation of privacy in the contents of emails that are stored with, or sent or received through, a commercial ISP, and the government may not compel a commercial ISP to turn over the contents of a subscriber's emails without first obtaining a warrant based on probable cause.

PEN REGISTERS

Pen registers are also referred to as dialed number recorders (DNR), which are electronic devices that record all numbers that have been dialed from a telephone line. These pen registers are used to determine whether or not a home phone is being used to conduct business, to check for a defective dial tone, and to check for overbilling. Based upon the characteristics and function of the pen register, it has been determined by the courts that there is no reasonable expectation of privacy in the numbers dialed by a telephone. Installation and use of a pen register at a telephone company offices did not violate the suspect's reasonable expectation of privacy and did not require the authorization of a warrant. Pen register orders for internet monitoring are virtually indistinguishable from pen registers for number dialed. Therefore, there is no Fourth Amendment violation.

MAIL COVERS AND POSTAL MAIL PRIVACY

The exterior of letters/packages are not entitled to Fourth Amendment protection because exterior appearance, size, and weight are exposed to the carrier and cannot support a reasonable expectation of privacy.

STORED ACCOUNT RECORDS

The government can obtain the records of how an account was used without triggering the warrant requirement. In this instance, if the government wanted to obtain information related to accounts, they would have to produce a subpoena and prior notice.

STATUTORY PRIVACY LAWS

The Wiretap Act addresses two privacy invading practices.

1. *Bugging*—use of a secret recording device in a room or physical space.
2. *Wiretapping*—the interception of private telephone calls.

* *The Wiretap Act regulates both government actors and private parties.*

- In 1986, Congress passed the Electronic Communications Privacy Act—Three basic parts.
  1. It expanded the Wiretap Act to include electronic communications *(i.e., computer)*.
  2. New statutory regulation of stored electronic communications.
  3. Pen Register statute—regulates the use of pen registers.

THE WIRETAP ACT

- Prohibits the intercepts of a wire, oral, or electronic communication.

  - *Wire*—communications that contain human voice that are sent over a wire (i.e., telephone calls).
  - *Oral*—"In person" recordings of the human voice that can be picked up by a bugging device or microphone when the person recorded has a reasonable expectation of privacy.
  - *Electronic Communications*—most computer communications that do not contain a human voice as most computer communications.

The Beginning and End of The Wiretap Act

- The collection of evidence that either has or will be sent over the network doesn't trigger the statute because it only regulates access to contents of information over the network itself.

**The message remains protected up and until it reaches the intended recipient.*

THE DUE PROCESS "VOLUNTARINESS" TEST

It is also referred to as the "the totality of the circumstances" test for admitting confessions. When questioning a suspect and determining whether or not they waived their rights against self-incrimination, law enforcement officers determined whether or not the confessions obtained were voluntary by the following criteria.

- Intelligence of the suspect
- Physical health of the suspect
- Emotional characteristics of the particular suspect
- Age

- Education
- Prior criminal record
- Whether sleep deprived
- Duration of police questioning
- Whether request for a lawyer was denied

SHORTCOMINGS OF THE "VOLUNTARINESS TEST"

When matters where criminals had voluntarily confessed had been challenged it was determined by the courts that few criminal confessions reviewed by the courts, if any, had been voluntary. This was largely in response to the values underlying the "voluntariness" and "coercion" rhetoric. There were accusations that it kept changing, as did the weight given by the court to the "totality of the circumstances test."

Police investigators made greater use of psychological techniques confronting suspects with improper interrogation methods. For instance, the suspect was frequently "inarticulate," which aggravated the following:

1. Atmosphere of police questioning;
2. Manner of appropriate advice involving suspect's rights;
3. Subsequent undermining;

DOUBLE JEOPARDY

The Fifth Amendment to the Constitution protects a defendant from being retried for the same offense jeopardy after jeopardy has attached. Double jeopardy arises when a defendant that is charged with a crime is charged with another crime that is based upon the same offense. However, an offense is "different" for purposes of whether or not double jeopardy attaches when an element of the offense requires proof of an element that is not included in the other offense. Jeopardy attaches during the course of a *jury trial* when the jury is empanelled and sworn in. In a *bench trial*, jeopardy attaches when the first witness is sworn in.

Once jeopardy has attached, retrial is permitted if there is a *hung jury* (jury verdict is not unanimous, or otherwise uneven), there is a *mistrial* due to manifest necessity (defendant is too sick to continue), there is a retrial after a successful appeal by the defendant (defendant can be retried unless the basis for reversal was insufficient evidence to support a guilty verdict), defendant breaches a plea bargain agreement, or a trial is brought in separate sovereigns. A defendant can be tried to for the same crime in different states without violating double jeopardy if the crime was committed across state lines. Additionally, a defendant can be tried in federal and state court without violating double jeopardy because they are different sovereigns.

WORKS CITED

Scheb

Police Interrogation and American Justice, Richard A. Leo

Bram v. United States

Malloy v. Hogan, 378 U.S. 1, 84 S.Ct. 1489, 12 L.Ed.2d 653 (1964).

United States v. Carnignan, 342 U.S. 36, 72 S.Ct. 97, 96 L.Ed. 48 (1951).

Nolo

Frazier v. Cupp, U.S. 731, 89 S.Ct. 1420, 22 L.Ed.2d 684 (1969)

State v. Cayward, 552 So.2d 971 (Fla. App. 1989)

State v. Patton, 826 A.2d 783, N.J. Super (2005).

Commonwealth v. Kichline, 361 A.3d 292, 290 (Pa. 1976).

Yarborough v. Alvarado

J.D.B. v. North Carolina

Rhode Island v. Innis (1990)

U.S. v. Turk,

Deal v. Spears

Wong Sun v. United States, 371 U.S. 471, 83 S.Ct. 407, 9 L.Ed.2d 441 (1963)

Segura v. United States, 468 U.S. 796, 104 S.Ct. 3380, 82 L.Ed.2d 599 (1984)

Minnick v. Mississippi

Maryland v. Shatzer (2010)

Berghius v. Thompkins (2010)

Montejo v. Louisiana (2009)

Moran v. Burbine

U.S. v. Katz, and *Berger v. N.Y.*

PRETRIAL ACTIVITIES AND THE CRIMINAL TRIAL
By Robert Aberle

Chapter 8

CHAPTER OVERVIEW

A person enters the criminal justice system when they are arrested and charged with a criminal act. Once the person becomes a part of the system, they become a defendant and their Sixth Amendment rights are immediately (and automatically) put into effect. This chapter will explain all of these rights and how they are applied from the pretrial phases through the actual criminal trial. The stages of a criminal trial will be examined and explained in this chapter, from jury selection until the verdict is rendered by a judge or a jury.

© Andrea Donti, 2011. Used under license from Shutterstock, Inc.

CHAPTER LEARNING OBJECTIVES

After reading this chapter you will be able to:

1. Understand the bail system and the alternative pretrial release procedures that may be used in different criminal cases.
2. Identify and explain the various pretrial activities that are used in the American court system.
3. Compare the grand jury system with the preliminary hearing and explain how they are both used to determine whether an arrest was lawful.
4. Explain what a plea bargain is and why it has become an important aspect of our judicial system.
5. List the rights that are afforded under the Sixth Amendment to the U.S. Constitution.
6. Identify the various stages of a criminal trial.

KEYWORDS

Booking	Bail
ROR	First Appearance
Preliminary Hearing	Grand Jury
Information	Arraignment
Plea Bargaining	Speedy Trial
Right to Counsel	Jury Selection
Venire	*Voir Dire*
Challenge for Cause	*Peremptory Challenge*
Opening Statements	Burden of Proof
Motion for Directed Verdict	Closing Arguments
Jury Instructions	Deliberation
Hung Jury	*Allen* Charge
Verdict	

© corepics, 2011. Used under license from Shutterstock, Inc.

ENTERING THE CRIMINAL JUSTICE SYSTEM

A person enters the criminal justice system when they are arrested and charged with a criminal act (a crime). When the police make an arrest, they will charge the suspect with a crime based upon the probable cause that they determined was present at the time of the arrest. The crime that the suspect is initially charged with is often changed by the prosecutor during the pretrial process (see plea bargaining).

BOOKING

After a person is arrested, they are taken to a jail facility where they are booked. The booking process consists of:

1. Filing of the arrest report.
2. Taking fingerprints of the suspect.
3. Photographing the suspect ("mug" shot).
4. Obtaining the personal information of the suspect (name, address, birthdate, and other identifiers).

Once the person is booked, they are housed in the jail until such time that they can make bail or are brought to court for their first appearance (see following section).

BAIL AND PRETRIAL RELEASE

One of the basic presumptions of the criminal justice system in America is that of the presumption of innocence. All persons arrested of a crime are presumed to be innocent until proven guilty by a court. It is this presumption that allows for the provision of bail. **Bail**, while not a guaranteed right, is provided for in the Eighth Amendment of the United States Constitution. The Eight Amendment states that "excessive bail shall not be required."

Bail

Bail is a way for an accused individual to be released from custody prior to trial by posting money or some other form of collateral.

Bail is a way for an accused individual to be released from custody prior to trial. Bail is the posting of money, property, or other collateral by the arrested person, as a way of guaranteeing they will appear in court to answer the charges against them. This is one of the foremost reasons for the allowing of bail in our system. This reason, release to guarantee appearance, has to be weighed against protecting society from the possible commission of more crimes by the suspect if they are released back into the community. Since bail is not a guarantee, certain charges are considered serious enough that no bail is allowed. Persons charged with capital offenses (those that could result in a sentence of death) and other serious offenses are routinely denied bail. The "excessive bail" provision also does not mean that a person cannot be given a bail totaling millions of dollars. This type of bail is routinely given in high level drug trafficking cases and in cases involving large amounts of embezzled or stolen property.

In many jurisdictions around the country, there are standard bail amounts that are posted in the booking facilities that will allow those accused to post a set amount of bail for certain crimes. These standard bails are usually agreed upon in advance by the judges within that jurisdiction. This type of procedure allows many of those accused of crimes to be released within a short amount of time without having to wait for an appearance before a judge or magistrate.

In addition to the posting of bail, there are other ways that an accused person can be released from jail prior to going to trial. Many factors are taken into consideration when making release decisions:

1. Prior criminal history of the accused.
2. The seriousness of the crime for which the person is currently charged.
3. Flight risk.
4. Job stability, family relationships, and other indicators that tie the accused to the community.

ROR

Release on recognizance (ROR) allows a person to be released from jail prior to trial on their promise to refrain from criminal activity and to return to court at the date and time specified without having to post collateral.

Many jurisdictions offer a variety of alternatives to releasing a person on bail. One of the most common of these is releasing on recognizance (ROR). **ROR** is allowing the accused to be released on their promise to refrain from criminal activity and to return to court at the date and time specified. The ROR release only requires the signature of the defendant. This type of release is often used for lesser crimes (certain misdemeanors) and is a way to alleviate overcrowding in the jails.

Another common alternative to bail is to be released on a program of house arrest. House arrest can be monitoring either electronically through the use of a bracelet and monitoring device, or with a curfew accompanied by a requirement of reporting daily to the jail or other facility for status checks.

ENTERING THE COURT SYSTEM— PRETRIAL ACTIVITIES

FIRST APPEARANCE

First Appearance

If an arrested person is unable to make bail, they must be brought before a judge or magistrate "without unnecessary delay" for their first appearance in court.

If an arrested person is unable to make bail, they must be brought before a judge or magistrate "without unnecessary delay."[1] Depending on the jurisdiction, the accused person must be brought to court within forty-eight or seventy-two hours of their arrest. This time includes weekends and holidays. While jurisdictions can vary the time lapse required for a **first appearance**, the U.S. Supreme Court requires courts to determine whether or not the arrest was valid and was based upon probable cause within forty-eight hours of arrest.[2] Courts throughout the country have set up a variety of procedures to insure that this requirement is met, particularly on holiday weekends when courts are not actually in session.

When the arrested person is brought before the court for their first appearance, they are given formal notice of the charges against them. They are also read their Sixth Amendment rights, and if they request an attorney (and they qualify) one will be appointed for them at this time. This is also the time when bail can be set or other pretrial release sanctions can be discussed and imposed.

PRELIMINARY HEARING

About half of all states utilize the **preliminary hearing** and the other half (and the federal government) use a grand jury system (see the following). The preliminary or probable cause hearing is a formal court preceding that is used to determine if there is probable cause to justify the arrest and to send the case over to the grand jury (in some jurisdictions) or to the trial court.

The preliminary hearing is held in a courtroom and has many similarities to a trial. The prosecution presents witnesses who are sworn, and may present other evidence. The defendant is present with his/her attorney and may or may not present any evidence at this time. The prosecution does not have to present their entire case, they only have to present enough evidence and/or testimony to convince the judge or magistrate that the arrest was legal and the charges are based upon probable cause.

THE GRAND JURY

The purpose of the **grand jury** is the same as that of the preliminary hearing; to determine if there was probable cause to justify the arrest and, if so, to send the case to the trial court. Grand juries usually consist of twenty-three citizens who have been subpoenaed to serve on the jury for a specified period of time. In most jurisdictions the grand jury meets in secret and the defendant is not notified of the hearing. The prosecutor calls witnesses into the grand jury room one at a time and swears them in. The prosecutor then asks the witness questions, after which time the jurors themselves may question the witness if they want. There is no cross examination since the defense is not even present. Similar to the preliminary hearing, the prosecutor does not have to present the entire case against the defendant, only enough to establish probable cause.

Preliminary Hearing

The preliminary or probable cause hearing is a formal court preceding that is used to determine if there is probable cause to justify the arrest and to send the case over to the grand jury (in some jurisdictions) or to the trial court.

Grand Jury

The grand Jury serves the same purpose as the preliminary hearing except that this is not a trial type setting. Instead the evidence is heard by a jury of twenty-three (usually) citizens.

When the prosecutor finishes presenting the evidence, the grand jury meets alone and deliberates. If the jury determines that there is probable cause, they will issue an indictment, or a "true bill." The case is then sent to the trial court. If the grand jury does not find probable cause, they will issue a "no bill" and the case is over.

INFORMATION

Information

The information is a formal accusation submitted to the court by a prosecutor and alleges that a specific person(s) has committed a specific offense(s).

Once a defendant has been bound over to the trial court, either by a determination by the judge in the preliminary hearing or by indictment of the grand jury, the prosecutor files an **information**. The information is a formal accusation submitted to the court by a prosecutor and alleges that a specific person(s) has committed a specific offense(s).[3]

ARRAIGNMENT

Arraignment

The arraignment is the first time the defendant is brought before the court that has the jurisdiction to actually conduct the trial.

The **arraignment** is the first time the defendant is brought before the court that has the jurisdiction to actually conduct the trial. The arraignment is a formal hearing where the defendant stands before the judge and is:

1. Informed or the charges for which they will be tried.
2. Read their Sixth Amendment rights.
3. Enter a plea.

When asked to enter a plea, the defendant has several options. The defendant may enter a plea of not guilty in which case the judge will then set a trial date. If the defendant enters a plea of guilty, a date will then be set for sentencing. Sentencing usually occurs thirty to sixty days after the plea in order to allow enough time to have a presentence report submitted to the court (see Chapter 10). The defendant may also enter a plea of *nolo contendere* (no contest). *Nolo contendere* has the same effect as a guilty plea; however, it is usually used in cases where there may be civil proceedings filed against the defendant at a later date because it is not an admission of guilt in civil court.[4] If the defendant refuses to enter a plea, they "stand mute" and the judge will enter a plea of not guilty for the defendant and set a trial date.

© Rafa Irusta, 2011. Used under license from Shutterstock, Inc.

© Cupertino, 2011. Used under license from Shutterstock, Inc.

*P*LEA BARGAINING

Plea bargaining is the negotiation between the prosecutor and the defendant (usually the defendants attorney) which results in the defendant entering a plea of guilty in exchange for a reduction of charges, or the prosecutors promise to recommend a more lenient sentence than the defendant would ordinarily receive.[5] The U.S. Supreme Court allowed the use of plea bargaining in the 1970 case of *Brady v. United States.*[6]

In 2006, state courts in the United States sentenced 1,232,290 persons for felony convictions and plea bargaining was used in 94 percent of these cases.[7] Plea bargaining receives a lot of criticism because it seems like the courts just give offenders a "slap on the wrist." The reality is, without plea bargaining, our entire criminal justice system would probably collapse. Our court system could not possibly handle 1.2 million actual trials every year. There just are not enough courthouses, judges, or staff to allow for that. An often overlooked fact is that 69 percent of those felons who do plead guilty under plea bargain agreements are actually sentenced to a period of confinement (41 percent to state prison and 28 percent to local jails).[8]

Plea Bargaining

Plea bargaining is the negotiation between the prosecutor and the defendant (usually the defendants attorney) which results in the defendant entering a plea of guilty in exchange for a reduction of charges or sentence.

*L*EGAL ISSUES

There are two very important legal issues, both of which are contained in the Sixth Amendment, that impact the court system in the United States: the right to a speedy trial and the right to an attorney.

SPEEDY TRIAL

The Sixth Amendment of the United States Constitution states: "In all criminal prosecution, the accused shall enjoy the right to a speedy and public trial." The U.S. Supreme Court has recognized that there is in fact a right to a **speedy trial** for all citizens accused of crimes,[9] however, they have never actually defined the time frame in which a trial must be commenced in order to comply with this provision. In the 1967 case of *Barker v. Wingo*[10] the Court stated that only in the case of delays that are unwarranted and prejudicial can the defendant claim a violation of their Sixth Amendment rights. The provision providing for a speedy trial was applied to the states in 1973 in the case of *Strunk v. U.S.*[11]

Many states have enacted their own statutes that define the time frames that courts must follow in order to comply with the provisions of a speedy trial within

Speedy Trial

While the Sixth Amendment of the United States Constitution states that the accused in any criminal prosecution is entitled to a speedy and public trial, the Court has left it up to the states to define the time constraints.

their respective jurisdictions. The United States Congress passed the federal Speedy Trial Act in 1974 (which was amended in 1979), which defines the time frames that federal courts must follow in order to comply with the speedy trial provisions. The federal Speedy Trial Act states that there can no more than[12]:

1. Thirty days between arrest and indictment.
2. Ten days between indictment and arraignment.
3. Sixty days between arraignment and trial.

RIGHT TO COUNSEL

Like most of the rights afforded by the U.S. Constitution, the Sixth Amendment guarantee "… to have assistance of counsel for his defense" has undergone a transition over the years by the U.S. Supreme Court:

- 1932—states must appoint counsel for indigent in capital cases.[13]
- 1938—indigent defendants are entitled to appointed counsel in federal criminal cases.[14]
- 1963—indigent defendants are entitled to appointed counsel in state felony cases.[15]
- 1972—states must provide counsel to indigents in any case where they may receive a sentence of imprisonment.[16]
- 2002—counsel must be provided to the indigent even for minor offenses if there is even a slight chance of the defendant getting a sentence of incarceration.[17]

© Andrey Burmakin, 2011. Used under license from Shutterstock, Inc.

The question of who qualifies for government funded counsel has been left up to the individual states and local jurisdictions. Generally the defendant who asks for appointed counsel will be required to fill out a financial questionnaire that will be reviewed by the court to determine if the person qualifies.

There are several ways that the state and local courts comply with the appointment of counsel for the poor. The most common is the use of public defenders. Public defenders are full-time, government-paid attorneys who are assigned indigent cases from the court during the pretrial stages of the court process. The public defender system has come under a considerable amount of criticism over the years because of their high caseloads and the fact that they are a part of the government run court system. Proponents, on the other hand, point out that public defenders know the local court system better than other, outside attorneys and handle only criminal defense cases.

Another system that some courts use to provide indigent counsel is that of court-appointed counsel. In these jurisdictions, the court assigns local attorneys cases as they come up and the attorneys are paid a fee for defending the accused.

Critics of this system are quick to point out that the fees paid the attorneys are generally very low and consequently they are very reluctant to take a case to trial.

The third method used to provide indigent counsel is the use of contract attorneys. Local attorneys and law firms bid for contracts from the local government in order to provide defense services for the court.

*T*HE CRIMINAL TRIAL

A trial is the examination in a court of the issues of fact and law in a case for the purpose of reaching a judgment.[18] There are two basic types of trials: bench and jury trials. A bench trial (or a nonjury trial) is a trial where there is no jury, just a judge. The judge is responsible for hearing the facts of the case and issuing rulings on matters of law. A jury trial is one in which a jury is empanelled and they are to determine the issues of fact in a case and render a verdict. The judge is still responsible for deciding and ruling on all issues of law.

JURY SELECTION

The first order of business in a jury trial is the **selection of the jury**. The jurors, or the jury pool, are selected randomly from the citizens of the community where the trial is going to be held. Depending on the jurisdiction, prospective jurors are usually selected from the voter registration lists or the driver license rolls. Once the jurors have been summoned, they form the *venire*. The **venire** is the group of prospective jurors summoned by the court to report at a specified date and time.

Once the *venire* has been summoned, the next step is to question the prospective jurors to determine their qualifications to serve on the jury. This questioning is called the **voir dire**. The defense attorney, the prosecutor, and the

Selection of the Jury
The first order of business in a jury trial is the selection of the jury.

Venire
The *venire* is the group of prospective jurors summoned by the court to report at a specified date and time.

Voir dire
The questioning of the prospective jurors by the defense attorney, the prosecutor, and the judge is called the *voir dire*.

© Ginae McDonald, 2011. Used under license from Shutterstock, Inc.

judge get to ask questions of the prospective jurors during the *voir dire* in order to determine if they have any relationship to any of the parties involved in the trial (the defendant, attorneys, judge, or any of the anticipated witnesses), or have any preconceived prejudices or bias.

Both the prosecution and the defense may challenge the jurors during the *voir dire*. Challenging a juror is a way of removing that juror from the *venire*. There are two types of challenges that are used; challenge for cause and peremptory challenge. A **challenge for cause** is a challenge where the attorney (either prosecution or defense) must state a reason why they feel that juror should not serve on the jury. Challenges for cause are usually used when the prospective juror shows any type of prejudice or bias towards the case, indicates that they have a relationship with any of the members of the trial, or state that they have already formed an opinion on the case. There is no limit to the number of challenges for cause by either side.

Peremptory challenges are also made by both the prosecution and the defense. The attorneys do not have to state a reason for wanting a juror removed from the jury pool when using peremptory challenges. Unlike the challenges for cause, there are limits to the number of peremptory challenges that are allowed. The number of these challenges is usually set by statute.

OPENING STATEMENTS

Once the jury has been selected, the trial begins. The first part of the trial is the **opening statements**. The opening statements are made by both the prosecution and the defense; however, neither side is required to make one. These statements are a brief outline of the case that they will present. The attorneys can talk about what evidence they intend to present and what they anticipate witnesses will say during the trial. Opening statements are not evidence, and jurors are not to consider these statements when they deliberate over the case at the conclusion of the trial. The attorneys are required to limit their opening statements to comments about what they believe will be presented during the trial.[19]

THE PROSECUTION'S CASE

Since the **burden of proof** is always on the prosecution to prove their case beyond a reasonable doubt, they always present their case first. The prosecution will call their witnesses to the stand and question them. When the prosecutor questions the witness it is called direct examination. During direct examination, the prosecutor may not ask the witness any leading questions. A leading question is one where the answer is implied in the question itself. "You saw the defendant leave the scene of the crime in a red car didn't you?" This would be an example of a leading question because the prosecutor is implying that the car was red.

When the prosecutor has concluded the questioning of the witness, the defense gets a chance to question that same witness. The Sixth Amendment of the United States Constitution states: "In all criminal prosecutions, the accused

---

Challenge for Cause

A challenge for cause is a challenge where the attorney (either prosecution or defense) must state a reason why they feel that juror should not serve on the jury.

Peremptory Challenge

Peremptory challenges are also made by both the prosecution and the defense; however the attorneys do not have to state a reason for wanting a juror removed from the jury pool.

Opening Statement

The first part of the trial is the opening statements. The opening statements are made by both the prosecution and the defense. These statements are a brief outline of the case that each side will present.

Burden of Proof

The burden of proof is always on the prosecution to prove their case beyond a reasonable doubt. The prosecution always presents their case first.

shall enjoy the right ... to be confronted with witnesses against him." This questioning is call cross-examination of the witness. Attorneys are allowed more leeway in the way they question witnesses during cross-examination.

This procedure of direct examination and cross-examination continues until all of the prosecutors witnesses have testified.

The prosecution will also present any physical evidence, documentary evidence, and any other type of evidence they may have during this phase of the trial. When all of the prosecutor's evidence has been submitted, the prosecution will rest its case.

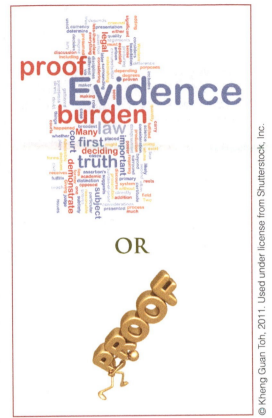

MOTION FOR DIRECTED VERDICT

After the prosecution rests, the defense will many times make a motion for a directed verdict. When this motion is made, the defense is telling the judge that the prosecution failed to meet its burden of proof and did not prove all of the elements of the crime beyond a reasonable doubt. This motion is rarely granted, but if it is the judge will find the defendant not guilty and the trial is over.

THE DEFENDANT'S CASE

Once the prosecution rests, it is the defense's turn to present its case to the jury. The procedure is the same as that used to present the prosecution's case, except that the roles are reversed. The defense attorney will call up any witnesses that they have and the defense will question them first under direct examination. When the defense is finished questioning their witness the prosecutor gets to cross-examine them.

The purpose of the defense during their cross-examination of prosecution witnesses and the direct examination of their own witnesses is to raise reasonable doubt in the mind of the jurors. They attempt to do this in a variety of ways, and if they are successful they can win the case for their client, the defendant.

One of the most critical decisions that the defense must make is whether or not to have the defendant take the stand and testify in their own behalf. One of the biggest reasons for not putting the defendant on the stand is the fact that they will be subject to cross-examination by the prosecution. It is important to note that the prosecution is not allowed to comment to a jury on the defendant's refusal to take the stand on their own behalf.[20]

CLOSING ARGUMENTS

When both sides have presented all of their respective evidence and have rested their case, the attorneys are given one more opportunity to talk to the jury in the form of **closing arguments**. Closing arguments are a summary of all of the evidence that has been presented during the trial. The prosecutor will attempt to persuade the jury that they have met their burden of proof, have proven each and every element of the crime charged, and that the defendant is guilty. The defense will attempt to convince the jury that the prosecution did not prove their case beyond a reasonable doubt and that they, the jury, should find the defendant not guilty of the crime charged.

JURY INSTRUCTIONS

The last phase of the trial before the jury deliberates is the charge to the jury, or the jury instructions. During this phase the judge gives the jurors the applicable rules of law that pertain to the case. If the defendant did not take the stand, the judge will explain to the jury that they are not to draw any inferences, positive or negative, from the decision not to testify. The judge will also explain about the possible verdicts that the juror can render, and will tell the jurors the proper procedures to use from selecting a foreman to writing the verdict.

DELIBERATION

Once the jury has been given their instructions, the will be taken to the jury room and begin their deliberations. The deliberation, which is where the jury discusses the evidence of the case, is done in complete secrecy. Criminal cases in most jurisdictions require that the jury reach a unanimous verdict. If the jury is unable to reach a unanimous decision, it is a hung jury. If the jury cannot come to a verdict and are a **hung jury**, the case will go back to the prosecutor and a decision will have to be made as to whether to retry the case and start all over again at a later date.

In some jurisdictions, if the jury tells the judge that they are "hung," the judge can send them back for further deliberation. If there are only a few jurors who are not in the majority, some states allow the judge to give what is called an *Allen* **charge**.[21] An *Allen* charge allows the judge to tell the jurors who are in the minority to reconsider their decision and see if they can change their mind and vote with the majority.

VERDICT

The jury can render one of three verdicts:

1. Guilty
2. Not guilty
3. Hung jury

If the jury finds the defendant guilty, the judge will set a sentencing date. If the jury finds the defendant not guilty, the judge will release the defendant from custody (if not on bail).

SENTENCING

If the defendant is found guilty, the judge will set a sentencing date. The sentencing process will be discussed in Chapter 10.

REVIEW QUESTIONS:

1. When a person is arrested, they are taken to a jail facility where they are _____.

2. The posting of money, property, or other collateral by an arrested person to guarantee that they will appear in court to answer the charges against them is called _____.

3. The first time an arrested person, who is unable to make bail, sees a judge or magistrate is during their _____ _____.

4. The _____ or _____ _____ hearing is a formal court preceding that is used to determine if there is probable cause to justify the arrest of the suspect.

5. Grand juries usually consist of _____ citizens who have been subpoenaed to serve on the jury for a specified period of time.

6. The _____ is the first time the defendant is brought before the court that has the jurisdiction to actually conduct the trial.

7. In 2006, plea bargaining was used in _____ percent of the felony convictions in the state courts in this country.

8. The _____ Amendment guarantees the right to a speedy trial as well as the right to counsel.

9. The _____ is the group of prospective jurors summoned by the court to report at a specified date and time.

10. The questioning of prospective jurors to determine their qualifications to serve on the jury is called the _____ _____.

11. The burden of proof in a criminal trial is always on the _____.

12. The last phase of a jury trial before the jury begins deliberations is when the judge _____

the jury.

CRITICAL THINKING QUESTIONS:

1. Explain the bail system that is used in this country. Why is it allowed? How does it work? What are some of the alternative ways that arrested persons can be released from jail prior to trial.

2. Describe the different options a defendant has when the judge asked them to enter a plea during their arraignment.

3. Discuss the concept of plea bargaining in the United States. Why is it used? Why is it a necessary component of the judicial system?

4. Explain the jury selection process that is used in courts in the United States. Include in your discussion the two types of challenges that are used during this process.

5. Explain why the burden of proof is always on the prosecution in criminal trials in the United States.

6. Describe and discuss the various stages of a typical criminal trial.

NOTES

CHAPTER 8

[1] McNabb v. U.S., 318 U.S. 332 (1943).

[2] County of Riverside v. McLaughlin, 500 U.S. 44 (1991).

[3] Connie Estrada Ireland and George E. Rush, *The Dictionary of Criminal Justice With Summaries of Supreme Court Cases Affecting Criminal Justice,* 7th Edition (New York: McGraw-Hill Companies, Inc., 2011).

[4] Ibid.

[5] Ibid.

[6] Brady v. United States, 397 U.S. 742 (1970).

[7] Sean Rosenmerkel, Matthew Durose, and Donald Farole, Jr., *Felony Sentences in State Courts, 2006—Statistical Tables* (U.S. Department of Justice, Office of Justice Programs, Bureau of Justice Statistics, December, 2009; revised 11/22/2010).

[8] Ibid.

[9] Klopfer v. North Carolina, 386 U.S. 213 (1967).

[10] Barker v. Wingo, 407 U.S. 514 (1972).

[11] Strunk v. U.S., 412 U.S. 434 (1973).

[12] 18 U.S.C. Section 1361.

[13] Powell v. Alabama, 287 U.S. 45 (1932).

[14] Johnson v. Zerbst, 304 U.S. 458 (1938).

[15] Gideon v. Wainwright, 372 U.S. 335 (1963).

[16] Argersinger v. Hamlin, 407 U.S. 25 (1972).

[17] Alabama v. Sheldon, 535 U.S. 654 (2002).

[18] Ireland, *Dictionary of Criminal Justice.*

[19] United States v. Dinitz, 424 U.S. 600 (1976).

[20] Griffin v. California, 380 U.S. 609 (1965).

[21] Allen v. United States, 164 U.S. 492 (1896).

SENTENCING

By Robert Aberle

Chapter

9

CHAPTER OVERVIEW

© Lou Oates, 2011. Used under license from Shutterstock, Inc.

Once a person has been found guilty of a felony in a federal or state court in the United States, a presentence investigation is typically requested by the court prior to the actual sentencing of the defendant. This report is a detailed background history of the defendant that is used to assist the judge in determining the proper sentence that should be imposed. This report is typically written by the probation department and also contains a recommended sentence that is based on the results of the report.

Sentencing in the United States has undergone some major reforms since the 1970s. Prior to this time the goal of sentencing was the rehabilitation of the offender. This philosophy of sentencing soon gave way to an emphasis on the punishment of the offender. This change came about because of increased crime rates and a new "get tough on crime" attitude that spread throughout the country. With this new reform movement came several new sentencing models that are now in use, in one form or another, in both the federal judicial system and those of the individual states.

The most severe sentence that can be imposed is that of the death penalty. This chapter will discuss the history of the death penalty in the United States as well as the legal issues that have been raised since the death penalty has been implemented. Methods of execution and the status of the death penalty today will also be discussed.

CHAPTER LEARNING OBJECTIVES

After reading this chapter you will be able to:

1. List the various sections contained in a presentence report.
2. Explain how sentencing in the United States has changed since the 1970s.
3. Identify various sentencing models that are currently in use in the United States.
4. Compare the indeterminate sentencing model with that of the structured sentencing model.
5. Understand the difference between aggravating and mitigating circumstances as they relate to sentencing.
6. Explain how the U.S. Supreme Court has dealt with the administration of the death penalty in the United States since 1967.
7. List the various methods that are legally used to execute prisoners in the United States today.

KEYWORDS

PSI
Truth in Sentencing Laws
Structured Sentencing
Mandatory Sentences
Sentencing Reform Act of 1984
Mitigating Circumstances
Consecutive Sentence
Georgia v. Gregg

"Three Strike" Laws
Indeterminate Sentencing
Determinate Sentencing
Presumptive Sentencing
Aggravating Circumstances
Concurrent Sentence
Furman v. Georgia

THE PHILOSOPHIES OF PUNISHMENT

One of the most controversial issues concerning the correctional system in the United States is the question "Why do we put criminals in prison?" Our correctional system has gone through several different philosophies concerning why we incarcerate criminals over the past two hundred years:

1. Incapacitation
2. Deterrence
3. Restorative Justice
4. Retribution and Just Deserts
5. Rehabilitation

INCAPACITATION

Incapacitation has taken on different meanings over time. Early use of incapacitation was banishment. When a person was banished, they were sent into the wilderness on their own and were never allowed to return. This accomplished the ultimate goal of incapacitation which is to remove the problem from society. The person could no longer be a threat to the community. The modern implication of incapacitation is putting criminals in prison with the ultimate goal of removing them as a threat to society so that they cannot commit any additional crimes. One of the inherent problems with this philosophy is that in most cases it is only temporary. Unless the criminal is given a life sentence or the death penalty, they will eventually return to society. Incapacitation is often referred to as warehousing.

Incapacitation

The modern implication of incapacitation is putting criminals in prison with the ultimate goal of removing them as a threat to society so that they cannot commit any additional crimes.

© James Steidl, 2011. Used under license from Shutterstock, Inc.

DETERRENCE

Deterrence is a philosophy that says we should punish criminals in order to deter others from committing crimes. There are two general theories of deterrence: general and specific. General deterrence says that we should punish criminals so that others see the punishment and will not want to be subject to the same penalties. Specific deterrence is based on the theory that we should punish criminals so that we prevent that specific criminal from wanting to repeat their criminal ways.

In order for deterrence to be effective, punishments must be swift and certain and must be severe enough to make potential criminals think twice before committing a criminal act. In some countries, deterrence seems to work quite well. European and Scandinavian countries do not have the problem with DUI (drunk driving) that we do in the United States. The punishments for driving impaired are severe and certain enough to deter citizens from driving under the influence. There is also tremendous peer pressure on those who are impaired to keep them from driving. In the United States, the punishments in most jurisdictions for DUI are relatively minor in comparison, and there is not the stigma attached to it in order to deter people from doing it. The stark reality is that about 1.5 million people are arrested each year in the United States for driving under the influence.[16]

Deterrence

Deterrence is a philosophy that says we should punish criminals in order to deter others from committing crimes.

Restorative Justice

The concept of restorative justice focuses on the needs of the victim and society, as well as the offender.

RESTORATIVE JUSTICE

The concept of **restorative justice** focuses on the needs of the victim and society, as well as the offender. This philosophy is in use, at least in part, in many jurisdictions around the country. "Making the victim whole" is the catch phrase of restorative justice. If a criminal steals the property of victim, restorative justice says that the offender must make restitution to the victim in order to reduce the harm caused by the act of stealing. Community service is another way that the offender can

© Andy Dean Photography, 2011. Used under license from Shutterstock, Inc.

make society whole again, by giving time and work to the community as part of the restorative sentencing. Restorative justice is often used in conjunction with other philosophies of punishment.

RETRIBUTION AND JUST DESERTS

Retribution

A more modern philosophy based on the concept of *lex talionis* that states the actual punishment should match the crime as closely as possible so that the offender can feel the same pain as they caused the victim.

© Dusan Jankovic, 2011.
Used under license from
Shutterstock, Inc.

Retribution is a philosophy that goes back over two hundred years in the United States, and is based on the concept of *lex talionis* or "an eye for an eye." This early philosophy was based on the idea that the punishment should equal the crime. If a person stole his neighbors horse, the neighbor could take the offenders horse. If a person killed his neighbor's wife, the victim could kill the offender's wife, and so on. The idea is that the actual punishment should match the crime as closely as possible so that the offender can feel the same pain as they caused the victim.

Lex talionis

The concept of *lex talionis* or "an eye for an eye," was an early philosophy based on the idea that the punishment should equal the crime.

Since the mid-1990s, there has been a movement back towards the concept of retribution; however, it is now referred to as "just deserts." **Just deserts** incorporates the idea that criminals are responsible for their own actions and their decisions, and that punishment is the natural consequence of those actions. The United States began "getting tough" on crime in the 1990s. Sentencing reforms, building of more prisons, and laws like the "three strikes and you're out," all contributed to this modern get tough with criminals model.

Just Deserts

Just deserts incorporates the idea that criminals are responsible for their own actions and their decisions, and that punishment is the natural consequence of those actions.

Many of the proponents of just deserts argue that this philosophy of punishment is one of the primary reasons that crime rates have declined in this country during the same period of time. Their argument seems to have validity when you consider that more criminals have been incarcerated for longer periods of time and have not been on the streets committing more crimes. While this philosophy is still popular, economics may bring this era to a rapid end. State governments have been experiencing very severe budget problems and many have been forced to reduce funding to corrections. This has resulted in the closing of prisons and the release of many prisoners long before the completion of their prescribed sentences.

REHABILITATION

Rehabilitation

Rehabilitation is the philosophy premised on the idea that criminals can be "cured" and made to change their criminal ways.

Rehabilitation is the philosophy premised on the idea that criminals can be "cured" and made to change their criminal ways. Over the past several decades, billions of dollars have been spent expanding and developing prison and community programs aimed at rehabilitating criminals. Counseling programs, job skills training, education, and a host of other programs have been geared toward reforming criminals who become a part of our correctional system. The proponents of rehabilitation argue that people can be forced to change their ways and criminals can be shown that crime is a poor alternative to a productive and successful life. They argue that we should not throw away a segment of our society just because they have made some poor choices.

Opponents to rehabilitation point to the fact that many studies have shown that rehabilitative efforts have had little or no effect on the overall recidivism rates of prisoners being released from prison. They also point out the fact that society cannot 'force' a person to change, if a criminal decides to end their criminal activity they will do so whether or not they have been in any program. The opponents also argue that many times the best rehabilitative programs are quickly forgotten when the prisoner returns to the same environment that he/she lived in prior to getting caught and going to prison.

*P*RESENTENCE INVESTIGATION (PSI)

When a defendant is found guilty of a felony by a judge or jury in a trial, or pleads guilty before a judge, a date is set for a sentencing hearing. This hearing is routinely set thirty to sixty days in the future so that there is time to obtain a presentence investigation (**PSI**). The presentence investigation is a detailed background investigation that is conducted on the defendant to assist the judge in determining what sentence should be imposed.

PSI

The presentence investigation (PSI) is a detailed background investigation that is conducted on the defendant to assist the judge in determining what sentence should be imposed.

In most jurisdictions, the presentence investigation is written by the probation department. The report looks into the defendant's background and includes:

1. Family history, including where the defendant lives, who they live with, marriages, divorces, number of children, etc.
2. Educational history
3. Employment history
4. Military history
5. Criminal history
6. A summary of the offense for which they are going be sentenced on
7. A summary of an interview with the defendant
8. A written statement of the defendant if they want one included
9. A written statement from the victim of the crime
10. A recommendation for sentence

© Maaike Boot, 2011. Used under license from Shutterstock, Inc.

The recommendation for sentence is one of the most important sections of the presentence investigation. The probation department takes all of the information that they have gathered about the defendant and develops a recommended sentence based on several variables, including sentencing guidelines, risks and needs of the defendant, and other factors. The recommendation could be for prison or jail time, probation, or a combination of both. The recommendation will also include any special conditions that should be imposed, such as counseling, community service, fines, electronic monitoring, curfews, etc. The judge is the final determiner of the sentence; however, the PSI has a tremendous influence on what sentence will be imposed.

$\mathscr{S}$ENTENCING REFORM IN THE UNITED STATES

"Three-Strike" Laws

Some states have enacted mandatory sentencing laws called "three strikes" that mandate long term incarceration for offenders upon conviction of their third felony.

"Truth in Sentencing" Laws

States that have enacted truth in sentencing laws have done so in order to reduce the possibility of early release from incarceration.

Starting around 1900, almost all of the states in the United States used an indeterminate criminal sentencing system. The primary goal of the system was to rehabilitate the offenders so they could re-enter society as productive and lawful citizens. The roles of the participants in the criminal justice system—the judges, correctional agencies, and parole officials—were clearly defined. This system provided for a relatively stable incarceration rate for almost seventy years.[1]

Sentencing reform in the United States began in earnest in the late 1970s. The emphasis on rehabilitation began to give way to an emphasis on punishment as the primary goal of imprisonment. States and the federal government initiated a very serious "get tough on crime" policy. New policies and laws designed to identify hard-core criminals and insure longer sentences of imprisonment for them were being adopted throughout the country. **"Three-strike" laws** which required mandatory sentencing and **"truth in sentencing" laws** all gained popularity, and were significant contributing factors to the dramatic increase in prison populations in the United States. Additionally, there has been a substantial increase in the construction of prisons since the 1980s. It is also important to note that crime rates in the United States began to decrease significantly during this same period of time.[2]

$\mathscr{S}$ENTENCING MODELS

Indeterminate Sentencing

Indeterminate sentencing is a sentence that that provides for a range of time and includes a minimum time that the person must serve before becoming eligible for parole consideration, and a maximum amount of time that indicates the completion or discharge date.

Since the sentencing reform movement in the 1970s and 1980s, there are now several sentencing models that are used in different parts of the United States:

1. Indeterminate sentencing
2. Structured sentencing
   A. Determinant sentencing
   B. Mandatory sentencing
   C. Presumptive sentencing

INDETERMINATE SENTENCING

Indeterminate sentencing is a sentence that provides for a range of time and includes a minimum time that the person must serve before becoming eligible for parole consideration, and a maximum amount of time that indicates the completion or discharge date. Indeterminate sentencing gives the sentencing judge considerable discretion in being able to adjust the sentence. Prior to the 1970s, virtually every state was using some form of indeterminate sentencing. States that have continued to utilize indeterminate sentencing also maintain parole boards. Once a person is sentenced to prison under an indeterminate sentence, they become eligible for parole after serving the minimum part of the sentence. The parole board then has the discretion to decide whether or not to release the inmate on parole.

STRUCTURED SENTENCING

There are many opponents to the indeterminate model of sentencing. These opponents say that indeterminate sentencing allows for too much judicial discretion, which in turn allows for too much sentencing disparity. Offenders who commit the same crime, even within the same jurisdiction, often receive completely different sentences. The system became very offender specific, rather than offense specific, when it came to sentencing. This disparity in sentences was blamed on limitless judicial and parole board power and the fact that they made their decisions without having to show documentation as to why. Additionally, rising crime rates, the public's fear of crime, and the social problems of the 1960s (civil rights, Vietnam War protests, the widespread openness of the drug culture, etc.) became concerns of elected officials that led to a sentencing revolution in the United States in the 1970s.[3]

A variety of new sentencing models were implemented throughout the country. These new methods of sentencing were designed to reduce judicial discretion and were part of a "get tough on crime" approach to dealing with criminals. These new models fall under a general category of **structured sentencing**, and included determinate sentencing, mandatory sentencing, and presumptive sentencing.

Structured Sentencing
Structured sentences were designed to reduce judicial discretion when it comes to sentencing. Determinate sentencing, mandatory sentencing, and presumptive sentencing all fall under the heading of structured sentencing.

DETERMINATE SENTENCING

Determinate sentencing is a fixed term of incarceration. When offenders are sentenced in a determinate sentencing state, they are given their anticipated release date from prison on the day they are sentenced. Each state has established their own statutes that dictate how much "good time" a prisoner can earn while serving time in prison and that is calculated into the anticipated release date. Determinate sentencing is an attempt to reduce sentencing disparity by making the sentences offense specific and not offender specific. Under this model, all persons convicted of the same criminal offense (burglary, robbery, etc.) would, theoretically at least, receive the same sentence.

Determinate Sentencing
Determinate sentencing is a fixed term of incarceration.

Determinate sentencing states have, for the most part, done away with parole boards because they are no longer necessary due to the fact that there is very little (or no) discretion concerning the release date of the prisoner. States that have retained parole boards have greatly reduced their discretionary decision making authority.

MANDATORY SENTENCING

Mandatory sentences are an attempt to severely reduce sentencing discretion by setting all punishments for specific crimes statutorily. It is a statutory requirement that a certain penalty will be set and carried out in all cases upon conviction for a specified offense.[4] All states have at least some form of mandatory sentencing for some crimes. Many states have enacted laws that mandate a specific penalty for a third conviction of DUI or domestic battery that the courts are required to impose upon conviction.

Arguably the most extreme form of mandatory sentencing would be the "three strikes" laws that have been adopted in one form or another by at least twenty-five states.[5] "Three strikes" laws are a type of mandatory minimum sentencing structure in which judges have little or no discretion and must impose lengthy terms of incarceration on defendants who have two serious or violent felony convictions on their record prior to being convicted of a third.[6] California has had the most visible form of "three strikes" laws in that it states that any felony could be charged and counted as the third strike. California saw a rise in their prison population of third strike offenders from 254 in 1994 to 7,234 in 2003.[7]

© matis, 2011. Used under license from Shutterstock, Inc

PRESUMPTIVE SENTENCING

Presumptive sentencing is a model that combines the use of indiscriminate sentencing with that of determinate sentencing. This model allows for more judicial discretion than the other forms of structured sentencing, but not as much as the indeterminate model allows for. The discretion is limited by sentencing guidelines that are set up by state sentencing commissions. The federal government passed the Sentencing Reform Act of 1984 that was a form of presumptive sentencing and became a model for the sentencing reform of several states. The Sentencing Reform Act of 1984 was established as a part of the Comprehensive Crime Control Act and set up the U.S. Sentencing Commission. The purpose of the Commission is to review and adjust the sentencing guidelines annually.

The goal of the **Sentencing Reform Act of 1984** was to eliminate sentencing disparity through the use of guidelines that were based on both offense and offender characteristics. The federal government, when they adopted this form of sentencing, eliminated the Federal Parole Commission, which in turn eliminated the need for federal parole officers. Federal prisoners must serve 85 percent of their sentence prior to being released from prison. When the prisoner has served the mandatory amount of time, they are "conditionally released" and are supervised by federal probation officers.

Under presumptive sentencing, the judge must take aggravating and mitigating circumstances (see later in this chapter) into consideration before sentencing the offender. Once these factors have been considered and applied, the judge must use the Federal Sentencing Guideline Manual to determine the actual sentence that will be imposed.[8]

ISSUES IN SENTENCING

Even with all of the sentencing reforms over the past three decades, several factors are often taken into consideration prior to the actual sentencing of a convicted person.

AGGRAVATING AND MITIGATING CIRCUMSTANCES

Aggravating circumstances are factors that relate to the commission of a specific crime that cause its severity to be greater than that of a typical instance of the same type of offense. Aggravating circumstances may justify a harsher sentence for the defendant. **Mitigating circumstances** are those that favor the defendant and tend to reduce some of the blame for the crime. These circumstances may justify a reduced sentence for the defendant.

Aggravating Circumstances

Aggravating circumstances are factors that relate to the commission of a specific crime that cause its severity to be greater than that of a typical instance of the same type of offense.

Mitigating Circumstances

Mitigating circumstances are those that favor the defendant and tend to reduce some of the blame for the crime.

TYPICAL AGGRAVATING CIRCUMSTANCES

1. Use of a weapon during the commission of the crime

© jules2000, 2011. Used under license from Shutterstock, Inc.

2. Prior convictions for the same type of offense
3. Causing serious bodily harm

© Smit, 2011. Used under license from Shutterstock, Inc.

4. Committing a crime for hire

© artkamalov, 2011.
Used under license from
Shutterstock, Inc.

5. Crime was committed to avoid or prevent lawful arrest
6. The victim was elderly
7. The victim was a child

© Olga Yarovenko, 2011.
Used under license from
Shutterstock, Inc.

8. The crime was gang related
9. The victim of the crime was selected because of race, ethnicity, sexual orientation, religion, or because of the mental or physical disability of the victim

TYPICAL MITIGATING CIRCUMSTANCES

1. The crime was committed while the defendant was under extreme mental or emotional disturbance

© robodread, 2011.
Used under license from
Shutterstock, Inc.

2. The victim was a participant in the defendant's criminal conduct
3. The defendant had no prior criminal history
4. The defendant acted under duress or under the domination of another person

5. The young age of the defendant

© Sascha Burkard, 2011.
Used under license from
Shutterstock, Inc.

CONCURRENT AND CONSECUTIVE SENTENCES

In cases where a defendant is found or pleads guilty to more than one crime or more than one count of a single crime, the judge, in most cases, has the option of sentencing the defendant to concurrent or consecutive time. If the judge gives the defendant a **concurrent sentence**, that means the defendant will serve each of the separate sentences at the same time. **Consecutive sentencing** means that the defendant will serve the first sentence and only then will the second sentence start.

    If the defendant is sentenced on two counts of burglary and given a five year sentence on each count, under a concurrent sentence, both five year sentences will be served at the same time. The defendant will complete the sentence at the end of five years (less good time). If that same defendant is given a consecutive sentence, the first five year sentence must be completed (less good time) before the second sentence begins.

Concurrent Sentence

Concurrent sentencing that means the defendant will serve each of the separate sentences at the same time.

Consecutive Sentencing

Consecutive sentencing means that the defendant will serve the first sentence and only then will the second sentence start.

*V*ICTIM CONSIDERATIONS

© Junial Enterprises, 2011. Used under license from Shutterstock, Inc.

Prior to the 1970s, sentencing decisions gave little or no consideration to the needs or concerns of the victims of crime. Since that time, the needs of the victim have become a major concern of the courts. Every state has written laws dealing with the legal rights of victims. In addition to the statutory rights of victims, thirty-two states have adopted state victims' rights constitutional amendments that have been made a part of their state constitutions. The federal government has proposed, on several occasions, a constitutional amendment dealing with victim's rights.

The victims' bills of rights that have been incorporated into the various state constitutions and/or state laws generally include the following rights[9]:

1. To be notified of proceedings and the status of the defendant
2. To be present at certain criminal justice proceedings
3. To make a statement at sentencing or other times
4. To receive restitution from a convicted offender
5. To be consulted before a case is dismissed or a plea bargain is entered
6. To a speedy trial
7. To keep the victim's contact information confidential

*D*EATH PENALTY

© Boris15, 2011. Used under license from Shutterstock, Inc.

The death penalty is, obviously, the most severe sentence that our judicial system can impose. The death penalty is reserved for only the most heinous of crimes. Prior to America becoming a country, in the 1600s a person could be put to death for such crimes as murder, adultery, sodomy, witchcraft, and blasphemy. The 1700s saw people put to death for robbery, forgery, and illegally cutting down a tree.[10] Today, the death penalty is reserved for first degree murder in the thirty-six states that still utilize the death penalty. The federal government also has a death penalty that is reserved for thirty-two separate offenses, most of which deal with the murder of various federal officials, treason, and terrorist related activities.[11]

THE LEGALITY OF THE DEATH PENALTY

Furman v. Georgia

A 1972 U.S. Supreme Court case that suspended all executions in the United States because the death penalty was often used arbitrarily and disproportionally used based on the race of the defendant.

Georgia v. Gregg

A 1976 U.S. Supreme Court case that reinstated the death penalty in all states that use a bifurcated (two-stage) process for deciding if a defendant qualified for the death penalty.

Over the years, there have been many Supreme Court challenges to the death penalty, with the majority of them raising the Eighth Amendment guarantee against "cruel and unusual punishment." In 1967, the Supreme Court reviewed the way the death penalty was administered in the United States and found several serious concerns in the process. As a result, the Court put a moratorium on executions that remained in effect until 1977, when it was lifted and executions were again allowed. In 1972, the court ruled in the case of *Furman v. Georgia*, that the death penalty was often used arbitrarily and seemed to be disproportionally used based on race and not on the seriousness of the crime.[12] The Court did not say that the death penalty was constitutionally invalid, just that the procedures used had to be restructured to provide a fair and equitable way of deciding who qualified for execution.

The State of Georgia developed new laws and procedures in an attempt to satisfy the conditions for applying fairness and equity in the death penalty requirements. Another Georgia case, *Georgia v. Gregg*, reached the U.S. Supreme Court in 1976. The Court stated that the new procedures as used in this case met the standards of fairness and equity, and reinstated the death penalty in the United States.[13]

The new procedures for applying the death penalty incorporated the use of a bifurcated, or two-stage, process for deciding if a defendant qualified for the death penalty. The bifurcated system is used in capital cases and requires that the jury first listen to the evidence, as in a regular trial, and then deliberates to determine the guilt or innocence of the defendant. If the defendant is found guilty, a second hearing is held using the same jury. This second hearing is used to determine whether to sentence the defendant to death or to give a life sentence. The evidence that is presented in this second hearing deals with the aggravating and the mitigating circumstances of the case. If the jury decides that there are statutory aggravated circumstances, and they outweigh the mitigating circumstances, they can decide to impose the death penalty.

Since 1977, the U.S. Supreme Court has made several rulings that have restricted the types of crimes that are eligible for the death penalty and the categories of offenders who can receive a sentence of death. In 1977 the Court ruled that the death penalty cannot be used in cases of rape if the woman did not die during the commission of the crime.[14] The Court banned the execution of "mentally retarded" persons in 2002[15] and banned the execution of persons who were under the age of eighteen (at the time the offense was committed) in 2005.[16] In 2008, the Court invalidated a Louisiana law that allowed for the execution of child rapists.[17] In this case the Court argued that the execution for a crime where the victim is still alive is not proportional.

METHODS OF EXECUTION

While many forms of execution have been employed throughout history, the only methods that are currently sanctioned are:

1. Lethal injection

© Anton Prado PHOTO, 2011. Used under license from Shutterstock, Inc.

2. Electrocution

© Linda Buckin, 2011. Used under license from Shutterstock, Inc.

3. Gas chamber

4. Hanging

© Iwona Grodzka, 2011.
Used under license from
Shutterstock, Inc.

5. Firing squad

Lethal injection is the most commonly used method of execution and has been adopted as the primary device in all states that employ the death penalty, as well as the federal government.

THE DEATH PENALTY TODAY

At year-end 2009, there were 3,173 inmates under a sentence of death in thirty-six states and the federal government. Of these inmates, 56 percent of these were white and 42 percent were black; and 98 percent were male and only 2 percent were female. In 2009 there were a total of fifty-two executions in the United States.

SUMMARY FINDINGS

THIRTY-SIX STATES AND THE FEDERAL GOVERNMENT HAD CAPITAL STATUTES AT YEAR-END 2009				
EXECUTIONS DURING 2009		NUMBER OF PRISONERS UNDER SENTENCE OF DEATH		JURISDICTIONS WITHOUT DEATH PENALTY
Texas	24	California	684	Alaska
Alabama	6	Florida	389	District of Columbia
Ohio	5	Texas	331	Hawaii
Virginia	3	Pennsylvania	218	Iowa
Georgia	3	Alabama	200	Maine
Oklahoma	3	Ohio	165	Massachusetts
Florida	2	North Carolina	159	Michigan
South Carolina	2	Arizona	131	Minnesota
Tennessee	2	Georgia	101	New Jersey
Indiana	1	Tennessee	89	New Mexico

THIRTY-SIX STATES AND THE FEDERAL GOVERNMENT HAD CAPITAL STATUTES AT YEAR-END 2009				
EXECUTIONS DURING 2009		**NUMBER OF PRISONERS UNDER SENTENCE OF DEATH**		**JURISDICTIONS WITHOUT DEATH PENALTY**
Missouri	1	Louisiana	83	North Dakota
		Nevada	80	Rhode Island
		Oklahoma	79	Vermont
		24 other jurisdictions	464	West Virginia
				Wisconsin
Total	52	**Total**	3,173	

Source: Capital Punishment, 2009—Statistical Tables

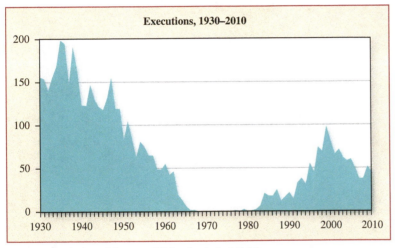

Source: Capital Punishment, 2009—Statistical Tables

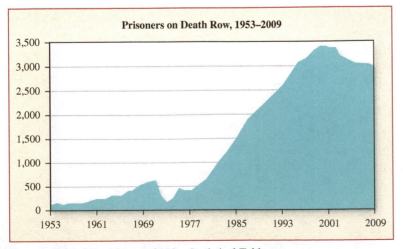

Source: Capital Punishment, 2009—Statistical Tables

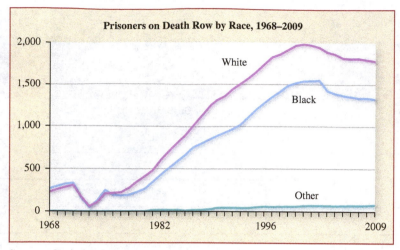

Source: Capital Punishment, 2009—Statistical Tables

REVIEW QUESTIONS:

1. The report that is filed with the court prior to sentencing by the probation department is called the

    _____ _____.

2. The two primary sentencing models used in the United States are _____ sentencing and

    _____ sentencing.

3. _____ sentencing is a fixed term of incarceration.

4. _____ sentencing is a model that combines the use of indeterminate sentencing with that

    of determinate sentencing.

5. _____ circumstances are factors that relate to the commission of a specific crime that

    causes its severity to be greater than that of a typical instance of the same type of offense.

6. _____ circumstances are those that favor the defendant and tend to reduce some of the

    blame for the crime.

7. If a judge sentences two or more counts to run at the same time, it is called a _____

    sentence.

8. If a judge sentences two or more counts to run one after another, it is called a _____

    sentence.

9. The _____ Amendment establishes the guarantee against "cruel and unusual punishment."

10. In 1972 the U.S. Supreme Court ruled in the case of _____ that the death penalty was

    often used in an arbitrary manner and was disproportionally used on race and not on the serious-

    ness of the crime.

11. The most common method of legal execution in the United States is _____ _____.

12. At year-end 2009, _____ states and the federal government had statutes that allowed for
    the death penalty.

CRITICAL THINKING QUESTIONS:

1. Discuss in detail the importance of the presentence report. What does it contain? Who writes it?

2. Compare and contrast indeterminate sentencing with that of determinate sentencing.

3. Discuss the effect that the Sentencing Reform Act of 1984 has had on sentencing in the federal judiciary.

4. Explain the difference between a concurrent sentence and a consecutive sentence.

5. Decide whether or not the death penalty should be abolished. Support your answer with good reasoning.

NOTES

CHAPTER 9

[1] National Council on Crime and Delinquency, *Criminal Justice Sentencing Policy Statement,* November 2005.

[2] Ibid.

[3] Ibid.

[4] Connie Estrada Ireland and George E. Rush, *The Dictionary of Criminal Justice With Summaries of Supreme Court Cases Affecting Criminal Justice,* 7th Edition (New York: McGraw-Hill Companies, Inc., 2011).

[5] NCCD, *Criminal Justice Sentencing Policy Statement.*

[6] Ireland, *Dictionary of Criminal Justice.*

[7] NCCD, *Criminal Justice Sentencing Policy Statement.*

[8] United States Sentencing Commission, *2010 Federal Sentencing Guidelines Manual & Supplement,* accessed June, 2011 at http://www.ussc.gov/Guidelines/2010_guidelines/ToC_PDF.cfm.

[9] National Center for Victims of Crime website, accessed June, 2011 at http://www.ncvc.org/ncvc/main.aspx?dbName=DocumentViewer&DocumentID=32697.

[10] Larry H. Gaines and Roger Leroy Miller, *Criminal Justice in Action—5th Edition* (Belmont, CA: Thomas Wadsworth, 2009).

[11] Tracy L. Snell, *Capital Punishment, 2009—Statistical Tables* (U.S. Department of Justice, Office of Justice Programs, Bureau of Justice Statistics, December 2010).

[12] Furman v. Georgia, 408 U.S. 238 (1972).

[13] Gregg v. Georgia, 428 U.S. 153 (1976).

[14] Coker v. Georgia, 433 U.S. 584 (1977).

[15] Adkins v. Virginia, 536 U.S. 304 (2002).

[16] Roger v. Simmons, 553 U.S. 35 (2005).

[17] Kennedy v. Louisiana, 129 S. Ct. 1 (2008).

CPSIA information can be obtained
at www.ICGtesting.com
Printed in the USA
LVHW051733121119
637074LV00001B/1/P